UNARMED
AGAINST
HITLER

UNARMED AGAINST HITLER

Civilian Resistance in Europe, 1939–1943

JACQUES SEMELIN

Translated by Suzan Husserl-Kapit

Foreword by Stanley Hoffmann

 PRAEGER

Westport, Connecticut
London

Library of Congress Cataloging-in-Publication Data

Semelin, Jacques.
  [Sans armes face à Hitler. English]
  Unarmed against Hitler : civilian resistance in Europe, 1939–1943
  Jacques Semelin ; translated by Suzan Husserl-Kapit ; foreword by Stanley Hoffmann.
    p. cm.
  Includes index.
  ISBN 0-275-93960-X (alk. paper).—ISBN 0-275-93961-8
(pbk. : alk. paper)
    1. World War, 1939–1945—Protest movements—Europe. 2. Passive
resistance—Europe—History—20th century. 3. Nonviolence—
History—20th century. 4. Europe—Politics and government—20th
century. I. Title.
D810.P76S4613 1993
940.53′161—dc20   92-32669

British Library Cataloguing in Publication Data is available.

Library of Congress Catalog Card Number: 92-32669
ISBN: 0-275-93960-X
      0-275-93961-8 (pbk.)

First published in 1993

Praeger Publishers, 88 Post Road West, Westport, CT 06881
An imprint of Greenwood Publishing Group, Inc.

Printed in the United States of America

∞

The paper used in this book complies with the
Permanent Paper Standard issued by the National
Information Standards Organization (Z39.48–1984).

P

In order to keep this title in print and available to the academic community, this edition
was produced using digital reprint technology in a relatively short print run. This would
not have been attainable using traditional methods. Although the cover has been changed
from its original appearance, the text remains the same and all materials and methods
used still conform to the highest book-making standards.

"The deeds of occupier and occupied alike suggest that there come cruel times when to save a nation's deepest values one must disobey the state. France after 1940 was one of those times."

Robert O. Paxton
Vichy France: Old Guard and New Order, 1940–1944

"When the Nazis stopped the Communists, I said nothing, because I was not a Communist. When they locked up the Socialists, I said nothing, because I was not a Socialist. When they came to get the Catholics, I did not protest, because I was not a Catholic. When they came to get me, there was no one left who could protest."

Pastor Martin Niemoller

Contents

Acknowledgments

The development of this book for publication was made possible by a Post-Doctoral Fellowship in the Program of Nonviolent Sanctions in Conflict and Defence in the Center for International Affairs at Harvard University. I am deeply grateful to the center's former director, Gene Sharp, for his encouragement and support, and also to Christopher Kruegler, Director of the Albert Einstein Institution (Cambridge, MA).

I am also grateful to Professor Stanley Hoffmann, Director of the Center for European Studies at Harvard University and Jean-Paul Charnay, Professor of Sociology at Sorbonne University, whose advice helped me to deepen my analyses.

Finally, I was fortunate to have the support of researchers at the Institute of History of the Present Time (Institut d'Histoire du temps présent, IHTP) in Paris. I would like to thank more particularly Jean Pierre Azéma, Claude Lévy, Henry Rousso, and Dominique Veillon who willingly answered my numerous questions and reviewed the whole or parts of my manuscript.

Foreword

Jacques Semelin's book is important and deserves to be widely read for a number of reasons. First, he has brought together, synthesized, and exploited a huge literature that deals with occupied Europe, with what went on in the vast area Hitler's armies had conquered or Hitler's allies were administering. Second, he gives us a balanced and thoughtful picture of the reactions—organized and unorganized—of people to Nazi occupation and repression: this is an essential aspect of the history of World War II, a necessary complement to the many military and diplomatic histories that have accumulated. Semelin has a fine sociological mind, and his analysis of the forms taken by popular opposition is discriminating and subtle.

Above all, he presents us with a comprehensive study of a phenomenon that may well be of lasting significance, beyond the case of World War II: what he calls civilian (as opposed to military) resistance. The many ways, passive and active, in which a public can make the life of the occupier, or that of the occupier's collaborators, more difficult, thwart his evil designs, protect his victims, sabotage his war effort, are rigorously documented here, and the fact that Semelin carefully avoids exaggerating their effects or presenting extravagant claims about nonviolent as opposed to violent forms of resistance makes his conclusions only more impressive. He evaluates the role played by what might be called public opinion at large as well as that of organized groups, social movements, and institutions. He shows that while all the acts of noncooperation, all the efforts at civilian resistance could not suffice to defeat the enemy, they played a key role in denying legitimacy to Hitler's plans and to his Quislings.

Semelin raises, at the end of his study, the fascinating question of the deterrent effect a carefully organized attempt at preparing a population for civilian resistance might have on a potential aggressor. In a world in which causes of violent conflict multiply, in which, in particular, nationalism breeds often horrible wars, but where the modern technology of warfare—displayed during the 1991 Gulf War—is likely to deter many actors from massive, overt aggressions, the danger of wars waged at lower levels of intensity, yet no less and sometimes even much more lethal for civilian populations—as in Bosnia—is frightening; and the costs of armed resistance are often prohibitive. In such instances, organized civilian resistance may well be a powerful deterrrent; for aggressors, ethnic cleansers, and expansionists today, the margin of maneuver at their disposal has an upper limit— the risk of nuclear war—and a lower limit—the risk of having to control a rebellious occupied population, especially when it receives external support. Semelin's admirable volume should help security studies in their badly needed reconversion from the fascination with the late bipolar conflict, to the discussion of the chaotic conflicts which have succeeded its demise, and of the ways of avoiding their spread. It also helps us to see that even in the worst of circumstances, the human spirit, the instinct of decency, all the spontaneous manifestations of what Judith Shklar has called the liberalism of fear, the revolt against cruelty, can provide ordinary men and women with ways of shaping their future and of confronting evil.

Stanley Hoffmann

UNARMED AGAINST HITLER

Introduction

A New Look at the "Resistance"

Works on World War II and the resistance to the German occupation of Europe abound. This book is still another contribution. Yet, it seeks to say something new. No synthesis of its particular subject—unarmed forms of resistance to the Nazi occupier—has yet been completely successful. The unarmed approach may seem surprising since the popular image of resistance to Nazism is of insurrectional violence. Recent historians have shown, however, that what is called *resistance* is a highly complex phenomenon in which armed and unarmed forms of opposition intertwine. Specific studies have been devoted to particular kinds of unarmed resistance: "intellectual," "trade-union," "religious," and so on. This study presents the principal cases of unarmed resistance involving thousands, even tens of thousands, of civilians. These cases include strikes, demonstrations, church or court protests, civil disobedience movements against the compulsory labor service (*Service de Travail Obligatoire*, or STO), and various kinds of opposition carried out by educational, medical, cultural, and religious organizations. They also include, of course, the most significant acts of the aid and rescue of Jews; because of the unique character of this genocide, however, this issue is treated separately. Cases like these took place especially in France, Belgium, Luxemburg, the Netherlands, Denmark, and Norway, but they also occurred in Poland, Czechoslovakia, and Bulgaria. The primary contribution of this book, which does not pretend to be exhaustive, will thus be to bring together succinct accounts of these particular forms of resistance, which are largely unknown among the public.[1]

This study was not motivated by historical curiosity alone. It was inspired by a profound ethical and strategic questioning about society's capacity for unarmed resistance against aggression from a military occupation or a totalitarian power. For several years, this issue has led me to explore the conditions under which "nonviolent" action is effective against oppression and tyranny. I was able to broaden this research through dialogue with high-ranking military men, whether in the framework of the Foundation for National Defense Studies (*la Foundation pour les Études de Défense Nationale*, the FEDN)[2] the General Secretariat of National Defense (*le Secrétariat Général de la Défense Nationale*, the SGDN)[3] or the War School (*l'École de Guerre*.)[4] One of the fruits of this reflection has been a work elaborating the concept of "civil dissausion" as a complement to Frances's military defense.[5] This volume follows that line of research. I wanted to test certain hypotheses concerning nonviolent action in the least favorable of circumstances: that of extreme violence under Nazism, one of the most horrible forms of violence in the history of mankind. To do this, I undertook the work of a historian.

This work seeks to propose a triple contribution to the field of sociohistoric thought. First of all, it presents a general interpretation of phenomena studied through the concept of civilian resistance. The idea of nonviolent action, indeed, does not seem relevant in the context of World War II. One of the fundamental characteristics of the resistance to Nazism was the great overlapping of armed and unarmed ways of fighting. Most of those who resorted to unarmed resistance did so for lack of better options, that is, because they had no weapons which remained the principal and ultimate means of those who were trying to oppose the German order. I therefore looked for a more neutral and appropriate concept than nonviolent action to reserve for cases that made explicit reference to a nonviolent philosophy or strategy. I have proposed the concept of *civilian resistance*, defined as the spontaneous process of resistance by civilian society using unarmed means, and mobilizing either its principal institutions or its people—or both at the same time. There will be objections that it seems insufficient to define civilian resistance only by its means. Under the German occupation, if individuals and groups really resorted to unarmed forms of action, these forms were in reality serving the goals of the war or of the paramilitary struggle (for example, information gathering, the masses' support of the Maquis, etc.). These actions of the civilian resistance, combined with the armed struggle, deserve an overall study, but they do not constitute the subject of this book. Rather, I have attempted here to study the autonomous actions of civilian resistance, that is, those that were oriented toward goals that were explicitly "civilian." Examples include maintaining the independence of various institutions outside the control of the occupying power, protecting people being chased, and so on. This choice explains why the study focuses principally on the period from 1939 to 1943, a period when the forms of armed opposition were still relatively undeveloped.

In the second place, the goal of this study is to propose "analytic guidelines" for cases of civilian resistance. My project is also to understand *why* and *how* men and women can accept and engage in unarmed combat against a heavily armed adversary devoid of morality. This goal led me to undertake comparative studies. All comparisons are debatable since events have to be "extracted" from their national context. Considering the diversity of each occupied country's history and its degree of occupation, there is a risk of developing analyses that are too general and that therefore apply poorly to each particular case. I hope, however, that I have established the relevance of several key concepts, such as "legitimacy," "social cohesion," and "opinion," that form the framework of this work. They make the bases of unarmed combat more understandable. I thus hope to present another perspective on the resistance, a new one, which in no way intends to exclude other approaches. I also think that the elements of reflection presented here, which sometimes use psychological and sociological analytical criteria, may offer tools that would help us to interpret contemporary events in Eastern Europe, the Philippines, or Chile. In this sense, this essay owes more to historical sociology or political science than to the discipline of history per se. Still, it corresponds to the challenge articulated by Stanley Hoffmann, summoning historians to a highly difficult task: "They must venture not only into fields already known by political scientists and sociologists but also into the much-debated fields of psychologists. An immense undertaking!"[6]

Finally, this work addresses a more general problem: can civilian society take part in its own defense? Some experts now wonder how civilian populations can contribute directly or indirectly to their own security. Examining the role played by the civilian resistance in Europe under the German occupation is quite revealing. Civilian resistance was rarely directed against the occupation forces openly; it did not have the means to drive them from the territory. The goal of this spontaneous struggle was instead to preserve the collective identity of the attacked societies; that is to say, their fundamental values. Civilian resistance very often arose in order to affirm an unstifled legitimacy in the face of the order introduced by the occupier and its collaborators. It was a legitimacy that would be embodied progressively by all the forces involved in the resistance, armed or not. "For us," a French resister wrote, "at a given moment in our destiny, the world 'resistance' will have meant: 'voluntary work carried out to affirm values we deem essential.' "[7] Civilian resistance offered a privileged means to dig a trench between military domination, which was the actual state of affairs, and political submission, which was a state of mind. When a society feels less and less submissive, it becomes more and more uncontrollable. Then, even if the occupier keeps its power, it loses its authority. This expresses how much the civilian resistance consisted primarily of a clash of wills, expressing above all a fight for values. The questions are contemporary ones: What do we have to defend today? What is the basis of our collective identity? What values deserve to be defended when a crisis threatens the security and integrity of our societies? The goal of this book is to look for the answers.

NOTES

1. The better part of this research took place while the author was completing a doctorate in contemporary history, which was defended at the Sorbonne in 1986. The book is based

primarily on investigations in different European countries, consultations with historians in these countries, and translations in French or English of previously unpublished texts.

2. The FEDN is a private foundation controlled by the state whose goal is to promote research in the field of defense.

3. The SGDN is an official organization, at the level of the Prime Minister, whose aim is to develop a global approach of defense.

4. The goal of the École de guerre, under the aegis of the École militaire, is to train young army officers for high-ranking positions.

5. Christian Mellon, Jean-Marie Muller, and Jacques Sémelin, *La dissuasion civile* (Paris, 1985).

6. Stanley Hoffmann, "Le désastre de 1940," *La France de 1939 à nos jours* (Paris, 1985) p. 33.

7. Alban Vistel, *Héritage spirituel de la Résistance* (Lyon, 1955) p. 63.

Chapter 1

The Main Traits of the Nazi Occupation in Europe

By the end of 1942, almost all of continental Europe had fallen under German domination. From the tip of Brittany to the mountains of the Caucasus, from the Arctic cape of Norway to the shores of the Mediterranean, Berlin reigned. Within three years, Nazi Germany had constructed an empire that it intended to rule for more than a thousand years. A new order had been born, and some believed that it heralded a "United States of Europe." In a lecture given in Prague in 1942, the German press director, Otto Dietrich, declared grandiloquently that this new order would be founded, "not on the principle of this or that nation's privileges but on the principle of equal opportunity for all of them"; he also promised "a grouping of nations according to their racial composition but that formed an organic whole."[1] Representatives of the nations of the anti-Communist or anti-Comintern pact gathered at the end of 1941 in a congress christened the "First European Congress," and this occasion inspired a "Chant of Europe."

Of course, this idea that the European nations would henceforth be equal and involved together in the construction of a common future was pure propaganda. The Nazi hold over the French was evident, but this hardly displeased Germany's great admirers; as the French collaborationist Pierre Drieu la Rochelle put it, "Only Germany can insure hegemony in Europe. She is at its center, her population is double that of any other European nation, she holds and can keep critical strategic points, but most of all, she possesses the greatest organizational, material, and spiritual resources in the world gathered together in one hand."[2]

But then came Stalingrad and the formidable American war machine. Who can say what would have become of Europe without England's ferocious insistence to continue the struggle alone until 1941 and the progressive mobilization of the United States at its side? It is difficult to answer, especially since German opinions about this have not really been made clear yet. Indeed, many emphasize that

Berlin seems never to have elaborated a serious plan aimed at building a true political, economic, and social European order. Nonetheless, the conduct of the Germans toward the conquered peoples conveys an idea of what might have been expected if Germany had won the war.

FUNDAMENTAL OBJECTIVES

Let us recall some key elements of Germany's foreign policy toward the European countries. It is not necessary to describe here the course of military events or even the global interpretations of the still-debated Nazi phenomenon.[3] Since this study aims to interpret the role of particular forms of resistance to the occupying forces, however, it is imperative to remember Germany's objectives with respect to the occupied countries.

Our first consideration is to examine the determination of Europe's new master, Adolf Hitler. We know that the Nazi nation was not a monolithic block; instead, it was a rather chaotic system in which major decisions were often the result of highly diverse pressures, not necessarily with any planning or any clear order from the top. But it is just as clear that the head of the Third Reich always retained control over the two areas that interested him most: the war and foreign policy. Hitler seems never to have specified his views on the political and economic bases of his empire. The first of his preoccupations was always to win the war that he himself had launched. He left the structure of this new Europe in the background. "Hitler's immediate objective," Gordon Wright has written, "was victory through weapons, not the reorganization of vanquished Europe according to a preestablished plan."[4] Within the conquered countries, Hitler's first concern was to insure *order and security* and to set up pragmatic formulas for the occupation that would impede the pursuit of the war effort as little as possible. This implied, if need be, dependence on aid from local administrations, whether for managing civilian affairs or repressing possible opposition movements. Once the war was won, the time would come to consolidate the fruits of the conquest.

Were these orientations a deliberate tactical choice that incited the Führer to conceal his plans for the postwar period, or were they a consequence of his passion for military strategy? Probably a little of both. But the image of Hitler that remains is above all that of an undeniably talented war leader rather than of an administrator bent on planning conquests. He knew how to make good choices for the reconstruction of the German army by equipping it with the most modern technology. He excelled at mystifying his adversaries and at galvanizing his people and soldiers by the magnetism of his voice. As for strategy, he had a gift for seeing ahead and for improvising, which led him to rapid military victories. As Arnold Toynbee has shown,[5] Hitler's drive for power, expressed especially in his drive to conquer, far outweighed his specific war goals, which were defined with more flexibility.

Still, some people believe that, despite its phraseology, *Mein Kampf* defined a course of actions and demands from which the future Führer never diverged.

That book demanded Germany's extension toward the East, especially toward the Ukraine and the Baltic countries but perhaps also beyond. Hitler declared the necessity of breaking France's military power but did not express a desire for territorial expansion in the west. He did not seem inclined to accept the challenge of British colonial and naval power. His idea was that a Reich, as the master of Eastern Europe, which was considered a potential "colonization" zone, would make Germany a world power. But what is striking in this book and in many other declarations by Hitler is the amount of space he reserves for his arguments on issues of race. This is, in fact, another clue to understanding Nazi politics on a national and international level: *racial considerations* play such an important role in foreign policy issues that they influence the policy's very direction. The foundation of this policy was the megalomaniacal vision of the German nation, of the "Aryan people," descended from the "race of the Lords." Because of this, the naturally vigorous and dominating German nation felt that it had to assert its right to "vital space"—*Lebensraum*,—a ritual term in the Nazi vocabulary. In Hitler's mind, Eastern Europe was the territory of preference, this *Lebensraum*. These lands therefore had to be "colonized" in the Nazi sense of the term; that is, they had to be emptied of their populations and then "Germanized", or peopled by representatives of the "master race." To facilitate this policy, an office of "Race and Population" was created in 1935 at the heart of the Schutzstaffel (S.S.) organization. In October 1939, Hitler attached this office to a State Commissioner's Office for the Reinforcement of Germanity directed by Heinrich Himmler. Its goal was to clean up the conquered areas and then repopulate them. This "germanization" was not conceived in the traditional sense, whereby a colonial power imposed its culture upon its colony. "Our task in the East," Himmler said in 1942, "does not entail germanizing in the old sense of the word, that is, imposing the German language and laws on the population, but making sure that only people with pure germanic blood are living in the East."[6] The colonization process did not target ethnic groups like the Scandinavians who were perceived as being racially close to the Germanic peoples; the policy limited itself to their reeducation. It did target others, however—the Russians first and foremost—for subjugation. And in 1941, at the same time as the attack against the Soviet Union, it developed a propaganda campaign to identify the inhabitants of Eastern Europe as subhumans—*Untermenschen*—a word hardly used until then.

The other fundamental theme of Nazi racism, equally obsessive and delirious, was Europe's "contamination" by "international Jewry." Jews were portrayed as responsible for everything bad that had befallen the conquered Germany in the 1920s. Nazi propaganda developed animal images to describe Jews, implying that it was necessary to cut off all relations with these dangerous and contagious beings. Before the war, the Nazi authorities had been content to deprive and banish the Jews. Indeed, from as early as 1939, Hitler declared to the Reichstag that "if international Jewish finance succeeded in plunging the countries once again into a world war, the result would be the elimination of the Jewish race in Europe,"[7] but few observers took this statement seriously. The war itself helped to make

this publicly flaunted threat become a reality. The systematic extermination of
the Eastern Jews started during the Russian campaign toward the end of July 1941.
In January 1942, an interministerial meeting in the Berlin suburb of Wannsee
planned the extermination of Jews of other countries, in particular those of Western
Europe. During the fall of 1941, special commandos behind the German armies
marching toward Moscow were already committing mass machine-gun executions.
Gas ovens were in operation in Chelmno, Poland, by the end of 1941, and four
large extermination camps (Belzec, Maidanek, Sobibor, and Treblinka) were
already being constructed in the same country. In 1942, a concentration camp,
Auschwitz, was also converted into an extermination camp.

Human barbarism has accompanied many wars. But after this war there was
a need for a new word to describe what had just transpired. The word was
genocide.[8] Some people are irritated by placing the extermination of European
Jews in a special category. Still, while it is true that many non-Jews disappeared
in Nazi camps—gypsies, homosexuals, Slavs, and, actually, people of all nation-
alities—the basis of this extermination process, the source of its dynamic force,
was inescapably Nazi anti-Semitism. The fundamental characteristic of Nazism,
its defining trait, consists of this industrial plan to eliminate certain categories
of civilian populations, principally Jews. In this respect, genocide must occupy
a central place in the interpretation of Nazi politics toward the nations that fell
under its influence.

But the war also had its economic imperatives, and, given the size of the available
forces, it was necessary to exploit the occupied countries' industrial resources
to the maximum in order to counter-balance Allied resources. The Germans came
up with what they called an "economy of large ensembles"—*Grossraumwirtschaft*
—for all of Europe. Theoretically, they had two options: either to strip the occupied
countries of their raw materials and food products in order to transport them to
Germany or to make the conquered populations work for the German war effort
in their home countries. In fact, they combined the two formulas, with emphasis
on the former. This policy consisted most notably of the forced transfer of millions
of workers into Germany, mostly as part of the Compulsory Labor Service (STO).
Although the methods varied with the countries, they were always crueler in the
East. The object was the same everywhere—pillage. Sending raw materials, food
products, and industrial equipment into Germany, confiscating goods (mostly from
Jews), and taking over financial companies were all common techniques to benefit
Germany economically.

PRINCIPAL FORMS OF DOMINATION

The absence of an overall plan was also noteworthy in the political domain.
Although the military victories mounted rapidly, they were not followed by internal measures that could have contributed to consolidating those gains. Hitlerian
improvisation piece by piece made Nazi Europe into a heterogeneous grouping.

When we try to analyze the structures of this political mosaic, we discern four basic forms of Nazi domination in Europe, after setting aside the neutral countries (Portugal, Spain, Ireland, Switzerland, Sweden, Turkey, and the Vatican). The word "domination," rather than "occupation," is used intentionally because certain countries were taken over by Berlin without being militarily occupied by the German army.

The first form was *annexation*, which was actually rather rare. The most important case involved the western part of Poland, the former Polish corridor (Gdańsk today), a territory that was divided into two new German provinces, respectively christened Wartheland and western Danzig-Prussia. Polish Silesia was likewise reattached to German Silesia, and western Prussia received some extra pieces of Polish territory. In 1940 after the French campaign, Germany took two small districts (Eupen and Malmédy) back from Belgium; these had been confiscated from Germany at the time of the Versailles treaty. Similarly, Berlin imposed an annexation statute on the Grand-Duchy of Luxemburg, Alsace, and a large portion of the Lorraine. After the fall of Yugoslavia in 1940, Germany also appropriated two–thirds of Slovenia and extended its frontiers along the Adriatic Sea. After the outbreak of war against the Soviet Union, the part of Poland formerly under Soviet control (part of the Ukraine, Lithuania, and Byelorussia [known now as Belarus]) was automatically reattached to Germany. Hitler hinted at other annexations but did nothing about them. These were probably just threats to pressure his subjects, but it is quite possible that he kept a variety of plans in mind that he hoped to carry out once the war was won.

The second kind of political domination, which was much more frequent, was *direct administration*, military or civilian, of the conquered territories. The term "administration," as used in this context by various historians, may lead to confusion, however. Indeed the term does not mean that the occupying authorities had the means to administer the country on their own. Quite the contrary: when a certain number of German officials came to a particular country, their function was to command directly the different services of the national administration that was composed of agents of that country. This second form was less important administratively than politically. It describes situations in Europe in which the Germans directed the occupied societies without a national political intermediary, because either the intermediary was weak or because the Germans lacked the desire to use one. Thus, after the departure of Norway's King Haakon VII and his government to London, Berlin created a commissary of the Reich, under the authority of Josef Terboven, whose task was to direct a Norwegian administration containing many pro-Nazi sympathizers. A similar scenario was played out in the Netherlands following the flight of Queen Wilhelmina and her government to London. Unlike the Norwegians, however, a team of Dutch secretaries of state, who were recognized by their government in exile, remained in Holland. They were directed by a civilian administrator, a Nazi of Austrian descent, Doctor Arthur Seyss-Inquart.

In Belgium, the government took refuge first in France, then in England, and denounced King Leopold III's decision to give himself up. Senior Belgian officials, the "General Secretaries," administered the country under the control of a German

soldier, General Alexander von Falkenhausen. In France, two-thirds of the
territory, known as the "occupied zone," was also run by German military
administration. The departments of Nord and Pas de Calais, which were considered
highly important strategic zones from both the military and the industrial standpoints
were isolated from the rest of the country and placed under the military
administration in Brussels. In the East, the part of Poland that had not been annexed
by either Germany or the Soviet Union was administered by General Hans Frank,
a Nazi soldier with a sinister reputation. This territory was named the General
Government of Occupied Polish Territories until 1940 when the name was
abbreviated to General Government. The invasion of the Soviet Union enlarged
the field for German administration considerably. Two enormous commissaries,
directed by civilians, were created there: the Ukraine and Ostland (including the
Baltic and Byelorussian states). Berlin also tried to establish two more: Muscovy
(including most of European Russia to the north of the Ukraine) and the Caucasus,
but was prevented from doing so by the Soviet resistance. Actually, the German
civilian administration in the Soviet Union was always somewhat formal since,
even in Ostland and the Ukraine, important combat zones remained until the end
of the German presence.

The third form of Nazi domination, also rather frequent, was the *guardianship*
of conquered countries through the maintenance of a more or less fictitious
autonomy for the state apparatus. In this case, a "national" government, made
up of recognized politicians or Nazi sympathizers, appeared to continue managing
its own country's affairs. Indeed, not only did such a government have the
responsibility of a civilian administration but it also could be considered a political
structure representing the defeated country. On the whole, instead of being in direct
contact with these populations, the German authorities meant to act upon them
through the intermediary of a "national" government that was willing to collaborate
with them. In such conditions, the scope for initiative by the "national" government
was highly limited, and, in any case, the German troops were already stationed
in the country.

Before the war, Hitler had experimented with this formula in Czechoslovakia.
After the Munich agreement that legalized the dismantling of the independent Czech
state, Berlin divided the country in two. The western part became the Protectorate
of Bohemia-Moravia, whose "government" had hardly any responsibilities. The
eastern part, however, was converted into a completely vassal state directed by
a Catholic prelate, Monsignor Jozef Tiso, who had an army and diplomatic status
at his disposal for dealing with the Axis countries. In France, Germany had the
benefit of Field-Marshal Henri Pétain, a great national figure, a first-rank
personality willing to take part in collaboration, but Berlin took the precaution
of limiting the Vichy government's authority to the southern part of the country,
the so-called "free zone." In Denmark, King Christian X, unlike his Norwegian
counterpart, refused to seek refuge abroad. Since the Germans hoped to maintain
a democratic façade in this country, the Danish government remained in place until
the crisis of August 1943. In the dismembered Yugoslavia in the south of Europe,

three different types of puppet regimes were established. A big new Croatian state, headed by the Croatian fascist, Ante Pavelic, was ostensibly placed under Italian protection; a tiny Serbian state was given to an old soldier of the Pétain mold, General Milan Nedić, while the small district of Montenegro was run by a group of local pro-fascists. Greece had collaborating governments that disguised the presence of Germany and Italy.

Finally, the fourth form of Nazi influence in Europe consisted of all the independent countries that declared themselves German allies. In appearance, there might seem to have been equality between them and Germany but, in fact, these were satellite countries of the Reich. Thus, Romania and Hungary managed to safeguard their fragile national sovereignty for some time by becoming armed auxiliary troops for Hitler. Bulgaria also declared itself allied with Germany, as did Finland, which thus abandoned its previous status as a neutral power. As for Italy, its ostensible status proclaimed it Germany's privileged partner in Europe's domination, Benito Mussolini did not have the resources to maintain this rank. His military failures could only remove his illusions. Actually, the Italians depended on Germany for war supplies and for the security of the peninsula. The myth of Italian independence was destroyed in 1943 with the fall of the Duce and the invasion of Italy by Germany's armies. Even until then, Italy had been no more than a rather cumbersome satellite country.

POLITICAL EXPRESSIONS OF COLLABORATION

Although Germany was the most populous country in Europe, it did not have adequate personnel to manage the territories that had fallen under its control within just a few months. It was therefore natural for Berlin to seek to depend on the occupied countries' local structures and especially on their administrative apparatuses. Moreover, the international convention of the Hague had stipulated in 1907 that in case of an occupation, the occupied country's administration must be placed under the orders of the occupying country's authorities.

In the spirit of this convention, certain countries adopted particular provisions. In Belgium, for example, railroad and electrical employees received a "Civilian Mobilization Handbook" in 1937; it called upon them not to offer any resistance in case of foreign invasion and to continue carrying out their services with professional conscientiousness and loyalty toward the occupying forces. The Germans could not have hoped for better psychological and technical preparation of the officials at their service. In general, they were actually able to obtain much more than this "simple" administrative collaboration. What makes actions specifically "collaboration" is a complex process whereby an occupied country becomes *politically* involved with the occupying country.

According to Hoffmann's classic definition, there are several forms of collaboration.[9] First of all, there is *national collaboration*, a tactic or strategy determined at the highest level of power, which aims to defend the national interests of the conquered country. This should be clearly distinguished from *collaborationism*, which is, by contrast, an ideological choice consisting of political action for the occupier's cause whose system one admires; this does not mean that such an attitude may not imply other motives as well. Collaborating is also, after all, a means of *social promotion* for opportunists hungry for recognition and a good—sometimes very advantageous—way to profit from *economic collaboration*. For a greater number of people, it is more a *state of mind*, a way of showing oneself to be "realistic," of trying to "look good" for the rulers of the time.

It is essential to point out that it takes two to "collaborate." If this simple truth is forgotten, serious misunderstandings or profound errors of interpretation may occur as to the nature of the relationship between the occupier and the occupied countries. Thus, Hitler did not always accept national collaboration. Polish historians have emphasized, for example, that it is to their people's credit that their government did not collaborate with the Nazis. If this fact is undeniable, however, it is because Berlin had no desire for such an arrangement. Since Poland was the first territory toward the East and was considered by the Germans as "vital space for the Aryan race," the Nazis wanted to administer the Polish "colonies" directly. The Führer felt the same about the Soviet Union, in spite of the opinion of certain Nazi dignitaries, such as the ideologue Arthur Rosenberg, who believed, on the contrary, that the German armies should depend on the cooperation of non-Russian minorities (especially Byelorussian, Ukrainian, and Caucasian) at the time of invasion. Rosenberg hoped to encourage separatist demands and especially advocated forming "liberation committees" in Berlin that would have reunited refugees from these areas. Such collaborating possibilities seem to have really existed. The warm welcome that the peasant masses gave the invaders, especially in the Ukraine, certainly attests to this idea. The abrogation of the collective farm system and the prospect of ending Stalinist terror would probably have stirred up much support. In 1942, the capture of General Andrei Vlassov also suggested the possibility of political collaboration through the reconstitution of a Russian state under German control. But Hitler always opposed such projects, and it was against his wishes that the Wehrmacht, in need of soldiers, enlisted many Cossacks, Caucasians, and men from central Asia.

Collaboration with the nations of the East was thus absurd. But how exactly did Hitler imagine it? Did the word itself—collaboration—have any meaning to him? As we have already pointed out, his natural penchant toward improvisation made his foreign policies seem somewhat incoherent. In spite of certain contradictions, however, one can discern some of their broad outlines.[10]

First of all, many collaborationists who were avowed partisans and admirers of the Nazi regime did not receive the signs of recognition from Berlin that they thought they deserved when the German armies arrived in their countries. These collaborationists were kept away from real power and relegated to secondary tasks. Their role was mostly ideological (organizing propaganda presses) and repressive (hunting for Jews and resisters). Some of them worked for administrations in posts of greater and lesser importance and served as recruiters for the German armies. Hitler did not have a lot of respect for Anton Mussert's pro-Nazi party in the

Netherlands, even though it imitated its German counterpart. Nonetheless, Mussert tried all the harder to glean favors from the Führer and, in 1942, got himself appointed "Leider." At its peak, his party had more than 110,000 members and provided more recruits to the Waffen-SS than any other European nation.

In proportion to its population, Belgium furnished one of the highest rates of collaborationists. Perhaps they could have played an important role in the political life of the party, but they fell victim to their own internal divisions caused by the old conflict between the Walloons and the Flemish. The competition was mostly between the Flemish VNV (*Vlaamsch National Verbond* [Flemish National Federation]), led by Staf de Clerg, and the Rexist movement, mostly Walloon, organized by one of the most influential personalities of the prewar period, Léon Degrelle. For racial reasons, the Germans probably felt closer to the Flemish groups, which were considering annexing their region to the Reich, but nothing concrete was undertaken. The collaborationists instigated ideological agitation and recruited for the Waffen-SS—more than 40,000 Belgians from the Walloon and Flemish legions, with the Walloons commanded by Degrelle himself.

In France, pro-Nazi movements had high hopes for collaboration with Germany in the "new Europe." Their principal representatives were the former communist Jacques Doriot and the former socialist Marcel Déat. Before the war, Doriot had founded the French Popular Party (PPF) to which many disillusioned members of the communist party gravitated, especially after the signing of the German-Soviet pact. Déat, who had been a socialist deputy and had worked personally with Léon Blum, created the Popular National Assembly Party (RNP). Although the French collaborationists were supported, financially and otherwise, by Germany (especially by Otto Abetz, Germany's ambassador in Paris), they were nonetheless distanced from power. Hitler preferred dealing with Field-Marshal Pétain's administration rather than with those smaller groups that he knew represented a minority. These smaller groups were supposed to put pressure on the Vichy government so that it would cooperate even more with Berlin. They also played an important role in the collaborationist press and as an auxiliary force of repression.

Only in Norway did Germany try to put its avowed ideological partisans in power, or more correctly, into the foreground. In 1942, Terboven, the Reich's commissar, decided to call on the head of Norway's national-socialist party, *Nasjonal Samling*, Vidkun Quisling. A former minister of defense from 1931 to 1933 and a great admirer of Germany, his name remains the symbol of unconditional collaboration with the Nazis. Quisling dreamed of building a corporatist country in the fascist mold in Norway, the heart of the Germanic empire, but with a strong nationalist base; this did not please Hitler. Since he had no real political solution for Norway, however, Hitler agreed to appoint Quisling Minister-President under the commissar of the Reich in 1942. This long-awaited promotion for Quisling changed hardly anything in the division of power, which remained in Terboven's hands. It only deepened the Norwegian people's hostility toward the regime, and the "Quisling experiment" was a political fiasco for both the Germans and for him.[11]

REASONS FOR STATE COLLABORATION:
A COMPARISON BETWEEN DENMARK AND FRANCE

Considering the general goals of Hitlerian politics, this Norwegian failure shows that the policy of not putting local pro-Nazi parties into power was well founded. If the goal was first and foremost to maintain order and public peace within the conquered countries while exploiting their economic resources to the maximum, it was not in Hitler's interest to place local pro-Nazi political leaders at the heads of their states; their local movements clearly represented too small a minority. Rather, Hitler would do better to gain the support of more neutral citizens, either politicians, who were more representative of national opinion but favored ''realism'' as the only way to save their countries, or technocrats, who thought it their duty to remain at their posts while continuing to serve the state and defend their countries' interests. In fact, Berlin often obtained the cooperation of both leading conservative and nationalist citizens and senior officials who were able to keep the administration functioning. Can we then say that, by doing this, Hitler meant to ''collaborate'' with them? Certainly not. His goal was always to get the most out of those whom he had conquered, not to propose a sort of partnership to them.

In this sense, the idea of ''collaboration'' is ambiguous. It implies a reciprocity that never existed in the Führer's mind. When it suited him, he maintained this ''misunderstanding'' on purpose in order to dupe those with whom he was dealing. In reality, though, the idea of ''collaboration'' did not come from the Germans but from the citizens of the occupied countries. They often believed that, in a situation as dire as foreign occupation, concession and cooperation with the occupier would avoid the worst, whereas resistance and breaking off communications would prove counterproductive. National collaboration was founded entirely on this paradox. In such circumstances, cooperating with the enemy and even serving his goals meant protecting one's fundamental national interests.

Denmark had recourse to such a strategy during the Nazi occupation. Because this small country could not resist the Nazi invasion militarily, it decided not to put up a fight. After a period of indecision, the government chose to remain in place, while vigorously protesting the violation of Danish neutrality. The German memorandum, presented on April 9, 1940 by Von Renthefink, justified the occupation for reasons of Reich security and simultaneously declared that the German forces' presence was the way to insure respect for Danish neutrality. Denmark would thus be allowed to retain its most important prerogatives: its own government, parliament (Rigsdag), and army. This memorandum served as a reference document for the entire occupation period. In the Nazi racial hierarchy, the Danes were de facto members of the Aryan brotherhood. That is why they could benefit from preferential treatment, the objective being to convince them eventually of the virtues of national-socialist ideology. But, in the short run, it was to Berlin's advantage to maintain a democratic-style regime under its control. Danish democracy was a good propaganda argument to use in response to the denunciations of the horrors committed in Eastern Europe.

The social-democratic team in power, which before the occupation had been led by Thorwald Stauning, was transformed into a national union government with the addition of representatives of the two biggest opposition parties. Together, the members of the administration team represented 95 percent of the population. The insignificant pro-Nazi party (DNSAP), led by Doctor Frits Clausen, was kept in the background.

Largely inspired by its Foreign Affairs Minister Munch, this government's political program was to take the German memorandum literally, both its demands and its promises. First of all, the Danes believed that deciding against the armed defense of their territory was not the same as a military defeat. Moreover, since there had been no declaration of war, there could be no talk of capitulation. The occupation was a most regrettable *fait accompli*. From then on, the important thing was to work out an arrangement between the countries. The Wehrmacht had to take charge of the country's security while in reality insuring its neutrality. In short, the occupation was certainly a new game that implied certain concessions from the occupied but also duties from the occupier. Acting as if the Germans would respect their promises, the Danish government was clearly trying to limit the damage of a particularly unfavorable situation. By continuing to function, it sought to act as a sort of screen between the Nazis and the population. The mere presence of such a government was an obstacle to the formation of a collaborationist puppet government and to Berlin's direct takeover of control. The goal was to preserve the democratic system and Danish culture while sparing the country too much suffering. Basically, the decision not to involve the Danish army in a fight that it could only lose was the first act of Denmark's policy of protection. In the days following the invasion, Danish leaders made this declaration: "The government has acted with the honest conviction that it has saved the country from a crueler destiny. We will continue to do our best to protect our country and its people from the disaster of war, and we are counting on the cooperation of our people."[12] The population, at this time, no doubt strongly supported the government's position, which also had the approval of King Christian X. Abroad, however, especially in Great Britain and the United States, comments like "lie down like a Dane" were frequent, indicating that this position was not very well understood.

It is true that Copenhagen appeared to be playing ball with Germany. The king and his government stayed in place, in contrast to other countries, which could be interpreted as a legitimation of the "new order." Moreover, the line chosen by the Danes was not easy to put into effect. It presupposed a skillful and complex mix of inevitable concessions and acts of firmness. The new prime minister and the principal master of this difficult enterprise, Eric Scavenius, showed undeniable talents as a negotiator. He often acted as an intermediary between the Danish government and the German authorities, whose relative confidence he succeeded in gaining.

Faced with pressures from Berlin, Copenhagen's usual tactic was to try to discuss, to win time, to delay executing orders, and, finally, to give way on certain points which did not seem essential. This led to a sort of flexible "cleavage" between Denmark's international and domestic policies: the country aligned its diplomacy to Germany's but managed to protect itself, up to a certain point, from Berlin's interference into its domestic affairs. Scavenius found the Reich's new plenipotentiary, Werner Best, very understanding. Best had arrived in Copenhagen at the end of October 1942, when a crisis was threatening. A member of the SS dynasty and a collaborator of Reinhard Heydrich, he was part of a group of Nazi intellectuals who thought that Germany should, above all, win the war. Once they reached this goal, they could devote themselves to the ideological education of the populations. For the moment, it was essential to convince the populations to collaborate. Overly brutal repressive measures were proving counterproductive to making this happen. Therefore, Best intended to act with prudence, which suited the Danish government. He even insisted on organizing legislative elections to the Rigstag, counting on their positive propaganda effects. These elections, which took place on March 23, 1943, were the only ones organized in German Europe. They emphasized the Danes' attachment to the parliamentary principle (89 percent voted) and their confidence in the traditional parties in government (which won 94 percent of the votes), a result that further confirms the insignificance of the pro-Nazi groups.

It is difficult to evaluate if Danish-style national collaboration really paid off for the country, especially when we take into account the major crisis of August 1943, which will be discussed below. A tally of the government's activity brings out both actions characterized by national collaboration and gestures of obvious or indirect opposition. On the one hand, Denmark expressed its wish to collaborate in the construction of a Germanic Europe through official declarations. It severed diplomatic relations with the Soviet Union and the United States, joined the anti-Comintern pact, and recognized several of the Reich's satellite countries. Economic relations with Berlin were very important, especially in the area of agricultural export to Germany. As for domestic politics, Denmark ended up yielding on an important point; it outlawed Communists, an unconstitutional decision nonetheless passed by the Rigsdag. On the other hand, the government succeeded in maintaining a reasonable level of economic life for the population and in preserving a certain political autonomy, even though, as early as October 1940, the Germans demanded the departure first of a conservative minister, Christmas Moller[13], and then of some social democratic ministers. Copenhagen managed more or less to put off the delivery of military war material and proved itself uncompromising on the question of Jewish deportations. The balance-sheet thus appears in half-tones, but without fully implicating the Danish authorities.[14]

The other major attempt at national collaboration was by Field-Marshal Pétain's regime in France. The methods and results obtained by the Vichy government seem very different from those of its Danish counterpart. France, of course, represented a higher stake for Germany than did small Denmark. Berlin had good reason for acting more intransigently toward the French. But even considering this, the tactics used by both these countries toward the occupier seem different: their spirit of collaboration was not the same.

After their lightning victory in May and June 1940, the Germans imposed severe conditions on France in a June 22 armistice enforced as of June 25. Hitler seemed to show clemency, by leaving a "legal" government with political autonomy in the southern part of the country; he probably wanted to get the war over with in the West and prevent the French fleet from reaching foreign ports. But, actually, the country was literally bound by the Führer's demands. In his mind, France did not need to be "polandized," for although the French were a "race of degenerates," they were not *Untermenschen*. Hitler preferred to score a major victory over France, prevent it from recovering militarily, and exploit it economically, but not exterminate its people. The armistice's Draconian clauses gave him several advantages toward this goal. Berlin took direct control of most of France's economic and industrial centers. France had to pay 400 million francs every day for the "upkeep costs of the occupation armies." Germany controlled 1,600,000 war prisoners—an excellent supply of hostages for future political haggling. The Reich also gave itself territorial wages. In August 1940, it annexed three departments in eastern France and set up a forbidden zone in the North, from a line that ran from the Somme to the Jura; this zone included an attached zone in the departments of Nord and Pas de Calais under the military administration of Brussels. As for the French government's particular role, Berlin expected limited but indispensable aid from it in terms of restarting the economy, administering civil affairs, and maintaining order. In this respect, article three of the armistice agreement, in which the word "collaborate" (*zusammenarbeiten*) appeared for the first time, is significant: "The French government will immediately invite all the authorities and administrative services of the occupied territory to conform with the rules of the German authorities and collaborate with them properly." That was already a lot. But the problem was that things went far beyond that. Vichy was more than a mere administration.

Indeed, out of concern for "realism," Field-Marshal Pétain, the symbol of France's military recovery during World War I who had been called to the head of the government by Paul Reynaud, the Council President, hoped to get France to collaborate politically with Germany. The latter was not at all impressed by Nazi ideology, but he judged that Germany had acquired a lasting advantage in Europe and that it logically had to win the war. It was sound politics and therefore sensible to try to get along with it. In this "new" Europe, France would be in a good position to become the Reich's most important partner. Its colonial and naval power, in particular, gave it useful cards to play. But France's moral and political reconstruction also had to be considered in order to rectify the errors committed under the Third Republic. According to Pétain, the country's moral and political recovery was indispensable and had to be based on the traditional values of authoritarian and conservative ideology. On July 10, 1940, he became a plenipotentiary, and the Third Republic was suspended. Then began the era of "national revolution" under the eyes of the Germans. French-style state collaboration was accompanied by a determination to regenerate domestically; one phenomenon cannot be understood without the other.

Hitler and Pétain's handshake in October 1940 symbolized this new era of Franco-German relations. On October 30, Pétain delivered a radio speech that created a sensation: "With honor and to maintain French unity, a unity of ten centuries, I step today onto the path of collaboration, to promote constructive activity of the new European order. . . . This policy is mine. . . . It is I alone whom History will judge."[15] With some variation, the successive governments of Vichy, the official seat of the new French state, worked toward this Franco-German rapprochement. When Admiral François-Xavier Darlan entered the administration in February 1941, France began the military collaboration and reinforced an already advanced economic collaboration. Much diplomatic activity was displayed in anticipation of a peace treaty with Germany, which would reserve a choice position for France in the new European empire. In June 1941, judicial and police collaboration began, with France accepting the creation of special sections to judge terrorists and all internal enemies. With Pierre Laval's return to power in April 1942, the Vichy government became a marionette in Berlin's hands, only to become a mere fiction after the Southern zone invasion in November 1942. Laval declared himself in favor of Germany's victory over Bolshevism; his team remained determined to fulfill the increasingly severe demands of the occupying forces. France became active in the hunt for Jews, organized the transfer of several hundreds of thousands of workers to Germany, and reinforced the methods of economic and industrial collaboration.

After the war, some French citizens argued that even if the Vichy leaders' politics were not free from error, their choice to remain in power was fundamentally good for French interests. Maintaining a government that tried to negotiate with the occupier was the only way to avoid a still worse fate—for example, the "polandization" of France. The French often called Pétain's France a shield, while Charles de Gaulle was France's sword. But more than 40 years after these events, this argument does not hold up to historical investigation. Far away from French infighting, Robert Paxton, an American researcher, wrote a study that has influenced knowledge of the records considerably.[16] While carefully searching the German archives, he drew up an overwhelming balance-sheet against Vichy.[17] Vichy fulfilled Hitler's expectations exactly, assuring the country's administrative management; German management would have been very difficult indeed, considering the complexity of French society. Vichy's repressive role (deportation of Jews, hunting for resisters, etc.) was important, since it saved Germany from getting directly involved in such activities for a long time. Vichy's economic performance was punishing for France. Paxton has shown how Vichy's politics, carried out by often brilliant technocrats, facilitated the exploitation of the country in all areas—industrial, agricultural, monetary—and made France the Reich's principal "milk cow" or food source. But the most serious element is that by remaining on duty and decreeing new laws under German protection, the French government committed an unpardonable error: it legitimized its country's occupation and made resisting the Germans illegitimate.

The originality of Paxton's work is his demonstration that, except during very brief periods, Hitler never asked for French collaboration on the political level.

Aside from Ambassador Otto Abetz's intrigues in Paris, the Germans had no particular interest in responding to the oft-repeated French offer. Vichy proposed its own services, going beyond German expectations, in the hope of winning political rewards that never materialized.

It is interesting to compare state collaboration in France and Denmark. While the Copenhagen government appeared to be on the defensive, making concessions only when it felt its back was to the wall, the Vichy government's strategy was offensive. When General Maxime Weygand declared, "Armistice, nothing but armistice," his attitude was comparable to the Danish government's position, which might be summarized as "The memorandum, nothing but the memorandum." Later, Laval moved in a very different direction: to earn himself a good position in the New Europe, he thought it necessary to forge ahead, make proposals, and take initiatives to show his good faith and loyalty.

The former reasoning—defensive—for national collaboration tends to immobilize the relationship between the occupier and the occupied from the outset. It is static, like a battle in a fortified camp. The second reasoning—offensive—tends instead to transform that relationship. It induces a dynamic of forward flight. A vicious cycle ensues: the more the occupier advances, the more the occupied slips away and eventually becomes trapped in the occupier's net, almost suffocating. This is the occupier's second victory: after his military success, he alienates the occupied population politically.

Once launched, this aspiring reasoning is hard to escape. In Vichy's case, however, it could have been broken, or at least restrained, if Vichy had really tried to defend French interests. One can indeed imagine that the country's leaders in such a situation might finally become aware of their errors and decide to turn back. But unlike its Danish counterpart, Vichy was not a national union government but rather the government of a political class seeking revenge against the Popular Front, a class that easily said: "Better Hitler than the Popular Front." Thanks to the occupation, they intended to settle accounts with their "internal enemy." Vichy initially led a "Franco-French war." Instead of presenting itself to the occupier as united, France displayed its internal divisions, which were those of its prewar political conflicts dating back to the Dreyfus affair.[18] The patriotic conflict with Germany was thus accompanied by an internal confrontation resembling a civil war. The Vichy regime, under the cover of defending the nation's vital interests against a foreign power, was actually a means of finally putting an end to democracy and installing an authoritarian regime.

This circumstance inspires two final reflections. First, one can discuss the advantages or inconveniences of a national collaboration strategy. By its nature, such a strategy implies a constant game of bitter negotiations that demands strong cohesion from the occupied population. It can claim whatever efficacy it may have only if the country is profoundly unified behind a national union government. In the alternative case, national collaboration is a form of political suicide, because the occupying power can gain advantages from the divisions within the occupied population. This is why the Danish government's position can be justified in the eyes of history and in terms of the interests of its country, whereas the French government's position cannot be justified.

The second observation has to do with the nature of the relationship between occupier and occupied. The extent of collaboration did not necessarily cause Berlin's internal presence or external pressure to trigger traditional nationalist resistance reflexes against the intrusion of foreign powers. In this sense, France's case is not unusual. The prewar governments of the three secondary Axis allies— Romania, Hungary, and Bulgaria—had already drawn much nearer to Germany. Except at the very end in Hungary, it was useless to put local Nazis into power. In Greece, a series of prime ministers succeeded each other from 1941 to 1944; they, like Laval, persuaded themselves that they were lessening the rigors of the occupation. As for little Serbia, led by General Nedić, it was a pale copy of Vichy France. Nedić's well-intentioned patriotism offered no more than a mediocre guarantee in the face of German demands. Most European leaders calculated, no doubt out of a sense of realism, that it was better to get along with the most powerful state on the continent. But it is also true that the Nazi regime's accession to power in 1933 had inspired admiration here and there and that, consequently, Germany's expansionist designs did not meet with universal disfavor. Without having out-and-out collaborators, Hitler did have friends. This is why Nazi domination in Europe was so unusual. Often it was not a case of the "bad" occupiers on one side and "good" occupied populations on the other. Their relationship was always complex and ambiguous—certainly not Manichean. Starting from that point, how can we be surprised that the resistance was so weak, at least at first?

NOTES

1. Otto Dietrich, *Die Philosophischen Grund Pagen des National—Sozialismus—Ein Ruf zu der Waffer Deutschen Geistes* (*The Spiritual Foundations of the New Europe*) (Breslaw, Hirt, 1934) 26.

2. Cited in Pascal Ory, *La France allemande* (Paris, 1977) 97-98.

3. During the last few years, a debate has developed among historians in Germany over the "verifiable nature" of the Nazi regime and the uniqueness of the Holocaust. See *Devant l'histoire: Les documents dans la controverse sur la singularité de l'extermination des juifs par le régime Nazi*, éditions du cerf (Paris, 1988).

4. Gordon Wright, *Europe at War (1939-1945)* (Paris, 1977).

5. Arnold Toynbee, *Hitler's Europe* (London, 1954).

6. Quoted in Alexander Dallin, *German Rule in Russia (1941-1945)* (London, 1957) 279.

7. Cited in Wright, *Europe* 113.

8. The word was coined by the jurist Raphael Lemkin. One of his first articles on this subject was "Le génocide," *Revue internationale de droit pénal* 10 (1946).

9. Stanley Hoffmann, "Vichy et la collaboration," *Preuves* (July-September, 1969).

10. For a general overview of collaboration in different countries, see Henry Rousso, *La Collaboration, les noms, les thèmes, les lieux* (Paris, 1987).

11. On the topic of collaborative movements, consult the Stein Ulgelvick Lansen, ed., *Who Were the Fascists?* (Bergen, 1981), an excellent collection.

12. Cited by Jorgen Haestrup, *Le Mouvement de la résistance danoise (1939–1945)* (Copenhagen, 1970) 5.

13. Moller became president of the Liberation Council, which was organized in London in September 1943.

14. See Erich Thomsen, *Deutsche Besatzungspolitik in Danemark (1940–1945)* (Dusseldorf, 1971); Richard Petrow, *The Bitter Years: The Invasion and Occupation of Denmark and Norway (April 1940–May 1945)* (New York, 1974).

15. Cited in Jean-Pierre Azéma, *De Munich à la Libération* (Paris, 1979) 110.

16. Robert O. Paxton, *Vichy France: Old Guard and New Order (1940–1944)* (New York, 1982).

17. One should also see the earlier works of Eberhard Jackel, *La France dans l'Europe de Hitler* (Paris, 1968); Henri Michel, *Vichy, année 1940* (Paris, 1966).

18. Consult the interesting study "Les guerres franco-françaises," *Vingtième Siècle* 5, (March 1985).

Chapter 2

Which Resistance?

Resistance against Nazism has become one of the modern archetypes of liberating violence. This is one of the founding myths of European societies. It embodies the legitimate recourse to armed force for a just cause—the struggle for democracy. The leaders of such movements are depicted as adventurous heroes and defiant warriors living in the shadows of an unacceptable tyranny. We cultivate their memory and use it as an example for younger generations. A kind of mythology has been created around resistance heroes, and movies and literature have helped to maintain it. Jean-Pierre Azéma has described it aptly: "Collective memory generally upholds a jumbled image of the resistance fighter as the combination of a secret agent, a lover of justice, and a machine gun-toting outlaw who resembles Western stars and knights in shining armor blowing up countless factories and trains. There have been many astonishing, even incredible, episodes, of course, but they were the exception."[1]

Armed combat was indeed one of the main characteristics of the European resistance to Nazism, and we do not mean to challenge the bravery of the groups and movements involved. It is depicted today, however, in a simplistic way, verging on caricature. Researchers often deplore the gap between the complexity of reality, whose multiple facets they are determined to describe, and the impressions or traces of reality remaining in the collective memory.

Historians are familiar with reconstructing historical facts. Beyond the facts are the ideas we make of them and the ways we talk or write about them. Many factors, especially political ones, lead to the distortion of facts. The manner in which history is written is of primary importance. Leaders justify the authority that they intend to keep by the way they describe their past conduct. By becoming the "good guys," they encourage their people to be eternally grateful for what they have done for them. Some writing on the history of the Resistance does not escape this tendency. Regarding France, Henri Michel has enumerated four political readings: the Gaullist one, the Communist one, the one emphasizing the first stages of internal resistance, and the one emphasizing the soldiers of the Armistice army.[2] In the East, they sing of "the masses' glorious struggle against Fascist tyranny." In the West, they celebrate "the surge of national unity in defense of our endangered country." Official history, with its oversights and the vocabulary used to recount it, varies according to regimes and eras. It reflects a community's present state of mind with respect to its past more than what really happened.

Although the elements making up collective memory may vary, one theme remains permanent: the role of violence. All communities need founding myths, and these are generally associated with images of redemptive violence, that is, violence perceived to be necessary.[3] The "resistance" mythology is based entirely on this idea. European countries no doubt want to be convinced that they were able to liberate themselves on their own from the horror into which they had sunk. Europe has certainly not finished settling its accounts with its past, especially with the genocide. We cannot consider the nations of Europe to be all the same. Nazism may have developed in Germany first, but Hitler's ideology stirred many minds throughout Europe. This painful past does not belong to Germany alone; it belongs to Europe in general. It is vital for the European peoples to maintain the image of their national unity and their recovery, both of which are exemplified in the image of a liberating violence springing from within them to destroy the evil that had been afflicting them. The "resistance" embodies the myth of rebirth by violence. All myths reconstruct reality. In this case, it is a way of recounting history to ask its forgiveness.

This is obviously only one interpretation among many of the collective memory of this tragic period in European history. But who can say that this common memory affects only the souls of peoples and not the souls of professional historians as well? Although historians try to keep from making value judgments in order to grasp facts more accurately, they also work with the spirit of their era and its view of the world. "Violence is the driving force of history," according to popular wisdom. True or false, this conclusion often leads us to study armed forms of opposition at the expense of civilian forms. Indeed, historians may be spontaneously attracted by what was "spectacular," what was seen, what made noise—in short, by what left an impression.

Even though civilian forms of resistance can sometimes have noticeable aspects, they often tend to be more discreet and harder to grasp. But are they not sometimes a more authentic expression of a community's profound state of mind? This raises the fascinating question of the visibility of historical facts and the role that history must play in interpreting them. Precisely because armed actions are often spectacular, historians may tend to pay more attention to them than to more discreet—because unarmed—actions.

WHICH HISTORY OF THE RESISTANCE?

In reality, the resistance is a very complex phenomenon that does not tolerate rigid categories. Whoever explores the subject soon realizes that *the* resistance is a misnomer; internal opposition varied in different countries and regions. An examination of the literature reveals three successive stages toward understanding the phenomenon that are like three modes of interpreting it.

The first shows the resistance as an important support for the Allied powers up until the final military victory. This resistance is understood as a contributing force in the broader context of the whole war. We are thus most interested in resistance activities directly related to the war goals. Unarmed demonstrations are therefore interpreted as subversive actions or psychological warfare. The objects of study are intelligence networks, parachuting and sabotage operations conceived in close connection with military staffs, the organization and actions of underground groups, and the contribution of underground "armies" in the final phase of the war in Europe. Writers try to show, for example, that these forms of resistance were effective because of the high quality of the intelligence given to military leaders or because the sabotage organized by resistance groups familiar with particular areas was often more effective than inaccurate air raids.

The second line of interpretation emphasizes the political significance of the formation of internal resistance rather than the development of armed resistance. It points out that the goal of resistance movements was to embody the legitimacy of a power other than that of the occupier and its collaborators. Its special subject is the political construction of resistance or what some call "institutional resistance." By studying the behavior of political parties, the role of national personalities in exile, and the development of resistance movements that represent the growing hostility of public opinion toward the occupier, this research seeks to show how this legitimacy was formed and played an essential role during the Liberation by reconstructing the state apparatus.

The third approach focuses on the moral and spiritual aspects of resistance. Unlike the other interpretations, it is less concerned with military or political dimension. It explores how men and women, in the name of their beliefs and ideals, were able to find the courage to resist tyranny, in spite of knowing that they were a minority. It stresses the intellectual and religious expressions of the spirit of resistance and the different manifestations of solidarity with people persecuted by the Nazi regime. This approach is determined to show that, even during the darkest hours of the "brown plague," people tried to live with values different from those imposed on them and that, by that very effort, they prove the indomitability of the human spirit.

Each of these briefly presented approaches to the resistance offers a limited grasp of the complex phenomenon called resistance. They seem to be somewhat complementary. They can also fit into a broader framework of analysis that may result in a dynamic vision of resistance*s*, in the plural. This framework would derive from analyzing the evolution of the *social shifts* through which resistance movements are born, developed, and structured. Indeed, whatever a movement's goal, whether military, political, or moral, the movement could not develop and maintain itself in the face of the denunciations and betrayals without some assistance from its social environment. We all recognize, for example, that the emergence of the *maquis* phenomenon in France cannot be interpreted without taking into account how opinion evolved after the summer of 1943. General Jacques Bollardière, a young military leader who had parachuted in to lead the *maquis* in the Ardennes region, liked to recall that draft resisters living in the woods and mountains depended entirely on the support that civilian populations were willing to give them.[4] Consequently, what should we emphasize? The armed aspect of the *maquis*, whose military effectiveness has been debated, or changes in the state of popular opinion, which had grown so exasperated by the occupier's pressures that many French young people finally resorted to civilian resistance, thanks to well-meaning assistance and support?

Thus emerges a fourth line of interpretation: Instead of analyzing resistance movements in and of themselves, this interpretation analyzes them in relation to the psychological and sociological contexts from which they emerge and which make their development possible. These movements are perceived as the clandestinely structured expression of an opinion that cannot express itself publicly. This line of research is evident in several recent works, such as Roderick Kedward's study[5], that are devoted to analyzing the motivations and behaviors of resisters and nonresisters during a given period. Works by French researchers like Étienne Dejonghe on the Nord department[6] and Pierre Laborie on the Lot department[7] focus on the evolution of opinion. In the introduction to his remarkable study, Laborie has stated explicitly that his study emerged from a "concern for an overall vision: the study of opinion assumes a global approach to history and intentionally overlooks the obvious, spectacular aspect of some leaders' actions in order to emphasize the population's state of mind."[8]

Although German resistance to the Nazi regime was very different from resistance to occupation, it is interesting to emphasize that new research on the occupation is also under way there. Klaus Jurgen Müller has distinguished three phases of German historiography.[9] The first, during the 1950s, was devoted to studying the forms of moral resistance, like that of the young Munich students from "The White Rose."[10] In the 1960s, historians leaned more toward efforts at military resistance, especially the different assassination attempts against Hitler; Peter Hoffmann's book is a good example of these works.[11] After this, many important studies appeared on the communists, the social democrats, and various layers of the population. These showed that the German concept of resistance, *Widerstand*, was rather limiting and should have been conceived in the much broader sense of *Resistenz*. The idea is that it is no longer appropriate to analyze partial forms of opposition—moral, political, military, or others—but instead to study the way that the whole social body—civilian society—reacts against aggression.

Thus, the Institute of Contemporary History of Munich became involved in 1973 in a vast research program aimed at studying the different expressions of resistance of the Bavarian population, whether at the individual, group, or mass level.[12] As Müller has pointed out, with such a line of interpretation, "it is possible to reach a broader view of attitudes: direct actions like strikes or illegal agitation, tract printing and distribution, or even civilian disobedience under different and varied forms, the refusal to collaborate, and efforts to preserve the coherence of communities of opinion."[13]

In short, to borrow an analogy from biology, one could say that civil society here resembles a living cell. One can observe the evolution of its defense mechanisms according to the nature of the aggression, whether internal or external. If a cell is the victim of an internal disorder, will it know how to reestablish its self-regulating mechanisms on its own? If a foreign body penetrates it, will it know how to produce antibodies able to digest or expel it? To answer these questions, it is important to study the behavior of each party, each function of the cell that is faced with aggression, and to learn whether it had immune mechanisms against the aggression ready at the outset.

THE FIELD OF CIVILIAN RESISTANCE

Continuing with this global approach, I propose the concept of civilian resistance to designate the phenomena of collective opposition that will be analyzed in this study. Although not often used, the term is not entirely new. The historian Jorgen Haestrup used it, although he was more likely to use the terms "passive resistance" and "civil disobedience."[14] The French historian François Bédarida also used it, distinguishing between civilian resistance and armed resistance.[15] I would like to introduce the concept of civilian resistance to denote the civil society's spontaneous process of struggle, by unarmed means, against the aggression of which it is victim. This general definition calls for an explanation of the nature of the *actors*, the *means, and* the *goals* of civilian resistance.

First of all, however, why do we use the word resistance? Some definitions of this word are too broad and therefore weaken its meaning. The term "resistance" refers to acts through which a determination to refuse is expressed collectively. To resist is first to find the strength to say "NO" without necessarily having a clear idea of what one wants. The act of resistance is characterized by the determination not to give in to the will of the aggressor. It is based on a radical attitude of noncooperation and confrontation with the adversary. If the resistance starts out as a clean break, we must add that it becomes one only when this refusal is expressed collectively. In the context of purely individual action, the concepts of dissidence or disobedience seem more adequate.

We should also emphasize the basic difference between resistance and defense. Whereas preparation is the essence of defense, this is not the case with resistance. By definition, the concept of resistance implies dynamic phenomena that occur progressively in reaction to an unforeseen situation. Improvisation and creativity thus always play a large role in the idea of resistance. Resistance implies adapting to the present, whereas defense implies anticipating the future. This does not mean, obviously, that a defense policy is devoid of imagination or principle. But it does imply that resistance is always reactive to an immediate situation, whereas defense is preventative of an anticipated situation.[16] The result is that resistance is characterized by its flexibility and its relative fragility, whereas defense is characterized by a certain rigidity of response that should also be accompanied by greater security.

The term "civilian" defines the nature of the actors of this particular form of resistance. It describes the civil society's capacity to resist by itself, whether by the struggle of its principal institutions or by the mobilization of its populations, or by both simultaneously. Civilian resistance is distinguished here from military combat just as a civilian institution is from a military institution. This does not mean that soldiers are "outside" society, for they are clearly part of it. This approach simply leads us to specify that civilian resistance and military combat are based on very different systems. Civil society may find itself forced to resist on its own precisely because soldiers have failed to fulfill their job—preventing and repulsing the assault of enemy armies.

Civilian resistance generally derives from both institutions and the masses. Institutional resistance applies to the specific action of the institutions that structure society as representatives of the *legitimate political power* (government and its administration) and as representatives of various *interest groups* and *currents of opinion* (parties, churches, unions, and associations). Popular resistance includes the spontaneous mobilization of populations at the grass-roots level, expressed through strikes, demonstrations, civil disobedience actions, and so forth. Institutional and popular resistance provide indispensable support for each other. In the best of all possible cases, this popular dimension of civilian resistance happens when society's legitimate institutions encourage struggle. For various reasons, however, this determination to act can be weak at the institutional level. In such a situation, civilian resistance can arise only from slow, deliberate work at the grass-roots level, aiming to organize groups and populations determined to resist. In the different historical situations studied here, we will find either one *and* the other of these dimensions, or one or the other. But theoretically, one can say that the complete picture of civilian resistance amounts to a dialectical mobilization of society from the top and the bottom in a strategy of noncooperation.

One may wonder about the utility of resorting to a new concept to designate phenomena that have sometimes been described expressions such as "psychological warfare" or "passive resistance." I believe neither one of these is appropriate. The first term is clearly conceived as a support for war that aims to hasten its success by persuasive, often dishonest, action against enemy populations and troops. The very words "psychological *warfare*" denies whatever nonmilitary elements an action may have that are not related to the rationale of armed struggle. As for the concept of "passive resistance," its meaning is too negative. The term is not completely misleading, since noncooperation consists first and foremost of withdrawing one's participation from the functioning of the aggressor's system. This voluntary withdrawal may cause inertia, but it generally requires a very active and risky attitude. Under the Nazi occupation, refusing to collaborate was not an act that could be called passive! Strikes were often met by deportation measures or even executions.

In the framework of Nazi occupation, the concept of civilian resistance is not without ambiguities, especially when one thinks about its means. One source of confusion may come from the fact that populations that were occupied between 1939 and 1945 did express their resistance by resorting to arms. The extent and intensity of armed forms of internal opposition varied, of course, with different areas and countries. It is nonetheless true that the recourse to weapons by civilian populations did constitute one of the major forms of the resistance struggle, one of the characteristic features of World War II. The concept of civilian resistance does not pertain to forms of action in which civilians take up arms. Civilian resistance denotes all kinds of opposition to the occupier and/or collaborators that are practiced without weapons; these include economic, legal, academic, religious, medical, and other forms of resistance. If the expression hardly ever appears as such during the Nazi occupation of Europe, certain elements directly or indirectly suggest its importance. In France, one of the first resistance movements in the occupied zone was called the Civilian and Military Organization (CMO). In Poland, where the word "resistance" was never used, the idea appeared a little more clearly through the creation of a board of civilian resistance (*Obrona Cyvilna*) that included underground activities by the press, teachers, and the legal corps. In Norway, resistance was divided into two branches: the military (*Milorg*) and the civil (*Sivorg*). After the war, Belgium recognized, in a somewhat limited way, the status of "civilian resister" for those who had had responsibilities in the underground press.[17]

Conceptually, these historic references allow us to identify civilian resistance as a movement using unarmed measures, as opposed to a movement based on armed measures (the French *maquis* or the Yugoslavian guerrillas, for example). We must not forget that, in reality, European resistance to Nazism very often overlapped with different forms of military or paramilitary actions. Without overemphasizing the paradox, the similarities between civilian and guerilla resistances are stronger than the differences. Both of them come from actions by civilian populations and belong to the ill-defined domain called "indirect strategies."[18] From this perspective, various authors have been able to show that the civilian resistance of occupied Europe was actually complementary to armed struggle. The creation of an underground newspaper served as a base on which to build a resistance movement, which then developed an armed branch. It thus seems artificial to separate one or another form of resistance from the context of its gestation. Furthermore, the relationships between the occupier and the occupied hardened with time and the progressing war; the radicalizing conflict made resistance evolve toward ever more violent means of expression.[19] In this perspective, some authors have depicted civilian resistance as so complementary that they hardly mention it at all or include it only peripherally in the context of armed struggle. Michel, for example, has depicted armed resisters as modern "knights" served by unarmed "pages."[20]

But civilian resistance is not always a simple complement to armed struggle. To respect the complexity of the facts, we must distinguish two fundamental forms of civilian resistance, based on the different nature of their objectives. The first form consists of resorting to unarmed measures to encourage or strengthen armed combat. This category includes the role of civilians in intelligence gathering for the military, as well as helping the *maquis*, supporting railroad strikes to slow down the advancing of enemy forces, and so on. On the whole, this kind of civilian resistance, integrated or combined with military or paramilitary combat, served *war goals*. This kind of activity seems worthy of study in its own right, since its role has not been sufficiently emphasized. Some studies, like the ones already mentioned, are finally getting around to it.

The second type of resistance refers to social mobilization and noncooperation to defend *civilian goals*. It develops outside of all military logic and appears somewhat autonomous. Its ultimate goal is not to destroy or paralyze enemy troops, but rather to maintain the integrity of civil society, the cohesion of society's social groups, the defense of basic freedoms, and respect for individual rights and for social and political attainments. This second category can include actions by diverse political or legal bodies aiming to assert their legitimacy, in spite of the presence of the occupying power, and by churches, unions, and professional organizations challenging the authorities in different ways. More generally, it includes populations trying to organize themselves locally in order to bring assistance to persecuted individuals. This second form of *autonomous* civilian resistance resembles what is commonly called nonviolent resistance. This latter term is not adequate, however, because this form of resistance has often been chosen for lack of a better alternative (that is, chosen for lack of weapons, which remained the ultimate and principal goal of most people fighting the German order). At the same time, the situation of being weaponless created conditions encouraging unarmed methods of action. These were sometimes very original and were able, in some circumstances, to defy the occupier and the collaborators. This autonomous civilian resistance includes spontaneous and pragmatic practices but does not reject violence as a strategic principle. It is by necessity that civilian resistance does not resort to physical violence and practices noncooperation. This book is dedicated to that resistance alone.[21]

NOTES

1. Jean-Pierre Azéma, *De Munich à la Libération (1938–1944)* (Paris, 1979) 169.

2. Henri Michel, *Bibliographie critique de la Résistance* (Paris, 1964).

3. Following this approach, Henry Rousso has analyzed the different ways in which the French were "sovereign" under the Vichy government. Henry Rousso, *Le Syndrome de Vichy (1944–1987)* (Paris, 1987).

4. See Jacques de Bollardière, *Bataille d'Alger, bataille de l'homme* (Paris, 1972), for a lively account of this and other stages of his military career. Also see the recent work of Jean Toulat, *Un combat pour l'homme: Le général de Bollardière* (Paris, 1987).

5. Roderick Kedward, *Resistance in Vichy France: A Study of Ideas and Motivations in the Southern Zone (1940–1941)* (Oxford, 1978).

6. Étienne Dejonghe, "Le Nord isolé: Occupation et opinion (mai 1940–mai 1942)," *Revue d'histoire moderne et contemporaine* (January–March, 1979).

7. Pierre Laborie, *Résistants, Vichyssois et autres: L'évolution de l'opinion et des comportements dans le département du Lot entre 1939 et 1944* (Paris, 1980).

8. Laborie, *Résistants* 2.

9. Klaus Jurgen Müller, "La résistance allemande au régime nazi: Historiographie en République fédérale," *Vingtième Siècle* 109 (July–August 1986) 91–106.

10. Inge Scholl, *The White Rose: Munich, 1942–1943*, 2nd edition. (Middletown, CT, 1983).

11. Peter Hoffmann, *German Resistance to Hitler* (Paris, 1984).

12. Martin Broszat, et al. *Bayern in Der NS-Zeit*, 6 volumes (Munich, 1977–1983).

13. Müeller, *La résistance* 100.

14. Jorgan Haestrup, *European Resistance Movements (1939–1945): A Complete History* (Westport, CT, 1981). "Passive resistance" and "civil disobedience" are the titles of sections of this work.

15. François Bédarida, "Résistance au fascisme, au nazisme et au militarisme japonais jusqu'en 1945," *Communication au 16ᵉ Congrès international des sciences historiques* (IHTP document) (Stuttgart, 1985) 22–23.

16. Hence the central concept of dissuasion: the capability of a defense system to prevent aggression determines its dissuasive value.

17. The decree of January 31,1948, promulgated "civil resister" status.

18. On this subject, one should see Anders Boserup and Andre Mack, *War without Weapons: Nonviolence in National Defense* (New York, 1974) chapter 4 ("The Analogy with Guerrilla Warfare"), 68–81.

19. This concept of a "civil resistance" that complements outright armed conflict is the topic of numerous works: see, for example, Marcel Rubby, *Résistance civile et résistance militaire* (Lyon, 1984).

20. See, for example, Henri Michel, *Histoire de la Résistance en France* (Paris, 1980).

21. To understand more fully the selection of cases of civil resistance analyzed here, review the appendix "Elements of Methodology." Within the text, I will, for the sake of convenience, use the expression "civil resistance" to designate this autonomous approach.

Chapter 3

The Complexities of Noncooperation

There is pre-Stalingrad and post-Stalingrad resistance. This battle, the first major defeat of the German armies, in February 1943 introduced a fundamental change in peoples' thinking. Of course, it is difficult to understand either the resistance or the passivity of populations toward the Nazi occupier without considering the histories of social group mentalities and of the political balances and imbalances in prewar European societies. Likewise, it has been traditional to declare that the geography and level of development of the occupied countries strongly conditioned the forms of their internal resistances. For example, guerrilla warfare was especially developed in mountainous regions, whereas civilian resistance was more common in major urban and industrial zones. As a result, we will tend to discuss the countries of Western and Scandinavian Europe a good deal and the Balkan countries very little.

But what made the European resistance so dynamic and determined its general evolutionary frame were the vicissitudes of the military conflict. Before 1943, realism was not on the side of those who opposed Hitler. Europe seemed to have become German for a long time to come. The future seemed Nazi. To resist was thus to wish to reestablish the old order with prewar values. The general dynamic of the resistance was thus of self-preservation. It started with rejection. Resisting meant, first of all, not submitting.

In the spring of 1943, however, the hope of ending Nazism finally became real. The military power struggle on the battlefield changed. The Soviet Union's entrance into the war with England and then the United States had of course been a decisive turning point in 1941. From that time on, the most lucid French thinkers predicted the Allies' final victory, since their accumulated economic potential surpassed that of Germany, Italy, and Japan. Still, this hope awaited proof. In 1942, the battle of El Alamein, followed by the Allies' reconquest of North Africa (November 8) showed that Germany was no longer invincible on the battlefield.

It was really the defeat of General Friedrich Paulus before Stalingrad which evoked the Napoleonic armies' downfall in Russia and led to a change in attitude toward Germany and its collaborators. Germany had just lost a decisive battle on European ground where it had reigned supreme for three years. Besides, people were starting to hope for an opening of a second front in the West; some were already waiting for the British-American landing of the summer of 1943. This shows how much the nature of internal opposition had changed qualitatively by this time. The general dynamic of the resistance then became one of liberation. The organization of clandestine structures was in the process of completion. From then on, it was a question of preparing the final victory. In most French minds at the time, this liberation resembled the popular insurrections of past centuries. The resistance leaders had requested arms from the Allies and, from 1943 on, felt the necessity to possess more and more of them. They intended to be in the right political position to play an active role in society's reorganization after the war. The resistance movements also tended to become increasingly radical, both through military combat and in struggles for power in competing groups, struggles in which each group tried to win lasting political approval.

The choice to study only autonomous forms of civilian resistance (i.e., those not overlapping with armed struggle) orients our research toward the period preceding Stalingrad. That is when the occupied countries were still rather weakly organized and not yet totally integrated into military plans. Does this mean that resistance efforts during this period were insignificant and that collaboration with the occupier was massive everywhere? Reality was too complex to divide it simply into these two categories. Let us remember some basic information on this subject.

THE COMPLEXITY OF BEHAVIORS TOWARD
THE OCCUPYING FORCES

The more one studies the files on resistance to Nazism, the more one discovers that the facts are astonishingly complex and bear no relation to the simplifying visions of ideological interpretation inherited from the recent past. First of all, despite the impressive speed with which Germany conquered Europe, to the point where its domination seemed irreversible, one cannot say that the majority of the conquered peoples spontaneously collaborated with Hitler. It is not because the European people were beaten militarily that they were willing to espouse the Nazi cause and to mobilize for the success of Nazi goals.

It is important to distinguish *collaboration*, whose principal political forms we have just described, from different attitudes of *accommodation* to a radically new and totally unexpected situation. When the shock of military defeat and occupation was over, life had to start over again. The occupied societies were absolutely unprepared to go through such an experience. There was thus a necessary adaptation time, more or less long and painful according to the nature of the new political situation. It was necessary to simply try to survive. Situations in which disintegration is followed by social restructuring often give rise to the development of opportunistic behavior. *A posteriori*, one can judge them with contempt, but they can be understandable when considered in context. As Stanley Hoffmann has observed, "Self-preservation is not the noblest of goals, but it is the most elementary."[1] Governments had to function minimally to ensure the management of civilian affairs and the restarting of economic activity to feed the people. These manifestations of elementary behavior, which form the basis of individual and collective life, should not be confused with those inspired by the spirit of collaboration. Of course, there may be some overlapping here, and it is actually the occupier's role to maximize it. Because of the English blockade and the diversion of most economic activity for the benefit of the Reich, it became more and more difficult to make an enterprise function without in some way serving German interests. But it is one thing to be constrained to such an attitude and another to encourage it voluntarily.

With the outcome of the war remaining uncertain, a majority chose to wait rather than to choose one camp over another. This "waitism" was often criticized because it indicated a lack of political courage. But how could the situation be otherwise? Many countries plundered by Germany were plunged into an economy of scarcity, and many people had to spend much of their time searching for basic food supplies. This physical and psychological exhaustion hardly encouraged the development of a resistance spirit. In the beginning of the occupation, the opening of a parallel economic market—the "black market"—made individual resourcefulness predominant over the almost nonexistent collective resistance spirit in most countries. In addition, most European populations did not have recent experience with foreign occupation. There were some exceptions, including Poland, which had known all kinds during the eighteenth and nineteenth centuries, as well as Belgium and northern France, which had been occupied by Germany in 1914.

Will power is not enough to resist, however, one also has to know how. In this regard, European societies had hardly any resistance knowledge to draw on. Nothing before the war had prepared them for such hardship. They were in this sense defenseless, as if naked before the enemy. Which is why their "waitism" can be justly interpreted as a collective reflex developed out of the most elementary caution. Whoever finds himself in a dangerous situation that he has not learned to confront on his own thinks it better to wait for help from the outside in order to stay alive.

In fact, to confront the situation and to stand up to the occupier, it was necessary to create new rules—adopt new behaviors, work out new social practices, and establish new institutions that could be adapted to the situation. Not all populations started from scratch or in the same conditions. But resistance was an innovation for all of them. It encouraged the most diverse individual and collective behaviors. One can thus speak of the creativity of resistance movements.

For the sake of clarity, it is appropriate to distinguish here between *resistance* and *dissidence*. Indeed, what is conventionally called resistance is often only the advanced phase of an internal social or political opposition that has managed to become organized and plan its goals. But beyond or concurrent with this process were all kinds of attitudes, behaviors, and even actions that mark a spirit of independence, of dissidence, regarding the new regime. Listening discreetly to foreign radio programs within the privacy of one's home, first from London, later from Moscow or Brazzaville, was the prototypical act in this quest for autonomy, which began with the search for different, unofficial information. Reading the clandestine press in secret, which was more dangerous because it left traces, stemmed from the same desire. These signs of dissidence were expressed publicly through codes of signs and symbols. For example, the way a person dressed or carried an object, which in part expressed his or her personality, also became a deliberate sign of support for political nonconformity. Thus, the French wore blue, white, and red clothing on national holidays, and the Dutch wore white carnations in their buttonholes as a sign of their attachment to the Crown. Norwegians wore staples inside their jackets as a sign of their resistance. Beyond national differences, the letter "V" for victory appeared all over Europe; proposed by a Belgian minister in 1941 as a common symbol of the desire for resistance, it was popularized over the BBC air waves. Different cultural signs thus progressively made up a language of distinction, a way of saying "no" to the values of the occupier and his collaborators and of maintaining a certain loyalty toward themselves.

This determination likewise manifested itself in the search for an attitude of distance and restraint toward the occupier. It is fascinating that in several places in Europe and in varying cultures, different texts of "instructions" to the occupied populations, written by unknown authors, appeared spontaneously. In France, one tract gave "Advice to the Occupied" that was sometimes naive and tinged with humor:

They are the victors. Behave properly toward them. But don't go beyond their desires in order to make yourself look good. Avoid haste. In any case, they will show you no gratitude. You don't know their language or you have forgotten it. If one of them speaks a German word to you, make a sign of powerlessness and, without remorse, go about your business.[2]

In Bulgaria, a Communist militant explained "How to Protect Oneself From the Enemy" in Marxist phraseology. He offered all who wished to resist instructions for security and prudence, often inspired by common sense: "Observe iron discipline. Be prudent when you speak of political problems in a milieu you don't know. . . . Don't keep illegal material at your home. . . . Don't take any unnecessary risks."[3]

"Ten Commandments from a Dane" gave not only good instructions for practicing the "cold shoulder" toward the occupier (*Den Skolden*) but also called with great terseness for acts of noncooperation:

1. You must not go to work in Germany or Norway.

2. You must do bad work for the Germans.
3. You must practice working in slow motion for the Germans.
4. You must destroy all the tools and machines that could be useful to the Germans.
5. You must try to destroy anything that can be profitable to the Germans.
6. You must delay all transports to Germany.
7. You must boycott German and Italian newspapers and films.
8. You must buy nothing from German shops.
9. You must behave with the traitors according to what they deserve.
10. You must protect whoever is pursued by the Germans.[4]

Such texts were often not read and did not have a great effect. They attest, nonetheless, to the desire of certain members of an occupied community to try, despite and even because of a lack of earlier references, to define a line of conduct valid for daily life and applicable for all, so that each person would compromise himself as little as possible with the occupier.

Thus, among the various kinds of voluntary or forced collaboration, accommodation behavior, forms of dissidence, and expressions of real resistance, one can discern a whole continuum of behavior of the occupied toward the occupier. In other words, an occupied society can generally be described by two antagonistic poles—the two minorities of declared collaborationists on one side and full-time resisters on the other. Between these two poles, there is a large range of behavior with complex and sometimes contradictory meanings. A people's general behavior under the yoke of a foreign power seems to be a result of simultaneous adaptation and rejection behavior toward the occupier.

From this perspective, certain historians of the Nazi period have maintained that the ambiguity of occupation situations often led to a joint practice of collaboration and resistance by the same individual or within one community.[5] For example, many "legal underground workers," that is, people participating in a resistance movement while keeping the official cover of their jobs, could collaborate a minimal amount of time during the day, because of their work, but still resist at night. The case of civil servants "working" for a resistance movement is particularly interesting in this respect.[6] They proved highly useful in the resistance struggle, for example, concocting "real-false" identification papers and food cards and warning people of imminent arrest or raids. Because of their jobs, however, these civil servants, who took considerable risks, could be implicated against their will in operations serving the occupier's goals, operations that they were nonetheless forced to carry out if they wanted to escape detection and keep their jobs. In fact, it was in the interest of the resistance itself that they be only minimally involved in collaboration.

In such situations, the boundaries between collaboration and resistance seem to blur. The main question is therefore in what state of mind and for what goals could one collaborate, given that tactical collaboration could in reality be a form of resistance. Everything depends, of course, on what is meant by "collaboration," and it is inappropriate to push the paradox too far, for it would risk legitimizing the actions of actual collaborators who claimed resistance motives. But it remains true that, in certain cases, various manifestations of limited noncooperation behavior—individual or collective—could have developed in a context of voluntary or forced collaboration.

On the institutional level, Denmark provides one of the best examples. The compromise politics of the Danish government sought to delay or thwart the application of certain German demands. Civil servants tried to obstruct or delay German orders with varying degrees of success. In January 1941, Berlin asked the Danish government to put eight torpedo boats at the disposition of the Reich's navy. The request was accompanied by the assurance that this "friendly gesture" would in no way affect Denmark's neutrality. Nonetheless, Denmark expressed its regret that it could not implement this action, since the request went against the agreement between the two countries. Indeed, in the April 9, 1940, memorandum, Germany had guaranteed that the Danish fleet would remain at the sole disposition of Denmark. Berlin responded to this unmistakably firm refusal by saying that its request had been misinterpreted: the Reich wanted the boats only for boat-schools and perhaps for patrolling the Baltic Sea, but in no way for military operations. Denmark did not change its position. The German ambassador in Copenhagen was then charged with requesting an audience with the king. Berlin was hoping for a final consent, and implied that, if none were forthcoming, Germany might interrupt its coal deliveries to Denmark. Christian X could only ask the German leaders for a written confirmation of what had become a kind of blackmail. Forced to agree to the Reich's demands, the Danes took care to disarm the boats while sheltering their artillery pieces, torpedo tubes, and precious navigation equipment. The ships were thus delivered but in a state that rendered them unserviceable.[7]

In isolation or with varying degrees of organization, many workers tried to slow down or sabotage production in factories producing for Germany. Although they felt they had to keep their jobs in order to earn a living, they knew that their labor power was furthering the Reich's war goals; they therefore were determined to lower the quality of their product and break the rhythm of the production process. What is commonly described as "passive resistance" (and should more appropriately be called "inertia force tactics") became increasingly widespread all over occupied Europe. In a work published in 1941, Jiri Hronek wrote about Czechoslovakia: "The wheels of industry are now turning very slowly in the factories and workrooms. This policy of slowed-down work has caused a considerable production reduction, just when Germany was trying to maintain the highest war production possible to keep up with the Allies."[8] Likewise, in the mining and industrial basin of northwestern Europe (France, Belgium, and Luxemburg), coal, iron, and steel production definitely seem to have been affected by this kind of procedure as of late 1940. From June 1941 on, European communist parties tried, through the unions under their control, to spread industrial sabotage techniques in the factories working for Germany. It is difficult to evaluate, however, how and to what extent these orders were applied by the workers. In a regional study devoted to Bergamo and its environs in northern Italy, Stefano Piziali has depicted the variety and ingenuity of these methods, which sometimes caused major problems for the occupier.[9]

These inertia force tactics were developed in all sorts of professional settings—factories, service companies (the railroad), administrations—and had thousands of variations. They ranged from "work *without* collaboration" (remaining at one's post while trying to do nothing that could aid the occupier) to the practice of "nonviolent sabotage" (removing an essential piece from a machine without destroying it), with "Schweikism" (the intentional misinterpretation of orders) in between.[10] These "soft" noncooperation techniques implied limited risks, which was not the case with strikes in which workers exposed themselves directly to repression. During the Nazi occupation, these techniques seem to have been put into effect only rarely in a concerted way. Rather, they were the result of isolated initiatives taken by individuals or small groups who wanted to "do something" within their work context when the work serving the cause of the occupier or its collaborators to varying degrees.

THE PROGRESSIVE RADICALIZATION OF RELATIONS BETWEEN THE OCCUPYING FORCES AND THE OCCUPIED POPULATION

The complexity of behavior of the occupied toward the occupier does not permit any simplification. It is impossible to divide all members of a society into two well-defined groups, one of collaborators and the other of resisters. At best, one can say that the conduct of each individual and social group had one dominating feature that determined its "camp" without this adherence being permanent.

But this variety of conduct must not make us forget the parallel existence of strong tendencies, whether sociological or political. Obviously, individual and institutional behaviors were integrated into a whole, into a social and political climate that varied with the country and the period of the war. In other words, although one can indeed observe mixtures of collaboration, accommodation, dissidence, and resistance in the behavior of various populations, one must also take into account the general state of opinion.

Time and events modified general opinion considerably. At the beginning of the war, opinion in many countries leaned more toward the side of accommodation with the new regime than toward a resistance that did not exist. By the end of the conflict, the general tendency was reversed: most occupied societies were hoping for liberation from the Nazism that had hurt them so much. Populations did not know what to expect at the beginning of their occupation; they could even hope for some improvements. By the end of four years of Nazi rule, however, they knew what they were dealing with. This shift of opinion provoked many transformations in individual and group behavior.

Actually, because of the reversal in the military power struggle and the ever-increasing German pressure on the occupied societies, there was a progressive radicalization of the relationship between the occupier and the occupied that forced each person to choose his or her camp. This polarization reached its extremes at the war's end and shattered all lines of political "compromise," especially of those who could be described as trying to resist while collaborating.

In such an evolving context, an attitude of both accommodation and resistance was no doubt always possible on an individual scale. In the factories, inertia tactics were a way of enduring. They were also a way of acting in the immediate present while waiting for the Allies to arrive. One can conceive of a civil servant, linked to a resistance movement but keeping his job, who played a double game. By the end, the exercise had become risky, but it was possible.

But can an institution sometimes be in a position of compromise or even collaboration and sometimes in a position of noncooperation over a long period of time? It seems that this double attitude was not viable during the Nazi occupation. Eventually, one had to choose, because the pressure of events inexorably forced one's hand. It was no longer possible to stall, looking for half-measures or yielding on one level while remaining firm on another. One had either to submit or to resign. But for the exception that proves the rule, the policy of compromise with Hitler led nowhere except to submission.

The evolution of Denmark's political situation, which led to the fall of the government at the end of August 1943, offers a significant illustration of this analysis. In this country, where Germany had sought to display an appearance of "human" behavior, of non-Nazi behavior, the relationship between the occupied and the occupier suddenly deteriorated, and the Danish experiment with the "democratic showcase" became a fiasco. The true nature of the regime reappeared: it could no longer tolerate the Danish will for autonomy. According to Werner Best, the Reich's plenipotentiary, however, the Danish situation seemed most favorable in the spring of 1943. In his Berlin semester report delivered in May 1943, Best proclaimed himself quite satisfied. The Danes were demonstrating realism, according to him, and Communism played practically no role in the country. He emphasized the fact that, with the support of the Danish government, 85 German officials and 130 German employees could manage a country of 4 million inhabitants, whereas in Norway, whose government had fled abroad, 3,000 German civil servants were needed to govern a country of 3 million inhabitants. Moreover, agricultural exports to Germany continued at a good pace. But Best put forward only the facts favorable to him. General Hermann von Hannecken, the Wehrmacht commander who disagreed with Best's political direction (von Hannecken thought more firmness was necessary), also wrote his superiors but expressed more somber views. He particularly emphasized the renewed incidence of sabotage.

In fact, during 1942, internal resistance really started to be organized. The small Danish communist party threw itself into immediate action. By the end of 1942, the number of acts of sabotage started to increase. British bombing raids were producing many victims. The increasingly dynamic clandestine press presented sabotage as a lesser evil. It would be better if the Danes themselves organized it for it would make fewer victims than the bombing raids. Opinion was changing, and there was a growing resentment toward the Scavenius government. The course of the war in Russia also had something to do with this change.

This emergence of internal resistance posed a new problem to the Danish government. How, indeed, should it behave toward the increasing sabotage? The Germans were demanding ever more severe measures of repression. Such an action would turn a large portion of the population against the government immediately. Thus, when Scavenius announced the creation of a special Danish corps to protect factories and other strategic points from sabotage, he aroused a current of hostility in public opinion that the clandestine press and the BBC promptly began to amplify.

During the summer of 1943, Denmark was suddenly seized by a large protest movement that led to a serious political crisis. No one, at least not the Danish government or the German authorities, had predicted it. The resistance organized a sudden outbreak of acts of sabotage: 93 in July, then 220 in August, which averaged three to seven acts per day.[11] This increasing agitation triggered a wave of strikes that made both political and social demands, in particular, for a raise in salaries and for the construction of air-raid shelters, whose absence had been cruelly felt during the British air-raids. The movement really took off in the beginning of August in the port of Odense and then spread over the whole country. In two weeks, most of the large cities had been affected, with the strikes sometimes accompanied by street demonstrations. Between August 23 and 27, the movement reached its greatest intensity, becoming an open revolt. Protesters came to blows with the German forces. A German officer was seriously wounded at Odense.

Best asked Scavenius to take immediate measures to stop the movement, but the Danish government seemed overwhelmed by the situation. It launched an appeal for calm. It went unheeded. Best's policy of moderation was failing. Called to Berlin on August 26, he was ordered by Hitler to set up martial law. The city of Odense was penalized with a fine of 1 million crowns and was threatened with severe reprisals if those who had mistreated the German officer did not give themselves up. Best was charged with giving the Danish government an ultimatum to do what it had always refused: suppress public freedoms, install a curfew, set up courts-martial sentencing anyone involved in sabotage to death, and so on. On August 28, Best conveyed the German demands to Scavenius and summoned him to give his government's agreement that very day. The Danish government met in special session and rejected the ultimatum. At first reticent about such a decision, Scavenius finally came around to the unanimous opinion of the other ministers: if the government itself became involved in unprecedented politics of collaboration and repression, the reaction of the Danish population would be uncontrollable. After having submitted the text to the king, the government made a declaration to the country. In a rather moderate tone, it declared: "Effectuation of the provisions demanded by the Germans would win the Government's possibilities of keeping the people calm, and the Government, therefore, regrets that it cannot find it right to help in carrying through these provisions."[12]

As soon as it learned of the news, the Wehrmacht took over operations. At dawn on August 29, German troops were deployed throughout the country, taking possession of strategic points according to plans prepared by General von Hannecken. Several limited battles took place against the Danish army, which had received the order to resist symbolically. One navy staff officer did not respect the order, however, and instructed the ships to flee or scuttle. Only a few boats managed to escape, most of them having been sunk or scuttled. The German police arrested certain civil servants, professors, journalists, and political personalities in their homes. Within a few hours, everything was finished, and the population had kept its calm. From then on, the Germans controlled the country directly, after the Danish government had resigned, so to speak, on its own. Martial law was installed, and from then on the occupier demonstrated great brutality.

Thus, after three years of an ambiguous political situation, the mask was peeling off. The actors' positions were suddenly clarified and would not change again until the end of the war. With the rise in power of the internal opposition, the Danish government was caught between two contradictory political paths: one of conditional collaboration, which was already highly complex to put into effect, and one of resistance, which was pressuring the government to make more radical choices. Eventually this contradiction proved untenable. Either the government would have to yield to Berlin's pressures, thus turning against the Danish population that it wanted to protect, or it would decide to make an act of deliberate political noncooperation and join the side of a more and more radicalized public opinion. By choosing to break, the outgoing Danish government not only helped to clarify a confusing situation but also legitimized the action undertaken by the resistance movements, thus giving that action an unprecedented dynamism. The first indication of this new situation was the creation on September 16, 1943, of the *Freedom Council*, a political organization that coordinated and energized the resistance and acted as a sort of temporary clandestine government until the Liberation.

The case of Belgium offers a different example. Wanting to avoid such a break, some administrative or judicial authorities chose to remain in place without becoming involved in full-time collaboration. They hoped to be able to put forward national legislation that would thwart pressure from the occupier. The tactic consisted of remaining active but in a way that would keep any German measures from being applied by using unconstitutionality as a pretext. After the government left Belgium, the occupying forces quashed the legislative power and increased the "executive" power that was entrusted to the General Secretaries (the highest government employee from each of the ministries). Because of the law of May 10, 1940, each General Secretary was entrusted with a particular ministerial power.[13] The pressure of events, however, led the General Secretaries to form a "college" based on the dismantled ministers' council. Each General Secretary thus ended up exercising all the prerogatives of a minister without political legitimacy.

Only the judicial power remained entirely in place, continuing to represent the legitimacy of Belgian prewar institutions. The judiciary thus constituted a sort of "high moral authority" to which citizens could turn for advice. Moreover, in the first days of the invasion, the highest magistrates of the kingdom, starting with the First President of the Supreme Court of Appeal (the supreme judiciary authority in Belgium), had helped to work out the June 12, 1940 protocol, defining the power of the General Secretaries.

The decision to keep the judiciary active in Belgium was founded in large part on the experience of World War I. Indeed, during the 1914 German occupation, the Supreme Court of Appeal had thought it no longer necessary to convene. The occupier then instituted German courts that issued extremely severe sentences.[14] Given this experience from 30 years before, many Belgian judges wanted to maintain a national judiciary up until the last possible minute. The magistrates' *Mobilization Book* explicitly stipulated that Belgian judges had to remain at their posts in case of an occupation. In short, the Belgian judges considered themselves the last resort of national legality and believed that justice had to be rendered by "Belgicists" who were especially attached to the country's traditional institutions. If they left, the risk was great that they would be replaced by collaborating judges, Flemish Rexists, or nationalists, who would not have the same scruples. When the German troops arrived in May 1940, however, some of the judges disobeyed the rules of their organization, in spite of their instructions, and fled abroad. A German order of July 18, 1940, prohibited those in this category from reassuming their functions.

All kinds of incidents between Belgian magistrates and German power marked the occupation period, and the complexity of the procedural battle defies succinct summarization. In the end, the credit side of the Belgian magistrates' balance-sheet seems rather meager, with their efforts at compromise failing to hold firm against the occupier's determination. The Supreme Court of Appeals sometimes tried to minimize *formal* Belgian involvement and responsibility in certain actions, but basically the country was powerless to block the course of the German steamroller. For example, the college of the General Secretaries sought to contest the fundamental basis of the October 1940 anti-Jewish orders, claiming the unconstitutionality of all discriminatory measures in the eyes of Belgian law. The Supreme Court of Appeals was in a position to give a deciding opinion in this affair. The Germans pressured the magistrates and the court declared that, if the General Secretaries would be satisfied with applying the orders without publishing them in the official log, Belgium would decline all responsibility. Although the texts of these orders were therefore not published, Mr. Adam, acting as Secretary General, did order the provincial governors to execute them. The Germans had succeeded in their goal of getting the Belgian government itself to take charge of registering the Jews and excluding them from certain professions.

The occupation experience tended to show that the General Secretaries were increasingly reduced to the role of executing German politics. In certain cases, the Supreme Court of Appeals and various other appeals courts tried to limit the effects of this policy with legal arguments. After several more or less important clashes, a serious crisis broke out in November 1942. Obeying the occupier's desire, the General Secretaries had passed a decree on the administrative restructuring of Belgium (called the large agglomerations decree) on November 5, 1941. In a rather minor affair, the Sixth Chamber of the Brussels Appeals Court was called upon to pronounce judgment on the legality of the decree of the General Secretaries. The magistrates underwent a great deal of pressure. But on November 30, 1942, the Brussels Appeals Court met in a general assembly to decide that its Sixth Chamber must rule in complete freedom and that, if by chance that chamber ran into any obstacle in the exercise of its mission, "such a hindrance would prohibit the entire Court from continuing to fulfill its functions."[15]

On December 10, what had been threatening for several weeks finally happened: the Sixth Chamber declared the General Secretaries' decree unconstitutional, stating as well that the Secretaries had exceeded their mandates. The German response was immediate: The Chamber president and his assessors were arrested the following night, with various magistrates and lawyers taken as hostages. On December 12, the Brussels Appeals Court unanimously decided to suspend its work temporarily, reasoning that it could no longer function under such conditions. Out of solidarity, the Brussels Council of the Order of the Bar called on lawyers to stop pleading in courts and tribunals. The conflict thus became open, expressed through an action of noncooperation carried out by one of Belgium's most important courts of justice.

The German administration threatened to take very severe reprisals against the judicial body and the population if the Court did not go back to work on December 17 at the latest. This ultimatum prompted a series of underhanded deals between the occupying power, the magistrates, and the General Secretary of Justice. On December 16, following a letter from the General Secretary to the Court that stressed the general interest and public order, the Court decided to suspend its "strike." The magistrates were freed but had made no progress on the essence of the legal problems raised. The resistance members did not understand the attitude of the Appeals Court. Commenting on these events, the clandestine newspaper of the legal community, *Justice Libre*, wrote of the abdication of the magistracy.

Belgian laws also protested measures on Jewish deportation and on the requisitioning of workers for Germany, but these conflicts never became as serious as the crisis of December 1942. In fact, it was as if the Belgian magistrates had never wanted to go the whole way in the confrontation with the occupier because of an initial choice to keep functioning. By seeking to avoid a definitive break at any cost, Belgium was forced to make more and more concessions to the enemy.

NOTES

1. Stanley Hoffmann, *Essais sur la France* (Paris, 1974).

2. Jean Texier, "Conseils à l'occupé," cited by Henri Noguères, *Histoire de la Résistance en France (1940–1944)* vol. 1 (Paris, 1969).

3. Émile Chekerdjiyski, *Oeuvres choisies* (Sofia, 1964).

4. Quoted by Lennart Bergfeldt, "The Danish Case, Program on Nonviolent Sanctions" (Cambridge, MA, 1988) (unpublished).

5. For example, Werner Rings, *Vivre avec l'ennemi* (Paris, 1981), shows the different ways in which people conducted themselves in Nazi-occupied Europe.

6. Beginning in November 1942, under the initiative of Claude Bourdet, there arose in France a secret organization devoted to recruiting officials who would provide help to the resistance movement. It was called NAP (Infiltration of the Public Administration).

7. Rings, *Vivre* 157.

8. Jiri Hronek, *Volcano under Hitler: The Underground War in Czechoslovakia* (London, 1941) 85.

9. Stefano Piziali, "Résistance non armée dans la région de Bergame (Italie, 1943–1945)," *Les Cahiers de la Réconciliation* (Summer 1986).

10. From "Good Soldier Schweik", Haselz, Viking Penguin, 1990, the legendary comic figure who never understood anything that could be used to exploit him; Schweik was immortalized in stories by Jaroslav Hasek (1883–1923).

11. Figures provided by Jorgen Haestrup, *Le mouvement de la résistance danoise (1939–1945)* (Copenhagen, 1970) 7–8.

12. Cited by Richard Petrow, *The Bitter Years: The Invasion and Occupation of Denmark and Norway* (New York, 1974) 92.

13. Article 5 of the ministerial decree of May 10, 1940, on "The law relative to the delegation of power in time of war" stipulated that "If as a result of military operations, a judge or an official, [or] a body of judges or officials . . . is deprived of all communications with superior authority to whom he reports, or if that authority ceases to function, he can exercise his official capacity and for urgent situations has all the attributes of that superior authority."

14. See Jean Jacqmain, "La résistance civile de la magistrature (1914–1918)," *Cahiers de la Réconciliation* (June, 1983).

15. Cited by L. Louveau, "La magistrature dans la tourmente: Les annnées 1940 à 1944," *Revue de droit pénal et de criminologie* (July, 1981) 635.

Chapter 4

The Question of Legitimacy

With the passage of time, it appears that the initial position of the institutional political authority played an essential role in the prospects for collective resistance by the population. In other words, civilian resistance by legitimate institutions was one of the factors that influenced civilian resistance by populations. The main question was whether military defeat necessarily meant that the conquered people had to give up all forms of combat. Many thought so; the signing of the armistice in France, for example, was a political decision that officially recognized a military defeat. But other governments made different choices. In Norway, for example, combat simply ended without any political agreement with the conqueror. In fact, two major strategic options were possible for those who wanted to continue the fight. The first consisted of pursuing *military combat from outside* the country; most of the governments that chose exile in London did it with this intention but without specific means. The second option was to wage a *political combat from within* the conquered country; at the beginning of the occupation, few people were aware of such a possibility, even though it was the very essence of what eventually became the Resistance.

In many minds, military capitulation inevitably implies political submission. As soon as a conquered people no longer has armed force as an option, it is no longer in a position to impose its own conditions and would therefore be automatically obliged to accept those of the conqueror. This position does not take into account the autonomy of politics. Politics, after all, cannot be reduced to the use of armed force. If war is "the pursuit of politics by other means," according to Karl von Clausewitz's famous definition, war is only *one* of the means of politics. Politics has a maneuvering area before the war and also after, even it that area turns out to be much narrower on the side of the defeated population than on that of the victor.

If the Hague International Convention of 1940, which was signed by Germany, foresaw that the administration of an occupied country had to submit to an occupying power, it certainly did not specify that the government of the occupied country had to do likewise. It is not appropriate to lend too much importance to this text, but remembering it can help us to understand why many political leaders and senior officials found it normal that all ministries and state services be spontaneously placed under the occupying forces' orders. An important space for political initiative by the governments of the militarily conquered countries remained, however. From flight abroad to national collaboration and various "administrative" situations, the range of historical choices shows that the game remained open. Governments thus had to decide among several political options that they had hardly considered. For the conquered countries, the drama of occupation was not simply the occupier's invasion; it also included the occupied country's complete lack of counter-strategy. In the 1930s, while Germany was becoming more and more threatening, no government seriously imagined a military defeat. It is human, of course, to avoid thinking about the worst case scenario. But is it not essential that all defense strategies deal with it? Lacking forethought, governments fell short by thinking they could compromise with Hitler and by persuading themselves that their arms were invincible. Confronted brutally with the trauma of occupation, they were forced to improvise pathetically because they had refused to imagine what might happen.[1]

Even if the situation had not been thought through in advance, it would still be important to know, after the fact, what particular political behavior of a militarily conquered nation would lead to its political submission. When we compare the histories of all governmental behavior, we find that it is obviously the process of national collaboration that favors this outcome. In the medium or long term, national collaboration leads to the political legitimation of the occupier's regime. It is fitting to add, however, that this "natural" progression is not inevitable, as demonstrated by the Danish government's spectacular "recovery" under the pressure of opinion and resistance.

One can thus affirm this general axiom: denouncing the illegitimacy of the occupier's power, which was acquired through force of arms, was the first way in which a conquered society could resist the conqueror's determination to control it. From this point of view, it is not coincidental that the Belgian magistrates' few struggles focused on the issue of constitutionality. Trying to articulate and defend the spirit of the law that had always prevailed in the country was the Belgian magistrates' principal means of preserving the identity of its society from the occupier's repeated blows. They could no doubt have shown a little more audacity in this fight. Still, we must add in their defense that this legal battle could hardly have been crowned with success in a context where the issue of political legitimacy was so ambiguous, with a king who had chosen to remain, a government in exile, and senior officials who did more than administer current affairs.

The battle to preserve the legitimacy of society's institutions after a military defeat cannot be won in the courtroom. The essence of the issue of legitimacy is political and thus calls for a political strategy. In a situation of occupation or something similar to occupation, this strategy rests basically on the legitimate political power's refusal to collaborate with the occupying power. The founding act of a resistance process against an occupation is basically an affirmation of the superiority of the *de jure* authority over the *de facto* one. To establish a true "Resistance" and to lay the necessary foundation for its development is to express, solemnly and publicly, the determination to preserve the legitimacy of the *de jure* power while refusing to collaborate with the *de facto* power. This reveals the degree to which the creative dynamic of resistance derives, above all, from this initiating and declaratory act of noncooperation politics. In this respect, the essential nature of resistance is not military.

Many may believe that it is unrealistic to undertake a policy without means. Demonstrating such determination would logically make sense only if supported by military strength, which would in some way be indispensable for transforming the desire to resist into action. Since this was not the case in the situations considered here, it would seem better to have done without such declarations of principle.

This point of view is based on a fundamental misunderstanding. The declaration of a political desire for noncooperation does not aim to engage in military resistance since, in any case, that can no longer be the response of the moment. Such a declaration aims to spur the political resistance of the militarily conquered society here and now. This consists of institutional resistance on the one hand and resistance of the people on the other. Another fight is starting. After the battle of the armed forces comes the battle to control civil society. It is as if the clearer the determination for legitimate political power, the greater the opportunity for civil society's resistance to become massive.

Concretely, in the historical context of 1940, no government clearly or consciously put such a political line into effect. The European leaders who were still determined to fight wanted first and foremost to pursue military combat. To this end, their choice was exile in England. These departures were far from being appreciated by the populations who interpreted them, at the time, as signs of cowardice. But the choice of exile had an inherent political meaning whose importance was revealed only with time. A government's going abroad was a way to continue its existence and thus to assure the permanence of the legitimacy of the conquered country's political institutions. The seeking of exile by a country's highest leaders was thus a first act of political noncooperation that expressed the refusal to legitimize all the occupier's power. This action was meant to inspire hope in the people that the situation was not irreversible and to spur or reinforce their desire to fight.

But such political determination had to be followed by immediate effects within the very heart of the state apparatus, that is, of the state's administration. As we have emphasized, an occupation situation supposes minimal accommodations with the occupier to manage ongoing affairs. Does this imply, however, that the highest national civil servants who have remained at home should serve the politics of the occupier? There is a great risk of sliding from a "technical" role into a political one. In the hands of a foreign power, these important government "technicians"—the high civil servants—can be transformed into virtual "ministers" without ever having wanted it themselves. The state administration then immediately becomes the main instrument of oppression and repression against the population of its own country. This is why the first arm of a political strategy of state noncollaboration is the state administration's noncollaboration, once the illegitimate character of the *de facto* power has been affirmed. In the context of the Nazi occupation, no government seems to have applied this line of action as such. This strategy is difficult to implement and is conceivable only if the civil servants have been seriously prepared. It is to be emphasized, however, that some of them spontaneously realized that the only way to remain consistent with the political choices of their legitimate government was to resign from their office. Thus, the problem is to know if administrative noncollaboration can be anything more than the sum of several cases of individual refusals—if, in other words, it can constitute a complete administrative community strategy. A comparative examination of the first year of occupation in France, the Netherlands, and Norway is particularly illuminating on all these points.

NORWAY'S STEADFASTNESS

The Norwegian government refused more than most to legitimize the occupier's power. We cannot say, however, that the Norwegian leaders had thought out this political conduct as strategy. It was more a line of action progressively imposed on them, especially by King Haakon VII's determination. This attitude gradually evolved almost completely by improvisation during the occupation's first few months. It could just as easily not have occurred at all.

It is surprising, after all, that we still remember the image of Quisling, a political personage symbolizing the essence of unconditional collaboration, rather than of King Haakon, who refused all compromise with the invader. In fact, Quisling headed a party whose pretentious name, "National Unity" (*Nasjonal Samling* or NS), poorly concealed just how unrepresentative it was of Norwegian opinion. The Germans knew the marginal character of this pro-Nazi movement full well. At the same time, Quisling was their main ally and could be very helpful to them. During the winter of 1939, Quisling had proposed to foment a *coup d'état* in Norway with Berlin's help. Hitler opposed the plan; he wanted to conquer the country himself and not have his hands tied. He thought, though, that once the military victory was won, the leader of the *Nasjonal Samling* could play an important role in converting Norwegian society to national-socialist ideology.

By dawn of April 9, 1940, when Germany attacked Norway (the same day as Denmark), Quisling had still not won Berlin's confidence. The occupation plan for Norway was immediately paralyzed when the ship transporting the operation's military and political general staff was sunk by Norwegian defense at its arrival in the port of Oslo. Taking advantage of the confusion in the capital, Quisling announced the constitution of a new government over the radio. He declared:

In the current circumstances, it is the *Nasjonal Samling*'s right and duty to assume government powers in order to defend the Norwegian people's vital interests and save their country's independence. I add that, in the situation we find ourselves in, resistance is not only useless but would mean criminal destruction of lives and property.[2]

Acting precipitously, Quisling announced the names of his ministers, several of whom had not even been informed! Dr. Braüer, the German ambassador in Oslo, thought his authority had been usurped and wanted to have Quisling arrested. But lacking a political solution, Hitler was ready to play the Quisling card, and Braüer had to yield. Several designated ministers, however, declined their appointment. Quisling was immediately confronted with the resistance of civil servants from various ministries who considered his government illegal. Many offices closed their doors, soon paralyzing the administrative functioning of the country. In any case, the absence of certain of its members made it impossible for the new team to hold council.

On that same April 9, a massive exodus left Oslo. The King and the government left the capital, and many precious state documents went with them. A general mobilization had been decreed, and the Norwegian army tried, for better or worse, to resist the enemy thrust. During its last session, the Parliament (Storting) asked the King to remain the "guardian of the nation's interests and, on behalf of the Storting and government, to carry out the decisions considered necessary for the country's security and future."[3] Confusion reigned in the capital, with Quisling unable to stabilize the situation. When King Haakon learned that Quisling was trying to hoist himself into power, he categorically refused to recognize Quisling's government. This failure reduced Berlin's chances for reaching a modus vivendi similar to the one being instituted in Denmark. Quisling was curtly dismissed on April 15, while the Germans searched for a political solution with some of the less controversial personalities who had remained in the capital.

Indeed, the isolation of the pro-Nazi party relieved most Norwegians and opened the path to the establishment of a more representative government. A solution was needed to manage the crisis shaking the country. Negotiations, particularly with Supreme Court members, led to the setting up of an Administrative Council in which the Supreme Court's president, Paul Berg, was involved. This solution seemed for a while to have the King's blessing; an important personality responsible for the only still-functioning constitutional body in Oslo, which was intended to be under the King's authority and without political function, was tempting. Simultaneously with these negotiations, however, Hitler appeared irritated by the "softness" of his ambassador, Dr. Braüer, who could not seem to control the situation. He decided to dismiss Braüer and appointed Josef Terboven commissar of the Reich. The arrival of this eminent member of the Nazi elite in Norway on April 24 meant the reinforcement of direct German pressure on the country. Conflicts appeared very quickly between him and the Administrative Council in which he wanted to play a political role.

Meanwhile, the war's destiny was unfolding. After the failure of the allied dis-embarkation in Narvik, the small Norwegian army had to capitulate on June 10.

Pursued by the Germans who had been trying to capture him from the beginning, the King finally decided to flee abroad after he was almost killed during a German bombing. Accompanied by his government and several hundred commissioned and noncommissioned officers, he embarked on a British ship bound for England. The Bank of Norway funds, withdrawn at the beginning of the German attack, took the same route. A declaration addressed to the country on June 7 explained the reasons for this departure to the population. Emphasizing the impossibility of continuing the fight on Norwegian soil, the text declared that:

The King and his Government had accepted the advice of the High Command to this effect, and had decided to leave the national territory.

However, they do not therefore abandon the struggle to regain Norway's independence. On the contrary—it will be carried out outside the country's borders. In this period of struggle, Norway's King and Government will be the free spokesmen for the national claims of the Norwegian people. They will to the utmost possible extent maintain the sovereign existence of the Norwegian Kingdom, in order that none of the rights pertaining to a free state shall go by default. It will be their task to defend the status and political rights of the country and its people, in such a way that the nation in the hour of victory can step forth and assert its national freedom.[4]

A certain number of Storting deputies remained in Oslo and became hostages in Terboven's hands. Beginning on June 13, 130 of them were assembled and summoned to appoint an authentic government to request the King's abdication. The commissar of the Reich exerted all kinds of pressure on the parliamentarians who showed themselves divided on how to react. Finally, an agreement was reached whose main thrust was the request to overthrow the King. The King obviously refused this demand and let it be known by letter and by a BBC radio address on July 8. He explained that the deputies were not constitutionally enabled to make such a request and furthermore, that since they were acting under constraint, none of their votes could be taken into consideration. This led to a stand-off. The King and the government, which had been enlarged to include prewar opposition members, asserted themselves as Norway's only legitimate political representatives.

During the summer, Terboven tried again to form a political team that would not be restricted to Nasjonal Samling members, but he had to give up on this plan. Instead he decided to create a State Council, made up exclusively of pro-Nazi party leaders placed directly under his orders. On September 25, he announced the suppression of all other political parties. Berlin had not succeeded in involving Norwegian authorities in the country's occupation process and was forced to govern the country directly with a handful of incompetent collaborationists who insisted on exerting direct pressure on the civil servants. The latter were left on their own, not having received clear orders from their administration. Some resigned, others remained on duty, trying to defend the country's interests, and still others collaborated with the new administration.

Meanwhile, the Supreme Court continued to function as the only true representative of Norwegian institutions still in the country. As in Belgium but with more force, the Norwegian magistrates tried to defend the constitution on different matters concerning the installation of the new administration. Conflicts with the commissioner of the Reich multiplied; they seemed unable to find viable solutions. In early December, the retirement age of civil servants was lowered from 70 to 65, in the hope that staunch supporters of the pro-Nazi party would join the new state administration. Moreover, Terboven addressed a letter to the Supreme Court forbidding it to discuss the constitutionality of his decisions. These measures stirred considerable agitation in judicial circles. During the preceding months, Supreme Court members had made efforts to arrive at a compromise solution with the occupier, in light of the gravity of the situation. But this time, they concluded that cooperation was impossible. On December 12, the Supreme Court sent a letter to the new Minister of Justice, declaring in substance:

It is the duty of the courts of justice to examine the constitutionality of decrees and decisions. During a military occupation, courts of justice must be in a position to examine the validity of orders promulgated by the occupying power with respect to international law. We cannot subscribe to the opinions expressed in this area by the Commissioner of the Reich. We therefore find ourselves in the position of no longer being able to maintain our functions.[5]

This resignation of the highest judicial authority in the country had important political consequences. Above all, it censured the illegitimacy of the new regime in a spectacular way. A corollary consequence was to advance the legitimation of a growing social opposition against the occupier. Indeed, the Supreme Court's decision had a galvanizing effect on a still-embryonic resistance in which Paul Berg, its president, held a leading position; other judges and lawyers followed him in this fight.

This does not mean that there was a direct cause and effect relationship between the political attitude of the legitimate representatives of Norwegian institutions and the development of resistance among the citizens. In the heart of occupied societies, resistance movements finally developed all over Europe, whatever the initial position of their prewar governments. In Norway as everywhere else, the first resistance fighters were on their own and could not count, at least at first, on the leaders exiled abroad. In this respect, there was a fundamental autonomy of the resistance phenomenon, regardless of whether it was armed or unarmed. Resistance was not created from outside the country but engendered from within occupied societies because of direct confrontations with the new power. The resistance was born on its own, so to speak, and completely improvised.

One can nonetheless maintain the thesis that, in Norway, social mobilization against the occupier happened relatively early, compared with Denmark and other Western European countries, because the legitimate Norwegian authorities refused to do anything that would legitimate the occupier's power. In Denmark, during the spring of 1942, the first resistance groups started to organize clandestine sabotage actions with the British secret services; the partial mobilization of civilian society did not occur until the summer of 1943 through the various strike movements. As we will see below, however, there was limited social mobilization in Norway as early as the spring of 1941 (all the athletic associations dissolved their groups, and 41 of the country's largest associations staged protests) and still more in the spring of 1942 (for example, the open resistance of members of the teaching and religious professions). These observations must not be interpreted as a condemnation of the Danish government's political position. The Danish government adopted a different attitude from its Norwegian counterpart perhaps because it had no choice. It is simply important to realize that different strategic options on the level of political institutions obviously affect the mobilization of the population differently.

In this perspective, one might suggest that the refusal of an occupied country's legitimate authorities to take part in a process of legitimizing the occupier's power is one of the key factors in the development of the people's resistance. If the occupier established an administration under its command when faced with this firmness on the part of political institutions, no one would be taken in. The more the question of legitimacy is muddled, however, as in Belgium or the Netherlands (see below), the less chance a civilian resistance has to develop quickly. Moreover, if a legitimate government chooses to deal with the occupier to the point of becoming involved in a national collaboration process, as in France, then the resistance dynamic on the civilian level seems neutralized. This attitude implies a legitimizing of the occupation situation, and it will take a long time before a collective opposition will form.

FRANCE'S ALIENATION

The French scenario makes an enlightening contrast with Norway's. French-style national collaboration had major consequences for the population's behavior and state of mind. Indeed, France went much further than Denmark in the national collaboration process, since it took advantage of a foreign occupation to establish a new French political regime on its own. No one will be surprised, therefore, that this process of legitimizing the occupier's power helped to paralyze popular resistance.

From this point of view, national collaboration was a determining factor in the citizens' passivity, or, at the very least, in their wait-and-see attitude. Whether or not we deplore it, the psychological mechanisms of submission to authority are strongly anchored in each individual. Especially in a crisis situation, like a foreign occupation, this is why the degree to which a state's power collaborates with the invader reveals a great deal about the population's behavior. The amount of firmness exhibited by those in authority is likely either to guide people in their daily behavior or to leave them on their own.

In the French case, an essential psychological factor is critical to interpreting this behavior of the population: the rise to power of Marshal Pétain, the hero of the Verdun victory in World War I. A character who had become a virtual legend, he had acquired such international renown that, from the very first days of Hitler's attack, many leaders saw in him the man of last resort. Pétain had saved France in 1916, and he was the one most likely to do it again in 1940. As Stanley Hoffmann has shown, we can understand nothing about Pétain's role, the armistice, Vichy, and all that followed without first considering the collective cataclysm of the French military defeat of 1940. It was a national trauma that was expressed by the population's massive and pitiful exodus to the south of the country. The Marshal's sudden burst onto the national stage was the first, most primitive step toward calming anxieties and tending to the debacle's most burning wounds. The signing of the armistice was welcomed with immense relief. The majority of the French people were deeply grateful to Pétain, who thus became all the more legitimized.

It was then that the cult of the Marshal started, to use Azéma's apt phrase. Pétain's glorification became one of the favorite themes of the Vichy press. After studying official newspapers, Laborie has made a remarkable analysis of the Pétainist mystique: "The means of information regularly use the necessity of blind rallying (to the Marshal) as a supreme argument in times of worry or doubt. The sentimental and irrational appeal finds its psychological roots in the act of trust in the savior."[6] We understand the reason for psychoanalyzing these emotional, almost carnal, links uniting Pétain and the French people during those black years; it is even more appropriate in light of another favorite Vichy theme—the exploitation of collective guilt feelings and the call to "repentance" to expiate the sins that the French had supposedly committed which had led their country to defeat.[7]

In such conditions, it is hard to see how a collective determination to resist could develop rapidly in France. Significant obstacles had to be surmounted before this stage could be reached. In the occupied northern zone, of course, the French were in direct contact with the occupier, causing a quicker radicalization of the resistance. But in the southern zone, as Kedward has shown, the resistance first had to "break" the "Vichy shield" myth to be developed. Pétain had to be demystified. More specifically, his façade of legitimacy had to be pierced to show that Vichy was only an illusion. For, paradoxically, the problem for the resistance was not the occupier. The French were not pro-German. The Great War of 1914 was not far behind them, and anti-Kraut feeling was still vivid. A majority of the French secretly hoped for a final victory for the Allies. In the beginning of the occupation, the French were mostly Pétainists. This was so true that even some of the first partisans were in favor of Pétain, such as the founder of the *Combat* movement, Henri Frénay.[8] The feelings of the French people were thus highly complex. Denis Peschanski has summarized this complexity: "From the beginning, only a minority accepted collaboration, whereas the majority transferred its hopes to England. Which in no way prevents a profound attachment to the Marshal, this conqueror who came to manage a defeat."[9]

So Pétainism was a fundamental perversion that helped greatly to chloroform minds and neutralize the resistance potential in civil society for a long time. How was it possible to think that Pétain, the "old warrior," was not once again serving

France's interests? The German invasion of the southern zone in November 1942 helped to break the collective illusion by which the French had allowed themselves to be taken in. The event was a psychological break, especially for many of the soldiers of the armistice army who had until then obeyed the Marshal both out of *esprit de corps*, and because, quite simply, they trusted him. But the turning point had already occurred in the summer of 1942. The return to power of the unpopular Laval, his speech in favor of a German victory over the Soviet Union, and the changing of the guard all contributed to deepening the rift between Vichy and French opinion. By the end of 1942, the French resistance had really started to take hold and represent something. Vichy then lost its *raison d'être* as a shield and was perceived only as a conduit for the execution of German orders. But the resistance still had to struggle for a long time to impose its *own* legitimacy and thereby establish the bases of a new power.

In such a context, it is truly fortunate that, at the very time of Pétain's rise to power, an obscure general also burst onto the political scene. From the start, Charles de Gaulle wanted to defend a political split that turned out to be beneficial for France. He tried to incarnate, in his person as well as in his acts, the continuity of a "Free France." The struggle that de Gaulle undertook was much more political than military. His combat consisted mostly of making the voice of a fighting France heard by the French and thus embodying a legitimacy different from Pétain's, one accompanied by freedom. Aside from their belonging to the same military institution, which had deeply marked both of them, the two men became involved in action to defend totally different political causes. This battle of leaders must thus be seen as a battle for legitimacy, with both claiming to speak "in the name of France." Pétain embodied the "legal" legitimacy of the new regime, whereas de Gaulle represented an "illegal" legitimacy, born from a serious act of disobedience to the state. In this respect, we have to recognize that, although de Gaulle spoke as a soldier, he nonetheless carried out a fundamental act of civil disobedience that served as a basis for his movement. As Paxton has emphasized in the last lines of his book: sometimes one must disobey the state in order to save what gives a nation its true meaning. In France, that time came after June 1940.[10] As the clandestine newspaper, *Témoignage Chrétien*, wrote in one of its most famous texts, "France, take care not to lose your soul."[11] France's political identity had been deeply alienated during the state collaboration process and had to be restored. De Gaulle had the political genius to understand this and to bring about this restoration.[12]

But it would be a serious mistake to credit only the general. All the internal resistance movements contributed to this restoration just as much. Internal French resistance did not wait for de Gaulle to develop. In his famous speech of June 18, 1940, which was broadcast by the BBC, de Gaulle called for military resistance. He was trying to rally the French colonial empire to his cause and did not then imagine the possibility of a resistance movement on his native soil. As has been pointed out with respect to Norway, the resistance phenomenon developed on its own, from within the occupied countries. Across its diversity and its divisions,

French internal resistance knew how to embody a new legitimacy—that of a fighting France. Its rapprochement with de Gaulle, negotiated by Jean Moulin, was laborious and fraught with conflict. Particularly difficult were the most uncontrollable resistance groups, the communists. The final rapprochement, however, was the result of a historic necessity.

Indeed, de Gaulle quickly realized that he needed France's internal resistance movement. He had too few armed forces at his disposal to be heard by the Allies or be taken seriously in military battle. The support of an internal resistance movement was just as important as the rallying of the French empire. By showing the Allies that his name was uniting all who were fighting within his country, de Gaulle took on political weight. To strengthen his own legitimacy, he absolutely had to show the whole world that he really did speak in the name of another France, a resisting France.

At the same time, de Gaulle imposed himself on the resistance little by little. For the France caught up in Vichy, it was vital that a personality or political body represent an alternate legitimacy. Unknown to the French in 1940, de Gaulle was eminently symbolic. His main weapon was the power of his words. It is hard to imagine him without the radio. It was the ideal weapon for him to lead a psychological campaign for the masses and to impose himself on them gradually. The presence of this distant voice opened up a new path and a new political future. Once they had an alternative to submission to the occupier's will, the French slowly dared to feel hope again. This forced the resistance movements to negotiate with de Gaulle, through whom, moreover, they could obtain financial support.

A dialectic thus developed between de Gaulle and the internal resistance. The resistance needed a de Gaulle just as much as de Gaulle needed a resistance. De Gaulle and the internal resistance movement prevented the smooth execution of the occupier's plans and soon became the two political poles around which the French countryside started to reorder itself.

THE NETHERLANDS' CONTRADICTIONS

As for the Netherlands, the political situation was halfway between those of Norway and France. It was characterized by a complex network of contradictions between the position adopted by the legal government in exile, which incarnated the refusal of all compromise with the occupier, and the collaborationist position of the General Secretaries, who were also legitimate representatives of the Dutch administration. On May 10, 1940, the small Dutch army proved unable to resist for long the breakthrough of the German armored cars. The terrible bombing of the port of Rotterdam and the impotence of the British forces to come to the aid of Holland were clear signs of the battle's outcome. Queen Wilhelmina decided to seek exile in London, along with her government made up of representatives of the main political parties of the country. General H. G. Winkelman, the highest army leader, was given full powers in her absence. He had to capitulate on May 15, because the military situation had deteriorated so badly. Germany controlled the Netherlands from this point on. In a speech broadcast by the BBC, the Queen expressed her determination to pursue the struggle and to maintain her country's legitimate institutions. As for the General Secretaries, they accepted the mission of administering the country according to the law of war determined by the rules of the Hague Convention.

From then on, Holland was led by a Commissioner of the Reich, Arthur Seyss-Inquart, assisted by several German soldiers and senior officials. Aside from Hans Albin Rauter, the Chief of Police and the SS, Seyss-Inquart appointed four German general commissioners who were charged with supervising Dutch administration (Security and Police, Administration and Justice, Economy and Finances, and a political Advisor without a specific function). From the beginning, Seyss-Inquart showed himself to be clever in his approach to the administration. He knew that he needed Dutch civil servants since he did not have sufficient competent German personnel. This is why he did not want to effect major changes in personnel, except for the police whose services were completely reorganized, especially with the addition of the pro-Nazi party, the NSB. He proposed that civil servants who wished to resign do it immediately and promised not to punish them for it. If they agreed to stay, however, he expected loyal collaboration from them in accordance with their country's new situation. Since the General Secretaries did not resign, except for those from the Justice and Finance offices, most other officials also remained at their posts.

In the next six months, German pressure on the state apparatus gradually increased. In June 1940, it suspended the Dutch Parliament. Then, an essential event took place: Seyss-Inquart gave the General Secretaries veto power over their subordinates' decisions, whereas their own orders would be law from then on. Under these regulations, as historian Werner Warmbrunn has pointed out, "the General Secretaries became virtual ministers who made policy under German supervision."[13] Starting in September 1940, when the German control and pressure apparatus was well in place, a flood of "decree-laws" dictated by the occupier took over. The Dutch administration thus worked to serve the occupier's goals. It was the Dutch administration that executed the first measures excluding Jews and enforcing obligatory labor in Germany. Later, however, when they realized the contradiction between their position and the political line of their government in exile, most of the General Secretaries quit their posts: out of the eleven General Secretaries who had participated in the prewar government, only three still remained at the end of 1943. Individually and separately, almost all of them resolved to leave.

To the Dutch servants' credit, it is important to add that they were not prepared to deal with the crisis situation in which they suddenly found themselves, since they had received no clear order of resistance from their government. As early as 1937, the government had worked out instructions to apply in case the territory became occupied. But the goal, according to a study written later by A. H. Heering, a senior official, was not to have the administration become a constituent element in a power relationship with the occupier, but rather to orient the civil servants so that they could act in the best interests of the population. The intention of these instructions was not so much to organize administrative resistance, as to adapt the administration during an occupation according to the planned dispositions of the Hague International Convention. Moreover, the content of these instructions was very vague on essential points and thus could not be of great utility in helping government employees to determine their conduct in difficult circumstances. For example, to the complex question of determining the conditions under which a civil servant must remain at his post during an occupation, the second paragraph of article 31 stated only: "If by remaining at his post, the civil servant's services benefit the occupier more than the population, he should leave his post." Heering has emphasized that

the investigation conducted after the war revealed that civil servants generally judged much too often that remaining at their posts benefited the population more than the occupying forces and that this illusion resulted in many civil servants, who were afraid of being fired, being too cautious in opposing certain of the occupier's measures, such as the hunt for Jews, obligatory labor, and other exercises of oppression.[14]

Whether the 1937 instructions were sufficiently clear or not, the civil servants would have had a hard time applying them, since most of these individuals were unaware of the very existence of the guidelines. Indeed, since the government had distributed very few copies within the administrative corps beforehand, most officials became aware of them only after the war.

As for Dutch judicial institutions, they were even less combative than their Belgian counterparts. Courts remained in session during the whole war without any apparent desire to resist. The highest among them, the Supreme Court, was hardly an example to follow. In November 1940, when its Jewish president, L. E. Visser, was excluded, his colleagues remained silent. In January 1942, the Supreme Court had a historic opportunity to pronounce its opinion on whether a German decree conformed to the rules of the Hague International Convention. Bogged down in contradictory opinions, the court refused to issue a judgment. Because of the Supreme Court's overly docile behavior, the government in exile dismissed its members in September 1944.

These contradictions within the state apparatus had similar effects within civil society. While the courts remained silent and even collaborated, Protestant and Catholic churches tried to express their opposition to the new regime relatively early. During the early days, most of the population accommodated itself to the presence of the occupier, toward whom it felt no historic hostility. At the same time, most of the Dutch people felt no attraction toward the National Socialist ideology, and the vicious behavior of the Dutch pro-Nazi party alienated the Dutch populace even more. As early as the first year of occupation, there were outbursts of anger; protest demonstrations and strikes broke out in support of the Jews. But these spontaneous movements expressed the pressures and tensions felt by civil society more than constructive forms of resistance.

Between the permanence of the government in exile and the attitude of the General Secretaries, the issue of the legitimacy of power remained muddled. Everything happened as if this confusion of powers had induced a certain ambivalence of behaviors on the part of the population. Until 1943, when Dutch opinion swung definitively toward the Allies, the history of the Dutch occupation was marked by phases of prudent accommodation and brutal demonstrations against the regime through massive, spontaneous actions of civilian resistance.

TWO POLITICAL RATIONALES FOR RESISTANCE

These limited comparative studies do not presume to produce a general synthesis that would apply to all the countries of occupied Europe and to other times and places. On the basis of the facts registered here, however, one can maintain a thesis whose generality and explanatory power would have to be verified. This thesis clarifies the underlying dynamics of the situations studied and the behavior of the people involved. We can state this in a very general way: it is possible to identify two distinct political rationales for internal resistance within an occupied society in conjunction with the initial position of the legitimate political authorities (in place before occupation) on collaboration or noncollaboration.

On the one hand, the choice of a noncooperation policy by the government of a militarily conquered country is an obvious factor (among others) provoking civilian resistance. The resulting direct contact between the occupied and the occupier makes a mass civilian resistance probable as a collective psychological defense mechanism against the foreigner—probable, but not certain. The resistance of civil society cannot be decreed. It obeys complex and unexplained laws and is all the more difficult to organize when the attacked society has not been prepared to submit to such a trial or actively to confront the occupier. We will say only that a noncollaborating state strategy is the one that best activates civil society's potential to resist.

On the other hand, when the legitimate government of a militarily conquered country chooses a policy of collaboration, this weakens civil society's resistance considerably. A possible resistance movement must then confront the power not only of the occupier but also of its own government. This is why civilian resistance is likely to remain embryonic and limited for a long time. But this general passivity does not necessarily mean that the majority of the population is in favor of collaboration. On the contrary, if civil society experiences the military aggression as a true foreign invasion, it is probable that it will not approve of its leaders' collaboration politics. Still, the fact that the legitimate government is in a position to act as a "screen" between the occupied and the occupiers neutralizes the immediate possibility of mass resistance against the aggressor. In other words, state collaboration limits the full expression of the resistance potential of civil society.

For the attacked country, the choices of noncollaboration and state collaboration involve very different costs. In the first case, direct contact with the occupier tends to harden the repression of efforts at resistance. Everything, of course, depends on the occupier's intentions. If he wants to set up a government that has a certain legitimacy, it is in his interests to moderate his policy of repression on his own. In the second case, since the national collaborating power is in the position of an intermediary between the occupier and the resisting sectors of civil society, one might predict that the repression would be self-limiting. State collaboration, however, makes a country prey to serious internal political conflicts that challenge its national identity. By contrast, a noncooperation strategy that emerges clearly on the institutional level preserves the political integrity of the attacked society. It is thus necessary to discuss not only the efficiency of a strategy but also to put its political and human costs into perspective in order to evaluate its validity. According to the historical situations, these parameters can apply to very different realities.

NOTES

1. On this topic, two works by Jean-Baptiste Duroselle describe a France without a strategy: *La Décadence (1932–1939)* (Paris, 1979), and *L'abîme (1939–1945)* (Paris, 1983). On Norway, see François Kersaudy, *Stratèges et Norvège: 1940* (Paris, 1977), and, by the same author, on German designs on Norway, *1940, la guerre du fer* (Paris, 1987).

2. Quoted in Paul Hayes, "Bref aperçu de l'histoire de Quisling et du gouvernement de la Norvège de 1940 à 1945," *Revue d'histoire de la Deuxième Guerre mondiale* 66 (April 1967). One should also read his penetrating study of the NS leader: Paul Hayes, *Quisling: The Career and Political Ideas of Vidkun Quisling, 1887–1945* (Bloomington, IN, 1972).

3. Cited by Magne Skodvin, "Norway in Exile," *Norway in the Second World War* (Oslo, 1974) 94.

4. Quoted in Skodvin 94.

5. Quoted in Tore Gjelsvik, *Norwegian Resistance (1940–1945)* (London, 1979) 26.

6. Pierre Laborie, *Résistants, Vichyssois et autres* (Paris, 1980) 169.

7. Gerard Miller, *Les pousse-au-jouir du maréchal Pétain* (Paris, 1975).

8. Henri Frénay, *La nuit finira* (Paris, 1973), provides a passionate memoir of the period.

9. Denis Peschanski, *Vichy 1940–1944. Quaderni e documenti inediti di Angelo Tasca: Archives de guerre d'Angelo Tasca* (Paris, 1986) 45.

10. Robert O. Paxton, *Vichy France: Old Guard and New Order, 1940–1944* (New York, 1972) 345.

11. Renée Bédarida, *Les Armes de l'esprit: Témoignage chrétien (1941–1944)* (Paris, 1977).

12. Jean Lacouture, *De Gaulle* (Paris, 1986). See especially the first volume of this great biography, "Le Rebelle (1890–1944)."

13. Werner Warmbrunn, *The Dutch under German Occupation* (Stanford, CA, 1963) 37.

14. A. H. Heering, "L'administration publique sous occupation étrangère," *Alternatives non violentes*, Summer 1989, no. 52, p. 57. This study has been published in the review *Bestuurswetenschappen* 4 (April–May 1983), under the title "Het openbaar bestuur onder vreemde bezetting."

Chapter 5

Elements of Social Cohesion

Fighting without arms is a complex matter. Without weapons one feels defenseless. No one is ready to take risks spontaneously. Tyranny succeeds because of the terror and isolation that it provokes among the population. Paralyzed by fear of punishment, people submit. Tyranny's peace is the peace of fear and death. Fighting without arms under these conditions thus requires going beyond fear. Only then can people claim to conquer the enemy or at least to hold their own. The deepest fear is always that of losing one's life. Confronting totalitarian violence barehanded starts with controlling this fear, which is really the anguish of one's own death. Since this control is one of the most difficult things that can be asked of a human being, unarmed combat is highly uncommon.

Faced with impending violence, one is likely to conclude spontaneously that counter-violence is the only worthwhile response. With weapon in hand, one tends to feel reassured—rightly or wrongly. One has the impression that one's own capacity to cause death somehow protects against one's own. Without a weapon, what can one lean on to confront the situation? There is nothing but one's own intelligence and determination. A ruse is one way to overcome danger, but it is never enough to stifle the menacing anguish of death. A man on his own without weapons, confronted with violence and refusing to flee or give in, has no alternative but to show exceptional moral courage. A moral ideal and religious faith are among the main supports that help him transcend fear. He has to be convinced that certain values are more important than his own physical life. He has to convince himself that the mind's strength is stronger than brute force. Only then will he be able to confront death by transcending life. There is a sacrificial element here that makes a person "gifted with nonviolence" often be described as a martyr or saint. Whether or not the description is correct, it is clear that not everyone has such a "gift."

On the collective level, the problem is completely different. Historians and military experts have wondered over the years if a civilian population itself could ever organize a nonmilitary civilian defense.[1] While drawing attention to the potential of such a strategy, they have not been optimistic about its outcome. They have had particular doubts about the apparently elitist character of unarmed combat. Since they saw this kind of struggle as reserved for "saints," they thought it unlikely to be carried out by an entire population unless it contained millions of saints. This argument has dissuaded many experts (though not General Bollardière) from further research on the possibilities for unarmed strategies, but it is because they did not understand the complex psychosociological mechanisms involved in such actions.

Fighting without weapons alone is very different from fighting without weapons in a group. The question of dealing with fear shows the most variation in these two different circumstances. In a group, and because of it, individuals can accept risks that they would not take alone, both because their feelings are shared and because belonging to a group usually fosters a feeling of solidarity. The military is very familiar with this basis of collective action. A shared fear is easier to bear. Strong ideological or religious conviction no longer helps to overcome fear; rather, it is as if the fear actually become diluted within the group. The rationale of collective unarmed action is thus different from that of individual combat—it becomes less necessary to believe in an ideal. This, of course, remains connected to the very idea of struggle. Fighting for something presupposes a belief in something. Within the context of collective combat, however, unarmed struggle loses the elitist, "saintly" element that it might have in the context of individual action. What makes unarmed combat possible is, above all, the feeling of solidarity within the group. A population's degree of social cohesion becomes the prime condition of its civilian resistance. Group cohesion in the face of aggression encourages collective noncooperation against the aggressor.

The idea of social cohesion should not be confused with that of the ideological control of individuals, which smacks of rampant totalitarianism. Social cohesion and its opposite, social division, describe the relative solidity of ties that bind individuals and groups to the heart of a given society. During peacetime, social cohesion can be evaluated first through how much a country supports its institutions. Social cohesion is not a synonym for political unanimity. There can be deep political disagreements within a society whose members still accept the same rules of the game—that is, the same institutions. In this sense, real political division within a given society occurs only when one part of the community intends to overthrow the institutional system that structures it.

Social cohesion should not be limited, however, to an institutional definition. It is based even more on the hard to objectify impression of really and completely feeling part of the society in which one lives. This presupposes that each person has the same civil rights as every other and also that each person "feels" the same as the others. It is thus a psychological way of recognizing others and feeling recognized by them. When all feel interconnected and integrated into the vast series of networks that make up society, good social cohesion is likely. As soon as one group feels excluded from the society in which that group is nonetheless formally present, social division is likely.

In times of crisis, social cohesion can be assessed by the degree to which an attacked society unites against the aggressor. If the aggression is external, this social cohesion should result rather easily from the society's polarization against the "foreign body" trying to penetrate it. The conditions of external aggression thus seem favorable to a civil society's expression of resistance on its own and of its ability to act as a whole against the intruder. Still, this retraction of the "social body" is not easy. It seems possible only if the bonds that bound the different groups before the attack were solid enough to support the shock. The greater the cohesiveness of a civil society, the more it can resist an armed attack on its own. One defends well only what one holds dear. One is really willing to take risks only for what one is attached to. It therefore follows that the deeper a society's internal divisions prior to an attack, the more difficult civilian resistance will be. It is likely that the "social tissue" will not be able to withstand the invader's repeated blows. Groups that had already felt excluded before will not feel that they have a lot to lose by going over to the occupier's side. Thus, preinvasion divisions will more likely lead a population to collaborate or to remain passive than to resist.

INTERNAL FACTORS

Faced with foreign aggression, social cohesion comes primarily from the occupied people themselves as a result of historical, sociological, or ideological factors inherent in the invaded country. If civilian resistance was more developed in Norway than in France or Belgium, it may be in part because there was initially greater social cohesion there than in the other countries. Of course, it is difficult to quantify this idea of social cohesion (which should not be confused, as noted above, with absence of conflict). As a young modern state founded in 1905, Norway experienced major social and political conflicts during the 1920s. But when the socialists were in power during the 1930s, they adopted social measures that reduced former differences, in spite of their closeness to the conservatives. When the Germans invaded their country, this consensus led the main political leaders to unite behind the King. These same leaders had been discredited in public opinion that reproached them for their earlier weakness and irresponsibility when faced with the increasing German threat. The King had been careful not to support this resentment, however, and always tried to involve the government in his decisions. During the time of crisis, Norway's national union government acted with strong political and social cohesion.

Indeed, the Norwegian resistance was particularly active. In February 1941, Terboven authorized the Norwegian Nazi party (NS) to create an organization to which all public service professions would belong. Protests by unions, groups, or associations of concerned citizens soon made themselves heard. Terboven likewise wanted to put all the country's athletic groups together in the NS because of their apparent neutrality. The groups reacted by ceasing all activity. They expelled their members, and athletic competitions in Norway stopped until the end of the war. This first action on the "athletic front" may seem tame, even insignificant. But by making young people aware of the danger of the new regime, this protest played an important role.

Other organizations also protested against efforts to control them. In May 1941, the movement culminated in a common declaration by 43 professional, cultural, athletic, religious, union, and other associations, which represented a total of 750,000 members. The declaration protested against the determination of the NS to control public life. Several leaders were arrested, and NS members were placed at the head of a few protest organizations. This *coup de force* triggered mass resignations from the organizations and, far from weakening them, gave them new vitality. In June 1941, their most prominent leaders decided to organize an underground Committee of Civilian Coordination and Resistance (Sivorg), which became the leading organization of the Norwegian resistance, along with Milorg, its military counterpart. This same month was a turning point for civilian resistance in Norway. Up until then, opposition was open and uncoordinated; afterwards, organizing the resistance went underground and followed the rules of collective bargaining.

In this climate of civil society's progressive mobilization, two other "fronts"—to use the Norwegians' own expression—soon appeared: the church and the school. This is not a coincidence. It instead demonstrates the society's collective determination to reject an ideological straitjacket. The civilian resistance struggle focused strongly on the fundamental *values* of Norwegian society in a country where the church and the school did not represent antagonistic currents of thought. In addition, the formation of a combined ministry of Education and Religious Affairs could only bring the struggle of pastors and teachers still closer.

At that time, 96 percent of the population belong to the national (Lutheran) church. In February 1941, Eivind Berggrav, the primate, who had been strongly influenced by the Supreme Court's recent resignation and shocked by the behavior of the *Hird*, Quisling's "police," addressed a letter to the country's new authorities. Signed by all the bishops, this letter reproached the authorities for their activities during the preceding months and particularly for a new decree abolishing a pastor's traditional right not to give police information gathered in the course of ecclesiastical functions. At the same time, Berggrav proposed that a sort of church council be created that would regroup the diverse tendencies of the Norwegian church into a broadened structure. The Norwegian church had experienced some major internal conflicts before the war, due especially to opposition by certain parishes in the west of the country. When the government did not deign to answer their missive, the bishops decided to address a pastoral letter to their congregations, informing them of the situation. On February 9, 1941, the document was read in most of the country's churches even though many copies had been seized by the police. Condemning the regime with great firmness, the pastoral letter articulated a true political stand:

When those who have authority in a community tolerate violence and injustice and oppress souls, the Church must be the guardian of people's consciences . . . . The Church bishops have therefore presented certain official facts and declarations to the Minister concerning the administration of the community . . . that the Church considers in conflict with God's law.[2]

To calm the church down, Terboven proposed that the bishops sign a declaration calling for "Germany's victory over bolshevism." The bishops refused to take part in his game, and, in June 1941, they let it be known that they had refused his request. Several bishops were dismissed in the following weeks.

A major conflict erupted when Quisling was appointed Minister-President in February 1942. The title was an honorific, since the real power remained in the hands of the Reich's commissar. But this promotion of the NS leader was a clear sign of Germany's determination to convince Norway eventually of the benefits of Nazi ideology. In fact, the news of Quisling's appointment brought an immediate negative response and upset the population. The church was the first to react. On February 1, the day of Quisling's official nomination, religious authorities and their congregations boycotted the service that was to be celebrated in his honor at the Trondheim Cathedral in Oslo. The Minister dismissed Deacon Fjellbu the next day. Reacting to this decision, the bishops then wrote another pastoral letter, which was read in the parishes on March 1, 1942. Disagreeing with the government completely, the bishops announced that they no longer considered themselves connected to it and called on the pastors to adopt the same position. The event had a considerable psychological impact, with the population strongly approving the church's intransigence. Some pastors were dismissed, and the primate of the church himself became quite worried.

On April 5, 1942, Easter Sunday, Norway's bishops and pastors officially broke all administrative ties with the state and thereby lost their salaries. They insisted nonetheless on continuing their spiritual responsibilities. Quisling considered this an act of "active insurrection" and threatened those who would not change their minds with worse censures. Of the 850 pastors, 50 gave in to this blackmail. Several dozen resisting bishops and pastors were arrested, and the primate was placed under house arrest. Hundreds of intellectuals and teachers signed a petition in favor of liberating Berggrav and others from prison. Karl Barth, the great theologian, addressed a warm letter to the primate, and the Archbishop of Canterbury praised the Church of Norway's firmness and endurance of which all of Europe soon became aware.[3] Several pastors were arrested and deported, but this changed nothing. Norway had no national church until the end of the war.

Quisling's promotion also radicalized the conflict between the new power and society through the teachers' struggle. Most teachers were already unionized before the war, since union membership was already deeply rooted at the time. During the first year of occupation, the three teaching unions (two for primary schools and one for high schools) decided to meet in a single clandestine structure. Several days after Quisling took over as head of the state, on February 5, 1942, he promulgated a law creating a new Norwegian teachers' union (*Norges Laerer-samband*). In his mind, this union would be a pilot organization for the building of a corporate fascist-type state, a foundation for the "New Norway." Toward that goal, Quisling also announced the creation of a national-socialist youth organization that all young people between 10 and 18 would have to join. The teachers reacted quickly to these measures. On February 11 and 12, the union leaders met in secret in Oslo and decided to reject them altogether. They still had to find a means for most teachers to express their disagreement. A strike did not seem like the best method. It would dangerously expose the most militant teachers and would risk being seen by the occupier as a provocation. A more direct action was needed—one that could be carried out by the greatest number of people. The leaders considered using the technique of individually mailed petitions. The brief text was written in collaboration with Eivind Berggrav: "I cannot take part in the education of the youth of Norway along the lines stipulated by the Nasjonal Samling Ungdomsfylking, as this is against my conscience. . . . I find it necessary to announce that I cannot consider myself a member of the Laerersamband."[4] Each teacher was to copy it, sign it, write his address, and send it to the Minister of Education and Religious Affairs. In order for the action to have a real mass effect on the authorities, it was decided to send all the letters on the same date, February 20. During the following two days, about 4,000 protest letters arrived at the Ministry, and hundreds more came later.[5] A remarkable fact is that almost 90 percent of the teachers in the cities are said to have answered the appeal. As for university professors, they sent their letter of protest against the creation of the new union on February 24. The Norwegian Church also supported the action and used its information networks to publicize it.

Confronted with this unforeseen collective initiative, the government was unsure how to react. On February 25, the Minister announced that all teachers who did not recant their declaration before March 1 would be dismissed. At the same time, he announced a decision to close schools for a month starting February 27 "because of the lack of fuel"—an explanation that revealed the authorities' discomfort; the chosen pretext was rather awkward in a country covered with forests. Offers of heating wood poured in from all over Norway. Many teachers decided to teach their classes in private homes. This "forced vacation" became in fact an opportunity to explain the teachers' movement to the population, especially to the students' parents. Indeed, no news had yet been released in the censored press. The school closings were the first sign that many citizens had that there was conflict between teachers and the new regime. The school closings upset the students' parents, who then also wrote individual letters of protest. Between 100,000 and 200,000 copies of the same letter from angry parents have been estimated to have arrived at the Ministry. Since the teachers stated that their salary payments had been interrupted and that some of them might be arrested, support funds were set up to come to the aid of teachers and their families.

At the beginning of March, only a few dozen teachers belonged to the official union. Terboven and Quisling decided to resort to strong-arm tactics. On March 20,

1,100 teachers were arrested and deported to different forced labor camps in the north of the country. The largest group arrived on April 28 in Kirkenes, a small village near the Finnish border, not far from the Russian front. Here, far beyond the Arctic Circle, teachers joined Russian prisoners and lived under horrendous conditions. After these arrests, on March 22, the bishops issued a public protest and declared their support for the teachers' fight.

These deportations had been intended to intimidate the teachers in order to bring them back to reason. Therefore, the Ministry announced that the schools would reopen on May 1, that teachers who returned to the classroom then would be considered members of the new union from then on, and that their union dues would automatically be deducted from their salaries. The teachers felt supported by the population, particularly by their students' parents and the Church. Although the arrests had weakened the movement a little, the determination of the majority remained intact. They still rejected obligatory union membership but saw no reason not to return to school. On the first day of classes, each returning teacher declared, according to union instructions:

These two things—being a member of the Norges Laerersamband and teaching—are incompatible. . . . Our task is to give each one of you the necessary knowledge and training to attain fulfilment as a human being, so that you can take your place in society for your own good and that of others. The teacher's vocation is not only to give children knowledge; teachers must also teach their pupils to believe in and uphold truth and justice. Therefore teachers cannot, without betraying their calling, teach anything that violates their consciences. . . . That, I promise you, I shall not do.[6]

This new firmness on the part of the teachers helped them to win their case. Quisling was afraid that he could no longer control the situation. Two weeks earlier, the ministers and bishops had resigned in a bloc. Terboven thought that Quisling's initiatives only aroused greater hostility in the population. On April 25, the Ministry of Education and Religious Affairs published a circular conceding that each teacher had the right not to recognize NS principles but insisting nonetheless on their automatic membership in the official union. Although the structure was thus formally maintained, it had lost its initial meaning. The teachers had succeeded in sabotaging Quisling's plans. He himself was not wrong when he said on May 23: "The teachers are responsible for the fact that we have not yet made peace with Germany. You teachers have destroyed everything for me."[7] This last sentence was repeated everywhere. It signaled the victory of the teachers' struggle.

In the months that followed, those who had been deported to the labor camps were freed. At the last minute, the Germans stripped certain prisoners of their NS membership. This changed nothing in the turn of events. The teachers had succeeded in mobilizing society in their favor and had inflicted a political defeat on Quisling. The teachers' fight became the symbol of Norwegian resistance. Quisling was never able to complete his plan for a corporate state. He had planned to take control of the unions once the school system was Nazified. But the population's recent involvement in the teachers' affair forced Quisling to give this up. Terboven thought that such an initiative would have risked triggering a general strike, which he certainly did not want. Magne Jensen, who was mainly responsible for drafting the "individual-collective" letters, commented on these events after the war; the letters "created the feeling of solidarity at a rather early stage, which was so necessary for civilian combat. They broke the feeling of individual isolation, the dread of remaining alone, which was the main weapon of Nazi terror."[8]

The remarkable group cohesion that was shown by most of Norway's teachers was also manifest in countries with a lower general level of resistance. Indeed, when a profession is strongly united by a high moral concept of its practice or by its own traditions, it often develops an esprit de corps that keeps it from being taken over in a crisis situation like an occupation. The fact that most members of a profession belong to the same organizations can strengthen their fight and make it more coherent. This ideological and organizational cohesiveness becomes an important factor in developing civilian resistance.

A case of civilian resistance comparable to Norway's took place in Holland, in spite of its politically weakened state that had resulted from the General Secretaries' collaboration. Dutch doctors played the role of Norway's teachers in many ways. In both countries, the issue was the fight against "Nazifying" a profession, in the name of the moral values that determined the groups' cohesiveness. In both cases, mass action was organized by individual-collective letters, with the precious support of churches and public opinion.

In Holland, things did not begin as they had in Norway. The leaders of the medical association with which almost all the country's practitioners were affiliated, the Dutch Society for the Promotion of Medicine (*Nederlandse Maatshappij tot Bevordering der Geneeskunst* or NMBG), started becoming involved in a dangerous compromise with the occupier.[9] The NMBG leaders wondered what posture a medical group should take in this new occupation situation. Like their countrymen, few of them were seduced by Nazi ideology; their strong moral or religious convictions distanced them from it. A handful of collaborating physicians linked to Anton Mussert's party had created a new organization, the Medical Front, in November 1940. A close collaborator of the Reich's commissar, Dr. Reuter, had engaged in negotiations with NMBG leaders who actually hoped to take control of it. On May 18, 1941, these leaders accepted the participation of one member of the Medical Front in the general direction of the NMBG. Once this decision was made, German authorities let it be known that the role of the Medical Front member would be to bring the Dutch medical corps into line. Among more purely administrative reform proposals, various provisions aimed particularly at excluding Jewish physicians.

The majority of doctors who had been passive until then reacted negatively to these measures. In June 1941, some physicians met and called on their colleagues to leave the NMBG. During July, a resignation movement began. It grew all the stronger when the Catholic medical association also called for a mass resignation on August 14. This decision was made with the agreement of the Dutch Episcopate.

By the end of the summer of 1941, most of the 5,700 NMBG members had quit. Confronted with this deep movement of defiance that it obviously could not control, the General Directorate of NMBG preferred to resign on September 27.

During the summer, the bonds between the resisting members became much tighter and more stable, to the extent that the physicians eventually decided to create an underground organization. On August 24, 1941, the more dynamic among them laid the foundation for this new association, which they called *Medisch Contact* (MC).[10] They then sent a letter to colleagues they thought might become regional leaders of the organization. The MC was officially established on September 14, 1941, during their first general assembly in Utrecht.

While the doctors were organizing clandestinely, the Germans were preparing a new health organization controlled completely by them, the Chamber of Dutch Physicians. In June 1941, they announced the project whose goal was to apply National Socialism to the practice of medicine. The first act of the MC was to make as many doctors as possible sign a letter dissuading the Germans from pursuing their plan. Addressed to the German authorities, this text declared particularly:

It cannot have escaped your attention that, having left the NMBG, we physicians are concerned with expressing our conviction that the therapist's function, invested with high moral and spiritual considerations, must remain removed from all political interference. . . . We have reason to fear that government employees unknown to us . . . could interfere with our patients' treatments and make us collaborate more or less directly. . . . Tied as we are to a professional oath, we feel obligated to declare to you that we will conform to the high values of this oath which has honored our profession since the beginning of its history. We will never recognize another path than the one recognized by our conscience, our professional duty, and our science.[11]

On December 16, 1941, the letter was delivered to a representative of the Reich's commissar; 4,261 physicians had signed it. This first action so impressed physicians that it established the *Medisch Contact's* authority. Furthermore, since the Germans seemed not to want to deal with reprisals, the success encouraged the physicians to continue the struggle. On December 19, 1941, three days after the petition was delivered, a decree pronounced the dissolution of the NMBG and the creation of the Chamber of Dutch Physicians. All the country's doctors were automatically enrolled. The MC's reaction was swift. It advised its members, purely and simply, to ignore the new organization, not to fill out the forms, and to refuse to pay the dues. In January 1942, around 3,000 doctors sent another letter to this effect. The new medical group was thus virtually still-born from its inception; its membership included only the few pro-Nazi doctors in the country.

The game was not yet won, however. After this affair, the German police started to take a serious interest in the medical field. They arrested and imprisoned some doctors for a short time, and, in September 1942, the official Chamber of Dutch Physicians once again decided to send membership forms to the doctors; the MC, in turn, sent another order not to fill the forms out, and only 700 of them were returned properly completed. On January 15, 1943, the authorities announced that doctors who did not join the Chamber by March 1 would be fined 1,000 florins. Some gave in to this new pressure but most persisted in their refusal. Resisting physicians were then summoned to pay their fines, but none did. Their sentences were pronounced nonetheless: a fine of 1,000 florins and the obligation to join the Chamber within two weeks. If a doctor gave no response, offenders would be hit with a new fine of 1,000 florins and so on until they gave in. The risks were serious: by multiplying fines like this indefinitely, the resistance could be weakened and even broken within a short time. The MC let it be known that it would answer for the payments of fines, but for how long?

To extricate itself from this affair, the MC hit upon the idea of relying on article 5 of the December 19, 1941, decree, which stipulated: "A doctor can declare his retirement from the medical profession. From then on, he loses the right to be called doctor." This text allowed doctors to give up the title "doctor" without prior authorization. Once he was no longer an official member of the medical profession, the "resigned" physician could not be forced to pay dues or fines to an organization to which he did not belong. On March 24, 1943, therefore, several thousand doctors sent in cancellation letters. They nonetheless continued to practice their profession *de facto*, in order to fulfill the population's health needs. They knew that they thus came under the "illegal practice of medicine" law, but the consequences of this act of civil disobedience seemed worth exploiting.

To make their gesture public, the "doctors" decided to cover their shingles and thereby inform people of their action. Public opinion clearly favored them, so colleagues who had cautiously removed themselves from the MC's activities until then did not want to be left behind; they also covered their shingles. Even some of the doctors who most strongly supported the Chamber did so. In all, more than 6,200 doctors, almost all those in practice in 1943, took part in this action. The affair took on a public and national dimension. The cabinet of the General Secretaries did not wish to express itself openly but also did not want to go against the movement. The General Secretary of Social Affairs let it be known that the doctors' act did not fall under the law concerning the illegal practice of medicine. Churches, especially the Catholic church, were also favorable to the movement and had actually been helping it from the beginning.

Faced with such a display of strength, the German administration agreed to negotiate. This resulted in an agreement. The doctors would no longer be forced to belong to the Chamber, provided they uncovered their shingles. But the Germans did not keep their word and demanded Chamber membership again on May 18. At that time, 360 physicians were arrested and their offices closed. Consequently, many of their colleagues went underground. The health system was paralyzed. As a result, new negotiations opened and renewed the preceding compromise. It was agreed that the official Chamber would be maintained since, according to the Germans, its suppression would harm the prestige of the Reich's commissar who had personally hoped for its creation, but no doctor was forced to belong. During the summer of 1943, the imprisoned doctors were released.

Dutch physicians engaged in other struggles until their country was liberated. For example, they fought against the control of medical funds by their German counterparts and forced labor in Germany. This battle against the official Chamber, however, marked the climax of the confrontation between physicians and the regime. According to historian Werner Warmbrunn, "The action of the medical profession may be considered an almost perfect example of noncooperation with the German war effort, which was made possible by the near-unanimous attitude and excellent organization of its members and by the fact that the physicians were irreplaceable; their wholesale imprisonment would have been a major disaster from both the German and the Dutch points of view."[12]

The outcome of the resistance by the Dutch physicians was strangely similar to what occurred with Norway's teachers. The collaborating institution was formally maintained but, in reality, no one was forced to belong to it.

In countries where social consensus was weaker, civilian resistance had a more limited scope. France and Belgium, for different cultural or political reasons, had deep internal conflicts before the war, which played into the hand of the occupier during their occupation. The first consequence of this lack of internal cohesion was the phenomenon of collaboration itself. Belgium had the highest proportion of collaborationists with respect to its general population. The virtual absence of organized resistance at the beginning of the occupation was another consequence. During the two years following the invasion, scattered groups representing different political tendencies and nuances blossomed. Henri Bernard has noted that "Belgian individualism led to the formation of an excessive number of groups."[13] This analysis applies equally well to France.

Should we conclude that there was therefore no consensus in these two countries? Of course not. France and Belgium are both too old *not* to have had within them, despite divisions, citizens with common values. The invasion and its resulting trauma totally confused the usual frames of reference, however. A new and completely unprecedented political situation resulted. France and Belgium were ripped apart internally. All opposition seemed completely utopian. Time was needed to build a new unity, even within the opposition. *Patriotic values*—that is, those defending their national identity against foreign intrusion—created the beginning of a consensus. In this sense, different studies have shown that those who resisted considered themselves, above all, as patriots. To recover their freedom, the conquered societies had to reclaim an identity that transcended the expression of their political divisions. For the most part, this identity was manifested in the patriotic ideal.

In this slow process of reconquest and repossession, consensus started to form on the occasions of strongly symbolic anniversaries. These celebrations brought back memories of national events that had marked the country's history and created a consensus. Popular and spontaneous protest marches that celebrated anniversaries of national founding events took place in many of the countries of occupied Europe.

The first occurred in Czechoslovakia on October 28, 1939, the anniversary of the foundation of the independent Czech state. Several thousand people, dressed in their national colors, demonstrated in the streets of Prague. They clashed with the Czech police and the Gestapo. A few days later, a student who had been seriously injured in those clashes died of his wounds. His friends decided to organize another demonstration on November 15, the day of his funeral. Nazi repression was ferocious, and thousands of students were deported. On November 17, all of the country's universities were closed until the end of the war.[14]

In Holland and Norway, there were also demonstrations of loyalty to the royal families. On June 29, 1940, which was Prince Bernard's birthday, many Dutch citizens wore a white carnation on their lapels, according to their custom. As for the Norwegians, they pinned a flower to their clothes on King Haakon's birthday, August 3, 1942. Many nationalist demonstrations took place in the more important cities in Belgium—Brussels, Antwerp, Liège, and Charleroi—on November 11, 1940, the anniversary of the end of World War I and the victory over Germany. The most widely distributed flyer announcing this celebration said: "Let's form a bloc, and may this day leave the memory of a unanimous demonstration in the minds of our oppressors."[15] In Brussels, where the largest demonstration took place on Sunday, November 10, sheaves of flowers and wreaths were gathered in front of the monument to the Unknown Soldier. The next day, several thousand people marched in the streets of the capital, singing the national anthem and shouting slogans hostile to the Germans. German repression was limited, but the occupier threatened the cabinet of the General Secretaries with severe reprisals if such incidents occurred again.

France had the greatest number of symbolic demonstrations, as if the repetition itself were urgently needed to heal the country's internal divisions. A veritable ritual of symbolic demonstrations took place in France, revealing a "fetishism for high festivals," according to Henri Noguères.[16] The first demonstration since the beginning of the occupation took place in Paris on November 11, 1940. On this day, several hundred students, shouting nationalist slogans and singing the Marseillaise, marched up the Champs-Elysées before being arrested. Too few have noted that General de Gaulle himself also called for demonstrations of this type several times from London. This was probably a means for the French leaders in London both to test their population's combativeness and to rouse their spirit of nationalist resistance. The radio became the ideal instrument for action toward this goal. General de Gaulle's first appeal, on December 23, 1940, asked the French to remain indoors and stay out of the streets for an hour on January 1, 1941. He declared on the BBC:

Next January 1, from 2 to 3 o'clock in the afternoon in nonoccupied France, no French person should be in the streets of our cities or our villages. Only the enemy will appear there. . . . All French people will remain inside behind closed doors either alone or among family or friends. During this hour of meditation, we will all think about Liberation together. It will be an hour of hope.[17]

It is difficult to conceive of the real impact of this appeal, repeated by de Gaulle in different ways several times before January 1. It seems that the order was observed especially in the occupied zone; in Paris, the Germans organized a free distribution of potatoes at the specified time in response. London radio launched many other appeals for demonstrations. "Free France" called for a one-day slow-down strike on September 5, 1941. De Gaulle called on the French as a nation to stand at attention on October 31, in a kind of lightning general strike that would last only five minutes, to protest the first execution of hostages in France (that of Chateaubriant, on October 22, in reprisal for the assassination of a German soldier). In his speech on the BBC on October 25, the general declared:

By shooting our martyrs, the enemy thought that he would frighten France. France will show that she isn't afraid. . . . She will give proof by standing at attention in total immobility. Next Friday from 4 o'clock to 4:05 in the afternoon, all activity must stop over the entire territory of France. . . . All French men and all French women will remain still, each right where he or she is—in fields, in factories, in offices, in schools, in stores. . . . This huge national strike will show the enemy and the traitors following him what a gigantic threat looms over them.[18]

In another speech, Maurice Schumann, the other famous spokesman for Free France, specified that the action should take place with the utmost calmness and with no shouts or unlawful assembly.[19] For the first time, the communists accepted the Gaullist order. This time, the order seems to have been followed so consistently that the Germans tried to provoke incidents to keep it from being carried out in several cities.

Internal resistance leaders of the unoccupied zone asked de Gaulle to launch an appeal for a demonstration on May 1, 1942. He made no objection and did indeed summon the French in the southern zone to "silently and individually pass in front of the statues of the Republic and the town halls of our cities and villages."[20] For the first time since the beginning of the war, mass demonstrations took place in several large cities in the south of the country, with tens of thousands of participants in Lyon and Marseille, several thousand in Toulouse, Montpellier, Clermont-Ferrand, and so on. They sang both the Internationale and the Marseillaise, booed Pierre Laval, the new Prime Minister, and cheered the name of de Gaulle. In an enthusiastic report, the personal delegate of General Jean Moulin wrote:

This is the first united demonstration of the Resistance. . . . It clearly marked the movement's communion of ideas and the determination of the Resistance to follow de Gaulle, whom everyone hailed as leader and symbol. Even if it did not meet the same success everywhere, it had a considerable effect on the activists who feel the coordination between London and local leaders for the first time.[21]

This provided a good opportunity for de Gaulle to strengthen his influence over the working class and to rally them to his side; for the local Resistance, it was a way to prove to itself that it was becoming a power to contend with, along with London.

Throughout nearly the entire occupation, France held demonstrations every July 14, its national holiday, and on November 11, which marked the end of World War I. From the first year of the German presence, these dates offered the opportunity for individuals or small groups to demonstrate their attachment to their national values. They displayed the tricolor flag at their windows or managed to dress in those three colors; families frequently dressed their first child in blue, their second in white, and their third in red. After the success of the May 1 demonstration, July 14, 1942, would be the stage of one of the largest demonstrations that France had seen since the beginning of the war. Once again, radio from London played an essential role. On July 5, 1942, Schumann called on the French in the nonoccupied zone to exhibit the national colors on July 14 and to gather in front of symbolic monuments.[22] These calls to action were repeated until "J–Day," concluding with a short speech by de Gaulle ending with these words: "Flags are our pride; parades are our hope; the Marseillaise is our rage. We need and still hold on to pride, hope, and rage. Tomorrow everyone will see!"[23] It is significant that the appeals emphasized the coordination between London and the internal resistance movement, and that furthermore, the orders became more precise and the tone increasingly solemn as J–day approached. On July 14, the prefect from Lyon himself counted more than 100,000 people in the streets of the city. Elsewhere, several thousands or tens of thousands of people came together in Grenoble, Toulouse, Valence, and Vienne, where the police intoned the Marseillaise along with the 4,000 demonstrators. Although these crowds usually gathered without incident, this was not the case in Marseille where people were killed by followers of General Doriot who fired on a demonstration. On July 19, the funeral of those killed was the occasion for another demonstration, which was once again launched over the BBC.

With the invasion of the southern zone on November 11, 1942, London radio stopped its appeals for public demonstrations. It continued mobilizing public opinion, however, so that each citizen could celebrate national events in his or her own way. These celebrations took other forms: sabotages, strikes, or spectacular eruptions into the streets by the men of the *maquis*, as occurred in Oyonnax on November 11, 1943, for a brief ceremony at the monument to the dead. On May 1, 1944, the Germans declared a national day off to keep the resistance movement from organizing a general strike on that day. But the July 14 demonstrations of 1942 were important, even if only one part of the country expressed itself openly. These actions marked an essential step toward the slow revival of the French citizens' patriotic identity on which the organized resistance could be built. Their numbers surprised both the public authorities and their organizers. They showed Vichy and the entire population that resistance movements really existed, could be influential, and were sufficiently structured to make their orders respected. Finally, the demonstrations marked the success of the coordination between the internal and external resistance movements. Indeed, through its nationalist symbols, through clandestine movements, which were drawing closer and closer together, and through a distant but increasingly respected leader, France was recovering its identity.

EXTERNAL FACTORS

In addition to factors based on convictions and on the typical behavior of an invaded society, there is a cohesion of occupied people based on the specific traits of the aggression and the occupation conditions accompanying it. Although it seems surprising from a theoretical point of view, aggression itself is a factor that contributes to cohesion, an event that can precipitate and crystallize cohesion. An occupied population suddenly has cohesion *because* of the occupier. Everything depends on the strategic objectives of the invader in relation to the invaded—what the former wants from the latter—and on the occupation tactics—the way the invader intends to behave.

Generally speaking, the occupier's attitude (for example, its degree of brutality toward the occupied population) partially determines the latter's cohesion. In this respect, repression seems to be a key factor of the development of social cohesion. We are accustomed to thinking of repression as the supreme means that a tyrant uses to spread terror among his subjects. It does not occur to us to contest the value of this observation, for which instances of historical verification unfortunately abound. But we have not adequately noted the other side of the phenomenon—namely, that beyond a certain threshold, repression becomes counter-productive with respect to its own objectives. Instead of shattering the society that it attacks, it unites it. By being too repressive, the invader creates unanimity against it. That is why, paradoxically, repression can create cohesion. Societies that may have been internally fragile before a war can thus witness a closing of the ranks to topple the invader.

That was the case with Poland, for example. The unbelievable brutality of Nazi repression created a new unity in this country. The extreme degree of repression by the occupier encouraged the development of noncooperation among the occupied population. This does not mean that all Poles were unwilling to collaborate. At the same time, however, the Germans were not automatically perceived with hostility within the Polish bourgeoisie and peasantry. Moreover, the complexity of the nationality question made the German and Soviet occupations strengthen the divisions within the populations. Thus, in eastern Poland, the Ukrainians moved closer to the Soviets and then to the Germans against the Poles and the Jews, whereas in the western part of the country, certain Poles of German origin played along with the occupier. In the General Government territory, however, Nazi brutality was so harsh that many who would otherwise have been predisposed to collaborate were dissuaded from it. In any case, the occupiers did not really try to set up a collaborating government. In fact, Berlin's opinion of Poland was never very precise except for one thing: Hitler wanted to destroy the intelligentsia and Polish culture in general.

The Polish resistance is known more for the insurrection of the Jewish ghetto in Warsaw in 1943 than for the insurrection of the city itself in 1944, when Stalin's armies were at the gates of the capital. These tragic events must not make us overlook the complexity and richness of the Polish resistance that succeeded in constructing a true clandestine state, an underground society with multiple ramifications within the interstices of official society. Resisting was called "serving." The Polish people served their fatherland in a wide variety of ways, both armed and unarmed. According to one of its most famous agents, Jan Karski, the resistance was organized from the beginning in this atmosphere of general complicity without unanimity around two main lines of action: "1. whatever direction the war would go in, the Poles would refuse to collaborate with the Germans in any way; 2. the Polish State would be perpetuated by a clandestine administration working with the government in exile."[24] This clandestine state, which was structured during the first three years of the occupation, in liaison with the government in exile of General Wladyslow Sikorski, consisted of five branches: administrative services, a secret army, political and parliamentary representation, a civilian resistance directorate, and a coordinating committee of economic, educational, religious, and other groups. An astonishing fact is that a true "parliament," which brought together the reduced political representations of the four principal parts of the country, continued to meet clandestinely during almost the whole occupation period. As for the secret army, it was famous for many sabotage actions, creating a climate of insecurity that led in turn to repression within the German ranks.

Within this context of total war against a population threatened with annihilation, one of the most remarkable cases of civilian resistance in the history of the Nazi occupation of Europe developed. One of the first measures of Poland's "Germanization" was the destruction of its intelligentsia and its culture. Hitler had said that the Germans had to eliminate the ruling elite of Polish society, to watch out for the younger generation who might replace them, and finally to liquidate them. From the first months of the occupation, the Germans went after the intellectuals and, in particular, the academics. At the beginning of the school year in Cracow, on November 5, 1939, all the professors at the prestigious university were arrested. There were also imprisonments and executions in legal, artistic, medical, and church circles. In November 1939, all academic institutions, except for primary schools and some technical schools, were closed. The teaching of the Polish language, history, and geography was also abolished. Scientific institutions, the radio, and the theater were likewise closed down.

In this context of generalized aggression against the culture of a people, the Polish resistance aimed at saving what little could be saved, especially in the field of art, and setting up underground courses at all levels. After all, Poland had a tradition of underground education dating back as far as the middle of the nineteenth century.[25] With the Nazi occupation, this historical reflex revived; underground courses were organized on a broad scale, mostly in the General Government territories. An education "ministry" was created within the clandestine state, and teachers were paid with funds from the government in exile.

Since primary schools were still authorized, the teaching of Polish language, history, and geography courses became even more crucial. In the countryside, where everyone knew one another, these additional courses were offered within the schools themselves. In the cities, children gathered outside the regular class hours in courses called *komplety* to avoid the presence of suspicious onlookers. According to Joseph Krasuski, in 1943–1944, about 37,000 students took the *komplety*, which had been organized by 2,352 teachers.[26] He figured that one pupil out of three or four took this kind of parallel course. This average does not take into account the large disparities between the different regions. In the colonized territories of the west, the strong German presence made organizing *komplety* almost impossible. In the Lublin region, the Ukrainian community created an obstacle by collaborating with the occupier.

In high schools, underground courses took place on a larger scale. All the high schools were closed from one day to the next, but many of the students were motivated to continue their studies. With the church's support, the teachers set up a broad organization of *komplety*, none of which was to bring together more than seven students. Since technical and trade schools (mechanics, sewing, etc.) were authorized, teachers took advantage of them, using their program hours for other purposes; for example, instead of studying the commercial correspondence course, the students did Polish or history. It is estimated that about 70 percent of all high school students of this period were taught in this way; out of 90,000 students before the war, about 60,000 are said to have taken the *komplety* in 1943–1944. About 18,000 are estimated to have taken their baccalaureate exam underground.[27]

Underground universities are probably the best known element of Polish underground teaching. Warsaw's was the first to be reorganized early in 1940. In the beginning, the universities were not inclined to work under such conditions, but the dynamism of certain students won them over. The theology school became active first in February 1940. The faculties of law, medicine, liberal arts, and others followed. Many university professors from Poznań, having been thrown out of their city, came to settle in Warsaw. Seeking to continue their courses and scholarly work there, they created "the University of the Western Territories" (*Uniwersytet Ziem Zachodnich* or UZZ). Without a specific geographical base, it consisted of *komplety* networks scattered throughout Warsaw and its suburbs. The first courses started in December 1940 and, by 1943, there were even elections for university rectorships. To have the right to participate, students had to take an oath pledging to respect the extremely strict security instructions. The UZZ first brought together the economics, agronomy, and liberal arts faculties, and later the faculties of political economics and the sciences. As for Cracow, the oldest university of them all, it became active again only in 1942. All these universities taught several hundreds of students, handed out degrees, and continued to publish scholarly works.[28]

A total of almost 100,000 students from all school levels took underground courses during the war. The difficult security conditions, the diversity of practices, and the small number of meetings among teachers certainly harmed the quality of the teaching. During this period, teacher training was also virtually nonexistent. Given the climate of terror pervading the country, however, underground teaching was no doubt the most widespread and best organized activity of the Polish resistance. One of its former leaders, Kozniewski, wrote of it:

Underground teaching on all levels of schooling was the most admirable work accomplished by Polish society. Neither tracts, nor violence, nor sabotages were as productive as this last manifestation of the national consciousness. It saved our society from a catastrophe equal at least to the destruction of Warsaw: the loss of five graduating classes of engineers, architects, doctors, teachers, and students who passed their baccalaureate exam.[29]

In countries where the Germans did not display such ferocity, the societies did not became so cohesive so early in the course of their political repression. On the contrary, in the Western European countries, the Nazi attitude of *Korrection* was even quite seductive. If the resistance of civil society was insignificant during the first year of the occupation in France or Belgium, it was due not only to internal divisions but also to the fact that the Germans did not yet behave too brutally. After June 1941, when the Germans entered the war against the Soviet Union, the communists took up armed struggle, and the first terrorists were executed in reprisals, the social and political climate became more oppressive with the bitterness of the terrorized populations constantly increasing.

It would be simplistic to conclude that physical repression was the only action by the occupiers that contributed to the progressive forging of civil society's cohesion against the occupier. Indeed, the deteriorating relations between the occupier and the occupied were generally due more to the occupying regime's ever-increasing pressure on civil society. Germany's determination to exploit the fruits of its conquests to the maximum was so great that populations were left desiring only one thing: an end to the constant drain that they endured every day of their lives. If the new situation had been relatively bearable in the beginning, it became less and less so as time went on.

Externally, attitudes toward the occupier changed considerably as the war evolved internationally. On the internal level of the occupied societies, everything that affected people in their daily lives was really the determining element in progressively changing their minds. The development of an economy of scarcity due to the war and to the endless exploitation by Germany played an essential role in it. If the scarcity of food and goods made fortunes for those who operated on the black market, it frustrated the majority. But above and beyond the seriousness of the economic situation, there was the pressure on the men. First, many young men were enlisted, to a limited extent, into the Wehrmacht; later, many young men and some of their elders were forced into obligatory labor in Germany. At this point, many families were affected. Being brutally and arbitrarily ripped out of their everyday milieu was what they found intolerable.

The whole history of the German occupation of Western Europe is marked by this slow deterioration of relations between the occupier and the occupied because of the occupier's excessive and arbitrary demands. It was as though the Germans, little by little and on their own, had lost the capital they had had when they arrived—not of friendship, but at least of prudent accommodation. In this context, the occupied societies used mass movement at various times to express their spontaneous resistance to the politics that were strangling them. These movements are analogous to the rejection mechanisms of a biological organism.

Food shortages in northwestern Europe, which was considered the war zone and therefore under German military administration, produced the first mass strikes in the occupation's history. In both Belgium and France, miners were the first to express openly the whole region's dissatisfaction. With the strong feelings of solidarity and internal cohesion for which they were known, the miners were particularly likely to air these grievances. Because their work was indispensable to the German war machine, miners, like metal-workers, had the power to go on strike, unlike professions that were less useful to the occupier and thus more exposed to repression in case of a work stoppage. To be sure, a German order prohibited salary raises, and striking was certainly not easy. Still, miners and metal-workers had a chance of being heard because they worked in strategic economic sectors. The movement took off on May 10, 1941, in metallurgy (Colkerill Establishments) and then reached the Liège mining basin. Salaries had not been raised for a year, contrary to the advice of General Eggert Reeder who was responsible for Belgian administrative services.[30] Food distribution functioned poorly, and people complained especially about the lack of potatoes, margarine, and soap. In spite of the abrogation of the right to strike, partial strikes began during the fall of 1940. At the end of January 1941, the movement suddenly grew. About 10,000 miners stopped work, protesting also against a tax that the General Secretaries had just imposed. Another strike broke out at the National Factory of Herstal, a munitions factory where 3,000 out of 4,000 workers asked for a larger potato ration. In this exuberant climate, tens of thousands of miners stopped work between May 10 and 20. The strike took off from the Liège industrial basin and reached as far as Hainaut and Limbourg. The strikers demanded better food distribution for the whole population, a raise in salaries, and a cancellation of taxes. Arrests were made, but the miners won partial satisfaction of their demands: an 8 percent salary raise and the distribution of additional food stamps. The occupier needed these workers.[31]

A week later, the same kind of movement took off in the mines of the departments of Nord and Pas de Calais on the French side. Sporadic strike movements also broke out during the fall of 1940. To the surprise of everyone, on November 11 (which had once again become an ordinary workday), 30 percent of the miners did not report to their mine shafts. In January and March of 1941, there were more partial strikes. On May 1, the Communist Party, which was very influential in the basin, succeeded in demonstrating its strength. In spite of an impressive police presence, dozens of red flags waved on the mining sites that morning.

The most important mass movement in the history of occupied France broke out in this tense climate on May 27, 1941. The communist leader, Auguste Lecoeur, has given an important account of this.[32] The movement started at the Dourges shaft, which was called "Dahomey," and slowly reached other mining operations. The demands concerned improving food distribution, salaries, and work conditions. The mine bosses had taken advantage of the German presence to challenge earlier salary agreements and the 1936 collective agreement. The next day, May 28, French authorities made arrests but the miners remained calm. The strike continued to spread despite the repression, with the women playing an important role in mobilizing the more reticent. On June 4, the day the movement peaked, about 80 percent of the miners (almost 100,000) stopped work. All operations were affected, as were dependent factories like coking plants. Workers from other industries in the region (metallurgy, spinning factories, tileworks) also started to mobilize.[33] The mining communities were placed in a virtual state of siege, and German troops intervened. Hundreds of people were arrested, including dozens of women. Courts-martial pronounced sentences of forced labor: 235 people were deported, and 130 never came back. Coal company bosses threatened not to pay salaries for the second half of May if the workers did not start working again very quickly. By June 10, everything was over. The occupier made some concessions during the days that followed, especially in terms of improving food distribution, but the price was still steep. Nonetheless, Stéphane Courtois, the author of a reference work on the history of the Communist Party during the war, has noted that it is to the "credit of the Communists that, whether or not they were aiming at a confrontation with the occupier, they triggered the first mass movement that challenged the very principle of the occupation."[34]

A little more than a year later, an important strike shook the Grand Duchy of Luxemburg, in response to the forced enlistment of young men into the German army. After the May 10, 1940, invasion, the royal family and government of this small neutral country went to England. With its mining and metallurgy industries, Luxemburg was of great industrial interest to Germany. But Berlin had other ideas for the people of Luxemburg as well. Since it considered them to be of Germanic stock, like the people of Alsace and Lorraine, Germany was determined to connect them to the Reich; the *Gauleiter* thus administered the two French provinces and Luxemburg directly. After the German offensive against the Soviet Union failed during the winter of 1941–1942, Hitler needed new troops. To recruit them, his general staff proposed making the annexation of these three territories official, by conferring German nationality on their populations. The young men of these countries would then be legally compelled to enlist in the German army. On August 24, 1942, the Ministry of the Interior in Berlin published an order to this effect. Thus began the tragedy of these forcibly enlisted men, who came to be called the *Malgré-nous* ("in-spite-of-ourselves").[35] From Alsace and Lorraine, they tried to flee to the Vosges or to Switzerland. In Luxemburg, the Gauleiter Gustav Simon announced the news on August 30. A strike was triggered the next day in the Esch mining basin and reached the city of Luxemburg itself. The students turned out to be particularly active in mobilizing the population. The movement lasted until September 4.[36] The Germans then decreed a stage of siege and promptly unleashed a fierce repression. Hundreds of people were arrested, 40 were deported, and 21 young people from various professional milieus were condemned to death. In a speech given over the few next days, the Gauleiter threatened the population with massive deportations. He also let slip this small sentence that the BBC and the Resistance picked up immediately: "In the West especially, Luxemburg represents constant danger, even if only of secondary importance, for the life of the entire German nation."[37]

This forced enlistment into the Wehrmacht affected only a small part of Western Europe's population. Starting in September 1942, however, measures requisitioning men and women from Belgium, Holland, and France for forced labor in Germany affected hundreds of thousands of people. After several months of passivity, during which populations were literally staggered by this shock treatment, public opinion became more and more negative. Starting in the spring and especially the summer of 1943, recruits went underground by the tens of thousands.

We will discuss below the forms of this spontaneous disobedience movement, especially in France. But it was in Holland that the German decision provoked the most immediate and spectacular reaction of popular discontent. Probably the largest strike in the history of the Nazi occupation of Europe was unleashed there at the end of April 1943; a half million people are estimated to have taken part in it.[38] To satisfy its need for manpower, Berlin had had the idea of "recalling to service" tens of thousands of Dutch soldiers who had been taken prisoner in 1940 and then liberated. The decision, announced on April 29 by General Christiansen, stunned the Dutch. A spontaneous strike broke out in the Hengelo region and soon reached the mining district of Limbourg and the Philips factories of Eindhoven. The movement spread mostly within the industrial areas of the country, where the owners did not seem hostile to it. An exceptional fact is that it also reached agricultural areas. In various places, peasants and delivery people refused to bring milk to cooperatives. On April 30, several hundred thousand people stopped working. Street protests broke out in several cities and were promptly put down. Completely surprised by the speed with which the strikes were spreading, the Germans declared a state of siege; dozens of people were executed after appearing before German courts-martial. The movement declined rapidly after May 3 but lasted until May 8 in Friesland and North-Brabant. Its psychological and political consequences were considerable, since the rift between opinion and the regime seemed definitive from then on. The strikes radicalized other social milieus, particularly in agriculture, and more and more people assisted and protected the labor conscripts throughout the country.[39]

The forced labor measures therefore had a disastrous effect on the very people who had imposed them. Germany provoked against itself a growing movement of internal cohesion that had not existed to such a degree before 1943. An objective indication of this new cohesion was the occurrence of many instances of solidarity shown toward the labor conscripts in most social milieus. From then on, organized resistance began to reach its true extent. Its numbers increased, and populations became increasingly receptive. In sum, the occupier bore the cost of his own politics.

LAWS OF REACTIVITY

Civilian resistance (although one should always phrase that in the plural—resistances) developed in a highly complex way. An occupied people first had to recover a certain cohesiveness, as a result either of its own prewar internal political balance or of the very nature or evolution of the occupying regime. This process of forming a civil society's "resisting cohesiveness" was often quite laborious. It was primarily the result of the progressive, sectoral mobilization of various social and professional groups. Many of the specific events reported here represented states of crisis through which the occupied society expressed its intolerance of a particular aspect of occupation politics. These crises, which could be spectacular, sporadic, or long lasting, mobilized specific social or professional groups for very different reasons. Generally, their scope surprised the occupier as much as resistance leaders.

These mobilizations more frequently resulted from the groups' "reactivity" to situations that were no longer tolerable rather than from being deliberately organized. Different groups each opposed the occupying regime in terms of their own histories and states of mind. Each group had a specific situation or event or symbol that triggered its mobilization. Thus, in Belgium, the protests on November 11, 1940, were due mostly to the bourgeoisie's attachment to nationalist values, whereas a few months later, the miners from the Liège basin reacted against the deterioration of living conditions. In Norway, the regime's attack on the school system mobilized the teachers, just as attacks on the church triggered the clergy's resistance. Many social groups experienced key moments that made them take up the fight with their own inherent styles and rhythms.

The growth of resistance followed a series of social chain reactions that precipitated certain elements of these groups into action, resembling the reactive process in chemistry. When these partial mobilizations came together, they formed the foundation of a national resistance movement. In this sense, civilian resistance movements were like specific stages along a difficult path leading to national organized resistance. This process did not necessarily take the same form according to the initial position of the legitimate political power with respect to the occupier. The reaction speed of a society's different elements was probably quicker, however, in countries where the legitimate political power refused to collaborate with the occupier. Still, we can observe three classic resistance phases in these countries as well as in the others: first, resistance is *spontaneous*, then *organized*, and finally, *unified*. Regardless of the initial situation, it has been proven that a society cannot be mobilized like an army.

Nonetheless, the mass character of the actions studied here should not delude us as to their true nature. Of course, the struggle around the school systems in

Norway or Poland and around the medical profession in the Netherlands may have been similar to a crusade to safeguard national values. But this was not always the case. For example, strikes that led to improved food distribution cannot be considered acts aiming to challenge the principle of the occupation but only to correct its most unbearable daily effects. This limited dimension of the protest action is also present in the Norwegian teachers' struggle; they fought more against Quisling, after all, than against Terboven. Still, the nature of the process of spontaneously mobilizing a particular group was radicalizing. A conflict, whether based on economic or civilian demands, can quickly reveal the political nature of the confrontation of the parties involved. Individuals or groups can then move from protest struggle to political action. This classic process of radicalization gave birth to what is usually designated as "resistance"—an organized political force working to end its country's occupation.

The brutality with which the occupier put down certain strikes or demonstrations helped to reveal, for example, that the true enemy was indeed the occupier himself. Furthermore, historians have often noticed increased distribution of the underground press and growing membership in resistance groups following such public protests. These are two objective indications of the growing radicalization. The press and underground movements appear to be two main "vectors" that tangibly embody the resistance phenomenon as an opposition political force. The variety of titles made the press the ideological expression of the resistance, whereas the diversity of movements was the institutional expression.

The central role of the underground press in the general development of institutional resistance must be emphasized. The existence of the underground press must not be considered as just one element among others in resisting Nazism. It does not belong in the same category as sabotage, intelligence activities, protest marches, and so on; nor was the underground press a simple instrument of counter-propaganda in the psychological war carried on by rival powers. This press was the central axis around which internal resistance movements could organize and develop. It was as if the resistance needed an initial ideological basis in order to develop combat structures. Early resisters therefore distributed pamphlets, bulletins, and various newspapers to formulate the values for which they were fighting Nazism. The underground press operated out of conviction rather than from the desire to disseminate information. Its function was not only to address those whom it wanted to rally to its cause, but even more to convince and assert a collective self on the basis of which the new ideological order—that of the occupation—could be rejected.

Underground papers fostered the construction of "ideological ramparts" that created a shelter for organizing resistance. The underground papers were often the core of a structured opposition that really gave birth to a group inspired by a common ideal. Once this core was formed, it acted like a magnet, attracting new candidates into action, while the international situation, German errors, and the social crises described above contributed to the progressive radicalization of more and more people. New activists made it possible for groups to diversify their actions and thereby respond to the needs of the moment. Aside from publishing newspapers, they became progressively more active in making false identification papers and even organizing acts of sabotage. The underground press thus guaranteed a kind of ideological cohesion of resistance groups, which then led to the development of concrete action against the occupier.

Two basic but confusing questions emerge from this analysis. If the growth of the resistance followed a logic of reactivity to particular aspects of Nazi politics, then one may say that it developed mostly because of the occupier's errors and clumsiness. This was particularly valid in the western European countries. As a Belgian historian has observed with a touch of humor: "The Belgian resistance was, above all, in whatever form one views it, an occasional reaction against the actions of the enemy who reached more and more people through his blunders— for example, by requisitioning the potatoes that no Belgian can do without."[40] Should we therefore think with hindsight that the resistance developed inevitably and that its growth was merely facilitated by the crystallization of the populations' discontent over the occupier's most unpopular measures? Or should we conclude that, if the occupier had behaved better and managed its occupation politics more astutely, the internal resistance movement would have remained as unassuming and harmless as in the beginning?

NOTES

1. Those whom one could cite include, in England, Basil Liddell Hart, the great military historian, and Francis Buchan, first president of the International Institute for Strategic Studies, and, in France, General Georges Buis, first president of the Foundation for the Study of National Defense.

2. Quoted in Tore Gjelsvik, *Norwegian Resistance (1940–1945)* (London, 1979) 35.

3. Subsequently, a copy of the pastoral letter found its way into the secret French journal, *Les Cahiers de Témoignage chrétien* in June–July 1942.

4. Quoted by Magne Skodvin, "Norwegian Non-Violent Resistance During the German Occupation," *Strategy of Civilian Defense* ed. Adam Roberts (London, 1969) 147.

5. There are no exact statistics on this. The figure of 12,000 letters that has sometimes been reported cannot be confirmed. It is estimated that a total of 6,000 to 8,000 letters arrived at the Ministry from a total of 14,000 instructors. The NS determined that in December 1942, 54.9 percent of the instructors were opponents of the regime, 36.9 percent were "loyal," and 3.7 percent were NS members.

6. Quoted by Skodvin, "Norwegian Non-Violent Resistance" 149.

7. Skodvin, "Norwegian Non-Violent Resistance" 149.

8. Quoted by Gjelsvik, *Norwegian Resistance* 31–32.

9. The NMBG included about 90 percent of the 6,300 physicians practicing in the Netherlands.

10. Philippe de Vries, *Medisch Contact (1941–1945): Van Het Verzet der Artsen dans Nederland* (Haarlem, 1949).

11. Cited in de Vries, *Medisch Contact* 24–25.

12. Werner Warmbrunn, *The Dutch under German Occupation* (Stanford, CA, 1963) 271.

13. Henri Barnard, *Histoire de la résistance européenne* (Paris, 1968) 200.

14. See Jiri Hronek, *Volcano under Hitler* (London, 1941), Jiri Hronek, *17 Listopad 1939* (Prague, 1959), and Vojtech Mastny, *The Czechs under Nazi Rule: The Failure of National Resistance (1939–1942)* (New York, 1971).

15. Quoted in J. Gérard-Libois and J. Gotovitch, *L'an 40: la Belgique occupée* (Brussels, 1976) 369–370.

16. Interview with Henri Noguères, *Dossiers de non-violence politique*, Montargis 2 (1984) 20.

17. Charles de Gaulle, *Discours et messages: Pendant la guerre (1940–1946)* Paris, 1970) 50.

18. de Gaulle, *Discours* 124.

19. Henri Amouroux, *La Grande Histoire des Français sous l'occupation*, vol. 4 (Paris, 1979) 255.

20. de Gaulle, *Discours* 183–184.

21. Cited in Henri Noguères, *Histoire de la Résistance en France (1940–1944)*, vol. 2 (Paris, 1969) 425–426.

22. The French in the occupied zone, for the sake of caution, limited themselves to public displays. In northern France, however, the communists did not hesitate to "celebrate" the national holidays by carrying out various acts of sabotage.

23. de Gaulle, *Discours* 213.

24. Jan Karski, *Story of A Secret State* (Boston, 1944) 132.

25. After the fourth partition of Poland, following the Treaty of Vienna in 1815, Prussia, Russia, and Austria each took control of Polish territory. While the Austrians gave a degree of autonomy to the Poles, the Prussians and especially the Russians suppressed the education of the population. Therefore, benevolent groups, often comprised of women, spontaneously organized study and language groups. They developed an intellectual tradition that was carried on in Russian Poland until World War I.

26. Josef Krasuski, *Tajne szkolnictwo Polskie w okresie okupaji Hielerowskiej (1939–1945)* (Warsaw, 1971). The author has estimated that his figures are on the low side.

27. Krasuski, *Tajne* 182.

28. Jean-Pierre Neveu, "Le fonctionnement de l'enseignement supérieur polonais sous l'occupation allemande," *Revue d'histoire de la Deuxième Guerre mondiale* 40 (1960).

29. Quoted in Alexandre Kolowski, *La Vie quotidienne à Varsovie sous l'occupation allemande (1939–1945)* (Paris, 1974) 182.

30. Gérard-Libois and Gotovitch, *L'an 40* 381.

31. Arlette Jolris, *Cohésion d'un groupe social sous l'occupation allemande (1940–1944)* (Liège, 1973).

32. Auguste Lecoeur, *Croix de guerre pour une grève* (Paris, 1971).

33. Étienne Dejonghe, *Chronologie de la grève des mineurs du Nord-Pas-de-Calais (27 mai–9 juin 1941)* (Seminar on the Communist Party from the end of 1938 to the end of 1941), the Center for Historical Research on Social and Labor Movements, Institute of Contemporary History and the National Foundation of Political Science, October 1983.

34. Stéphane Courtois, *Le PCF dans la guerre: De Gaulle, la Résistance, Staline . . .* (Paris, 1980) 199.

35. Pierre Barral, "La tragédie des malgré-nous," *L'Histoire*, no. 80, special issue of "Résistants et collaborateurs," 1985, p. 121.

36. G. Trausch, *Le Long Combat des incorporés de force luxembourgeois* (Metz, 1984). See also his general work, *Le Luxembourg à l'époque contemporaine* (Luxembourg, 1975).

37. Quoted in W. Bosseler and R. Steichen, *Le Livre d'or de la résistance luxembourgeoise* (Esch-sur-Alzette, 1952) 505.

38. These large forbidden strikes were combined with the activities of urban guerrillas who knew that liberation was at hand; the uprisings were massive, particularly those in northern Italy.

39. B. A. Sijes, *De April-Mei Stakingen in Twente* (Bijlage, 1956).

40. Léo Lejeune, ''La résistance belge (1940–1944),'' *Cahiers d'histoire de la Guerre* (1950) 17.

Chapter 6

The Role of Opinion

Resistance is effective only in a social environment that stimulates and protects it. Without the complicity of a favorable environment, all forms of resistance are necessarily fragile. Many resisters have testified that their lives were saved by a door opening at just the right moment or by a stranger discreetly gesturing imminent danger. Resisters had to be "like fish in the water,"[1] to use the stock Maoist expression that French historians have applied to the period of the Nazi occupation. In a certain way, a society's state of mind determines whether or not a resistance movement will form organically. Recent research has started to explore the close relationship between opinion and resistance.

Some of the era's documents give us an idea of how opinion evolved during the course of the war. In Belgium, the notes that Paul Struye made regularly about every six months during the occupation constitute a valuable text for understanding how the reactions of the Belgian population evolved. The fact that his observations were written on the spot and in a relatively impartial style adds to the value of this document, which was published after the war.[2] But texts like this are the exception. We have had to wait until recent years for objective studies by researchers who did not live through the period. The work of Pierre Laborie is certainly one of the most remarkable contributions in this field.[3] Turning away from studies of the institutional dimension of resistance (movement and network structures, actions by political parties, etc.), Laborie has proposed an overall study of the evolution of the state of mind of the French inhabitants of the department of Lot, with respect to the main events of the war and the occupation. Although this regional approach might have limited the impact of this study, it in fact created a deeper understanding of human reactions and behavior in the exceptional situations of war and occupation. The author has also proposed a method of analyzing opinion by studying the official and underground press, police reports, mail and official declarations, and texts by the main organizations and associations representing the population. The difficult methodological problems involved had, until then, made people doubt the feasibility of such research.

From the period of the phony war in 1939 up through the Liberation in 1944, Laborie followed the evolution of the state of mind of various social groups in a region of "la France profonde," with respect to their own collective histories and mind–sets. According to him, "opinion is formed as a result of complex ramifications between the profound states of mind, the experiences, and the ideological orientations of social groups." One obviously cannot understand a population's opinion without first taking into consideration the past of the social groups it involved, especially the history of their states of mind. These diverse groups may have had very diverse perceptions of the same reality. This is why "particular circumstances are needed for these divergences to be erased in favor of a broader, more homogeneous expression."[4] Borrowing an image from chemistry, one could say that the opinion forming at a given time[5] is like the "precipitate" resulting from the "shock" of more or less exceptional events on collective states of mind. The study of opinion modifications and of the accompanying behaviors becomes an indispensable key for understanding the phenomena of collaboration or resistance and the various attitudes toward the invader—in short, the basic features of the occupation situation.

We must emphasize a distinction, however, which Laborie does not always make clear, between a population's state of mind on a specific question (defining its opinion on a particular problem at a given time) and the different concept of public opinion. The latter assumes that civil society has a plurality of means of expression and of information independent of the regime, which is certainly not the case in authoritarian or dictatorial political systems. It is therefore confusing to speak of "public opinion" in the context of the Vichy regime and the German occupation. During this period, one can describe public opinion in the sense of an opinion that was not private and that was expressed officially in the press, for example. Since the press was subject to censorship, however, it is more a question of "authorized" or "directed" opinion. Such an approach to the concept of "public opinion" would lead to a formal definition that hardly fits with the idea of counterpower associated with it.

There is thus an important difference between what one might call a population's general state of mind about a particular event (under a dictatorship, the public expression of this state of mind can only be distorted) and the fact that an opinion differing from the regime's may be authorized (or take the right) to express itself publicly. From the perspective of the political logic of power struggles, the open expression of a resisting public opinion is particularly likely to modify the attitude of the dictatorial power toward civil society. In the case of the Nazi occupation, one can show two different trends: that the evolving state of mind of popular opinion generally helped the formation of resisting behaviors and that the emergence of an authentic "public opinion," in spite of pressures from the occupier, may also have influenced the occupier's behavior.

FROM OPINION TO RESISTANCE

The opinion issue arose less in countries whose legitimate leaders were not involved in legitimizing the occupier's power. For different reasons, this was the case in Poland and Norway. At the heart of these nations, the development of resistance was not so much a question of agreeing with the state of opinion (which was rather favorable to resistance) as a question of the means of action. The institutions and populations of these countries tried, in the most creatively improvised ways and under the worst conditions, to invent techniques of resisting that would be best adapted to the situation of aggression of which they were victims.

In France, the departments of Nord and Pas-de-Calais displayed a rather similar state of mind from the beginning of the invasion, unlike the rest of the country. As Étienne Dejonghe's regional studies have shown,[6] the atmosphere of this region was more one of war than one of occupation. Considered by Berlin to be a military and industrial zone of prime strategic importance, the region was subjected to a particularly severe regime. This brutality could only revive the already existing bitterness against the "Krauts" from the preceding German occupation of 1914. Because so many troops were present, the black market could command its highest prices, which further aroused the hostility of people confronted with difficult food shortages. In addition, the Vichy government, which was separated from Lille and Calais by two demarcation lines, hardly exercised its administrative authority over the region. That is why the "Pétain effect" had little influence over the people and why local combativeness was not weakened. The departments of Nord and Pas de Calais were thus unusual in their refusal to accept the lost battles of 1940 as a definitive defeat. In spite of the collaboration of leading citizens, public opinion condemned the signing of the armistice. In August 1940, a German report had to declare that

the population felt no need for a radical change of politics, that, on the contrary, its majority hoped that the English would retain control over the course of the war and would thus succeed in liberating it . . . , it was necessary to explain to the population in full detail that it had to give the *Wehrmacht* all necessary respect, conform without restrictions to its rules, and maintain the highest discipline.[7]

We can thus understand why spontaneous forms of resistance appeared in these departments comparatively early, in contrast with the general passivity of the French population at the beginning of the occupation. Sabotaged telephone lines were quite frequent, and some of the first escape routes were worked out for fugitive soldiers. The communist party, which was particularly well established in the industrial basin, restructured itself underground with remarkable speed. Its local newspaper, *L'Enchaîné*, distributed several thousand copies in the fall of 1940. Mining strikes during the same period likewise reflected this early combativeness.

We know that this spontaneous readiness to fight was rare. For the most part, the state of mind of popular opinion tended to accommodate the invader. Even if populations remained secretly hostile to the occupier, they were not favorable to open resistance. As a result, open resistance had to remain limited. Only a change of opinion in its favor could bring one of the indispensable conditions for its development. It is ⌐. ⌐ ⌐ ⌐sting to follow the way in which opinion, attitudes of disobedience, and resistance were able to evolve both jointly and consecutively.

In France, the general factors for the evolution of opinion were the ones already mentioned for most of western Europe. Laborie has shown, however, the parallel importance of factors specific to the French situation: mistakes by the Vichy government; Pierre Laval's return to power on April 18, 1942; his speech in favor of Germany's victory against the Soviet Union; and the anti-Jewish roundups of the summer of 1942. From that time on, the Vichy government seems to have been greatly discredited in the eyes of French opinion. But resistance had to wait until the spring of 1943 to mobilize. At that point, French society felt directly attacked by the establishment of conscription for compulsory labor in Germany (the Service du Travail Obligatoire or STO), which affected most families. This confluence of factors favorable to resistance principles allowed the movement to become a truly representative force of opinion during the summer of 1943. In this sense, the various initiatives of Germany and Vichy first to incite and then to force the French to go work in Germany provide an excellent way to observe the evolving links between opinion and the resistance.

From the beginning of the occupation, the Germans had tried to recruit labor with the slogan "Great Germany offers work for laborers and the unemployed." The French government intervened at this first stage only to smooth out legal difficulties and to encourage the publicity campaign. This encouragement, which was voluntary at the beginning, produced few results. As Dominique Veillon has noted, "a large part of public opinion rather quickly acted with severity toward those who left willingly."[8] By June 1, 1942, or about the midpoint of the French occupation, only 70,000 people had left for Germany voluntarily, most of whom performed semi-skilled labor: manual laborers, agricultural workers, maids, and so on. But on March 24, 1942, Fritz Sauckel was appointed Minister of Labor for the occupied territories. He called for contingents of hundreds of thousands of French workers on four different occasions.

Pierre Laval, the new prime minister, invented the clever system of *La Relève*, or the relief draft, to satisfy the first demand for 250,000 workers, 150,000 of whom were qualified. In his speech of June 22, 1942, he announced that French workers who left to work in Germany voluntarily would go to "liberate" the prisoners of war from 1940, since three departures would result in one return. Aside from the fact that this ratio was never respected, this fool's bargain was based on a kind of moral blackmail that was reflected in the government slogan, "They give their blood, you should give your labor." In spite of enormous publicity, the campaign failed: instead of the hundreds of thousands of people expected, only 17,000 knocked on the doors of recruitment offices on September 1, 1942.

To convince the French to go to Germany, the departures therefore had to be made *obligatory*. On September 4, 1942, Vichy promulgated its first law concerning the "use and orientation of manpower," which mobilized men from the ages of 28 to 50 years and single women from 21 to 35 to work in Germany. The minister of labor took charge of personnel registration in companies. Within a few weeks, departure numbers rose dramatically. By the end of 1942, they had reached the 250,000 demanded by Sauckel.

At that time, resistance to departures was limited, if it existed at all. Noncooperation orders were issued by the BBC, and Maurice Schumann called on the French "to organize the national flight from the labor draft."[9] Some resistance movements, like *Libération*, asked company presidents "to tie up the enormous Vichy administrative machine"[10] in order to paralyze the worker requisitioning process. In the fall of 1942, limited strikes broke out among the workers, who were the main victims of the requisition measures, especially in the Lyon region. The workers' departures sometimes resulted in public demonstrations of thousands of people, as in Lorient on October 27, 1942, or in Montluçon on January 6, 1943. But despite this agitation, protesting workers could not drum up enough support within public opinion to be able to refuse to leave. The Catholic church, whose influence remained strong, preached obedience to the state. Certain movements, like the Boy Scouts of France, even openly approved of the departures as "acts of charity." Jacques Evrard has pointed out that

actually, one can say that, aside from certain Catholic movement militants and local circumstances, of course, young people in their time of confusion were rarely able to find what many of them were waiting for—unconditional guarantees and support from the country's highest moral authorities for what the young people felt, at the bottom of their hearts, to be the only correct behavior: disobedience of an order that wiped out the most sacred rights of human beings.[11]

If a young man intended refusing to leave, he could not count on solid support from public opinion. He was left to find his own expedient, like trying for a medical exemption. During the autumn of 1942, many labor conscripts thus had no real options. That is why Veillon has concluded that "In the beginning, some isolated individuals were discreetly assisted in their efforts to avoid forced departure. Whether with rage in their hearts or painfully resigned, the majority obeyed because they had no choice. The general climate was not yet one of mass resistance."[12] In fact, the relief draft measures still affected only the working-class community and, although the Vichy government was already unpopular, the relief draft was not enough to make French society as a whole move.

But new German demands made the French government hastily promulgate a new STO law that went into effect on February 14, 1943. This time, all young people born in 1920, 1921 and 1922 were called to serve in Germany for two years; exceptions were made for a few professional categories, such as farmers, policemen, or railroad workers. The new STO law thus struck at a wider range of social and professional milieus than the earlier one had. From then on, many people believed that Germany was losing the war. From the spring and especially the summer of 1943 on, French youth who did not want to leave had statistically many more chances to find covert assistance, not only from within the French administration but also from the population itself. Such a youth was much more likely to meet understanding police, compassionate mayors, and welcoming farmers. "Once public opinion finally chose its side, refusing became easier and less dangerous."[13]

The labor conscripts' determination not to leave was also much stronger than it had been in 1942. Their decision to disobey was not inspired by major political or strategic considerations. They just found the idea of leaving intolerable, and they were determined to say no. With tens of thousands daring to transgress the taboo of illegality, a broad, spontaneous, civil disobedience movement now appeared in France. In a still largely agricultural country, the rural community's covert assistance was decisive. Many young people sought refuge in the most out of the way places, like the forests and especially the mountains, forming the *maquis*. The neighboring rural populations could not ignore these groups of resisters and the resistance movements that backed them. The formation of the *maquis* was thus carried out with the implicit and sometimes very active consent of country people. Laborie has stated that "The fate of the young resisters gave rise to the first acts of complicity between the population and Resistance organizations. The establishment of the *maquis* was carried out with the tacit agreement of the majority of the rural community."[14]

Contrary to a still widespread idea, however, many of these resisters to the STO did not join the underground or any resistance movement at all. Regional studies conducted by the Institut d'Histoire du Temps Présent (IHTP) have shown that those who did join were the minority. In the Tarn department, only 19 percent of the young people not wanting to go to the STO entered the organized resistance, whereas 50 percent sought refuge in agriculture, and 12 percent left the department; in the Isère, between 27 percent and 30 percent joined the resistance, while only a fifth of them joined the underground of the Jura, the Savoie, the Drôme and the Saône and Loire. This is why disobeying the STO must not be confused with the occasional or permanent militancy of a resistance movement member. It would be more accurate to say that the STO law was the key factor that triggered French civilian opposition to the Vichy regime concretely and en masse. The formation of the *maquis* and the development of institutional resistance movements were only two of the many manifestations of this refusal. In truth, these manifestations had thousands of facets, all demonstrating civil society's new mobilization and giving meaning to the concept of *civilian resistance*. The implications had already become apparent in peasant communities but now showed up among government employees and state representatives. The STO resisters were thus able to escape with the covert assistance of their countrymen who worked in municipal buildings or prefectures and who helped in obtaining false papers. Ministry of Labor inspectors sometimes took great risks by failing to carry out requisitions or by assigning labor conscripts to factories whose employees were exempted from the STO (mines or arms factories, for example). Some heads of companies ignored orders requisitioning their personnel. Police were also known to warn targeted citizens that they were scheduled to be arrested so that they would have time to flee. In the countryside, when the mayor and the police worked together, potential labor conscripts could feel safe.

In short, as the international context of the war was turning to the Allies' advantage, the STO law, which was thoroughly disliked, helped put French society in a state of resistance that must not be confused with the organized resistance movement, whose numbers were always limited. Civil society had become generally open to the practice of disobeying the collaborating state and of protecting this disobedience with an opaque cloak woven of the strands of many discrete new solidarities.

THE PUBLIC EXPRESSION OF RESISTING OPINION

One can compare a society's state of opinion with an ocean. Depending on the time, the nature of the sea bottom, and the configuration of the stars, the ocean can be either calm or very agitated. It is criss-crossed by currents, some on the surface and some on the bottom. Every sailor knows that to control the sea, he has to come to terms with it. To follow his route, he knows he must take sea currents into account. A politician must do the same with opinion currents. When the sea is agitated, it becomes harder to hold the helm; waves can capsize the boat.

When outraged by certain government decisions, public opinion can also make waves that seriously challenge aspects of the state's politics or seriously disturb their application. This is the case when more and more submerged opposition currents come to the surface and express themselves publicly. The public expression of a resisting opinion is indeed apt to disturb the pursuit of the goals of a collaboration policy. This phenomenon, which is easily observable within democratic systems, can also be spotted under certain circumstances in authoritarian or totalitarian societies. In any case, the history of the Nazi occupation of Europe provides several examples, both in the occupied countries and in Germany itself.

Of course, no single public word here or there creates a problem for the occupier or his collaborators. Generally, resistant public opinion was expressed through three main channels: statements by moral authorities, especially churches; writings in the opposition press; and different demonstrations by the general public (strikes, marches, etc.). Of these three modes of public defiance, the first was without doubt the most influential. In the context of the period, churches, because of their great hold over minds, were factors of either order or disorder for the occupying power. Churches determined moral legitimacy. Their silence meant support for the new regime, whereas their criticism was a means of defying or establishing distance from it.

We know that the behavior of Christian religious authorities toward Nazism, regardless of their sectarian persuasion, varied widely. The Norwegian Protestant

Church's rebellious attitude differed completely from the French Catholic Church's great complicity with the Vichy regime, of which it was its most solid pillar. Still one can say that when high-ranking prelates publicly manifested their disagreement with Nazi politics, they disrupted these politics and helped to arouse or strengthen the population's will to resist. Such observations have been made about the genocide,[15] but they also apply to the occupation politics of the conquered societies.

Here is one example among many—the protest of the Belgian Catholic Church, through the Confederation of Christian Unions, against forced labor in Germany. In 1940, Belgium was one of Europe's most Catholic countries. Virtually the entire population had been baptized, and the Catholic Church had several institutional advantages. Almost half the school population received a Catholic education, from primary school to the university. The Christian press was firmly implanted, as were Christian unions, which were more powerful in membership numbers than social unions. This very structured set of diverse organizations and associations, heir to late nineteenth-century Catholicism, constituted a social force of prime importance with which the Germans had to deal.

The Catholic attitude toward the occupier was varied and contrasting. Some Catholics became involved in collaborationism through Rexism or within nationalist Flemish movements. But many priests and nuns became involved in resistance organizations and paid for it with their lives. Rectories and convents frequently offered refuge for clandestine opponents, fleeing soldiers, Jews, and pursued resisters. In the beginning, the Catholic hierarchy was cautious. Cardinal Joseph van Roey preferred to act with moderation, unlike his predecessor, Cardinal Mercier, who had made resounding anti-German declarations during the 1914 occupation.[16] Van Roey wrote several confidential protest letters to General Alexander von Falkenhausen, the country's *Militarbefehlshaber*. Some of these letters were leaked, so that Catholics involved in resistance activities could feel comforted in their choice. This caution of Catholic authorities, combined with a certain firmness of tone, seems to have been appreciated by many of the congregation. Struye, the observer of public opinion, wrote on this subject: "Although one still meets a certain number of Belgians in 1941 who regret that the Episcopate's interventions did not draw their inspiration from Cardinal Mercier's vengeful instructions, the large majority allows that circumstances have changed and command a less spectacular attitude."[17]

As the war progressed, the Belgian Catholic Church gradually adopted an attitude of more open opposition. Cardinal van Roey's public declaration against forced labor in Germany on March 15, 1943, was a turning point in this respect:

The measures of human requisitioning are absolutely unjustifiable; they violate natural rights, international rights, and Christian ethics. They do not take into account any consideration, either of the human being's dignity and essential freedom—annihilated by constraint, threats, and serious sanctions—nor of the good and the honor of families painfully wounded by the violent dispersal of their members, nor of the supreme interest of society that will suffer fatally from feelings of anger and muted hatred, sowed in thousands of oppressed hearts. They tell us that these measures are necessary to protect European society. But . . . doesn't applying procedures that violate essential principles of all civilization rather wipe out society? Human reason and Christian ethics condemn and stigmatize this iniquitous and barbarous behavior; all collaboration with the execution of these measures is seriously inimical to the conscience.[18]

It is hard to imagine a more vital or clearer public position, and the Cardinal's entourage feared it would get him imprisoned.

General von Falkenhausen was worried, since certain German communities thought him responsible for the Church's hardening stance. This declaration actually did have considerable impact on public opinion. The head of the military administration, Eggert Reeder, complained to one of the Cardinal's close associates: "I must say, this letter has had very great repercussions; since its publication, we have seen a considerable increase in active resistance, the number of STO resisters has increased enormously; likewise in the world of industry and commerce."[19] In his diary, Struye confirmed this rather disillusioned comment by occupation authorities:

The extent of the repercussions (from the Cardinal's declaration) shows that, by taking this position, religious authority has accomplished an act that many had long awaited and now welcome with all the more enthusiasm. . . . There is no doubt that the Episcopate has translated the firmness and the rising feelings of a whole people into a language whose dignity we have been unanimous in praising.[20]

Thus, the position of the Belgian religious authorities evolved from calculated caution to an equally considered public opposition. Some Catholics regretted its initial "timidity," whereas those who had become involved in collaborationism reproached it for taking political positions. In general, the Belgian Church helped to create, by its words and actions, the Belgian population's "resisting conscience" of which the historian Henry Bernard has written.

Too few people are aware that in Germany itself the churches succeeded in making Hitler change his mind about one of his crazier projects: the extermination of the mentally ill. It would not be appropriate, of course, to idealize the German Church's battle. Generally, its opposition to the national-socialist regime remained rather weak, similar to that of the majority of the German people.[21] As soon as Hitler took power by exploiting left–wing party divisions, he was quite capable of manipulating every means to annihilate his main political adversaries quickly, especially the communists and socialists; the first concentration camps initially received Germans. But this ferocious repression does not explain everything. German resistance was not like resistance elsewhere. In Poland or Norway, resisters fought against the invader; in Germany, resisters confronted their own government. Many factors explain the weakness of the German resistance—its divisions, its organizational difficulties, it lacks of support from abroad, and so forth. But the main factor, which cannot be emphasized enough and which Nazi propaganda naturally exploited, is that Hitler came to power legally. During the first years of his reign, from 1933 to 1936, the Führer was supported by a large part of his people. It is hard to imagine how a vigorous resistance could be organized in those conditions.

After the beginning of the war, the persecution of the Jews, and the growing deterioration of the economic situation, one might have hoped that German opinion might wake up. This was not the case. War rarely encourages internal opposition movements. Everything leads to the conclusion that popular approval of the regime instead became more and more reserved or, at least, went through major fluctuations. Deprived of means of expression and of organizations likely to convey its concerns, German opinion could not play a counter-power role. But one case was an exception. If there were still a potential opposition force in Germany after 1939, it was in the church. Hitler knew this; as early as 1933, he tried to get the German Church to support him or at least to refrain from openly criticizing his regime. About 60 percent of the population was Protestant and 30 percent Catholic. The Nazi party tried to manipulate the Protestant churches, most of them decentralized and autonomous, and largely succeeded. But some contested this development, and German Protestantism was divided. Many members of Protestant churches believed that Christianity was compatible with national-socialism. Those who participated in the German Christian branch were even enthusiastic partisans of Hitler's cause, and many of them belonged to the state apparatus. Some Protestants, however, joined confessional churches to try and resist this evolution and thereby became Hitler's opponents. The Catholic Church did not have the same divisions, since its centralized structure does not facilitate its division into cells. Moreover, Catholics, grouped mostly in the *Zentrum* political party, were no doubt less conservative than their Protestant brothers, who were generally hostile toward republican ideas. For a time, the Catholic Church was linked to Hitler by the Concordat that Pope Pius XI had agreed to sign in 1933; from then on, German Catholics were obliged to accommodate the Nazi regime. But this alliance quickly proved very difficult. In 1937, the encyclical *Mit Brennender Sorge* denounced the Concordat violations and criticized Nazi ideology. The publication of this document increased repression against priests and nuns, but the hierarchy was not disturbed.[22] Still, they showed no real desire for resistance, even though they would have had many opportunities to become involved. As Klaus Scholder has emphasized:

There is no doubt (and Hitler understood this from the beginning) that the two major churches represented a potential for resistance against the theory and practices of the national-socialist regime. But this potential for resistance was at no time seriously activated by the leaders of the two churches.[23]

The emotion aroused by the program to eliminate the mentally ill demonstrates, furthermore, that when some of the country's highest moral authorities decided to declare their disagreement with the regime publicly, the latter felt obliged to revise its plans. Research in the Gestapo archives reveals that the regime feared church activities much more than those of the communist party. In fact, the regime concluded that protests by religious authorities were likely to mobilize the German masses.[24] The issue of euthanasia was one to which Christian communities had to be particularly sensitive. Before Hitler came to power, authorized voices in the medical field had pronounced their approval of euthanasia for the mentally ill and, more generally, for patients with physical ailments that were diagnosed as incurable.[25] Hitler himself had explicitly declared the necessity of "purifying the race." It could thus be assumed that his rise to power would seriously threaten the mentally ill. Fearing the reactions of the religious community, the Führer did not arrange to have his project carried out immediately. In 1935, the promulgation of the sterilization law for the mentally ill showed that his worries were well founded, since they provoked church protests. He had to wait for the more favorable circumstances that the war provided. In this sense, it is significant that the decree ordering "deliverance by putting to death ill people who, within the limits of judgment and after a thorough medical exam, are declared incurable" was dated September 1, 1939. Hitler concluded that he could risk executing his plan on the basis of a report by theologian Josef Meyer, who evaluated the position of the religious authorities on the euthanasia issue and whose conclusions were rather vague.

Because this decree was issued by the Chancellery in the highest secrecy and was never made public, only a limited number of people were aware of it; for a long time, even many of the ministers did not know it existed. The head of the Chancellery, Philip Bouhler, and Hitler's personal doctor, Kurt Brandt, were appointed to implement it. They created several organizations with inoffensive titles to take charge of the operation. The main one was in Berlin, at 4 Tiergartenstrasse, which explains its code name, "T4." The T4 headquarters worked with a committee of about 25 psychiatrists, including seven tenured university professors. All the country's psychiatric establishments soon received a questionnaire to evaluate the number of their inmates and the nature of their diseases. Several weeks later, the head of each institution received a letter from the Ministry of the Interior, ordering that certain patients be transferred for military reasons. A hospital transportation company made up entirely of SS men, the GEKRAT, was set up especially to pick up and deliver patients to "euthanasia institutes." After several trial runs, an asphyxiation process using carbon monoxide was adopted by the end of 1939. During the next year, five centers began operation, and the cadavers were incinerated in a crematorium. The Ministry of the Interior then notified families of the death of their relative, adding that they could receive the ashes on request. Families received proper, official death certificates in any case. The circle was closed. Murder was legalized.

When the directors of the psychiatric institutions received questionnaires in the fall of 1939, they were not unduly alarmed. They filled them out, and the GEKRAT buses came to pick up the first patients. During the spring of 1940, however, when the families received the death notices, many understood what had happened for the first time. Those who became the most hostile were generally the heads of private institutions (representing about 35 percent of the German psychiatrists) that were run by the Internal Mission of Evangelical Churches. Still, they did not know quite how to react. Some of them tried to negotiate a 10 percent reduction in the number of patients requested, for example, but when the GEKRAT came for its next visit, those who had been spared once appeared on the next list. Because of their isolation, doctors also did not know what tactics to attempt. Some refused to fill out the questionnaires, but the T4 headquarters simply dispatched a commission of experts to fill them out in their stead. A considerable amount of energy was necessary to save a few patients through the invention of all kinds of pretexts. One of the most effective tactics was simply to ask the families to take their relatives home, but a ministerial order soon forbade directors from doing that. Some appealed to those in high places, which had little chance of success. There were exceptions, however: the greatest success was achieved by Pastor Fritz von Bodelschwingh, the director of the Bethel center for epileptics in Westphalia. With relentless spirit, he managed to establish personal contact with Kurt Brandt and thus succeeded in saving the 8,000 residents of his institution.[26]

Those who had thought up the operation underestimated family reactions. Relatives who could not understand why their dear ones had suddenly died were determined to find out and ended up guessing the horrible truth. The T4 services were also harmed by their own gross blunders. For example, one death certificate cited an appendicitis attack as the cause of death, although the person had already had his appendix removed; some families received two urns instead of one; others received a death certificate, even though their ill relative was still alive, and so on. In the obituary columns of the local press, the numbers of death notices for residents of local institutions finally began to look suspicious. As a result, T4 forbade the publication of death notices in the press. Eventually, the comings and goings of the GEKRAT buses could no longer go unnoticed. They always arrived full and left empty. The fumes escaping after their departure soon left no more doubt as to the reasons for their trips. A feeling of terror gradually overwhelmed the German population. The people were frightened by a state so powerful that it could take the lives of innocent people with such impunity. Old people began thinking that they would soon follow the mentally ill. After the fact, we tell ourselves the German population could not have failed to react to such unprovoked assaults. Yet this strong general opinion, which was already intense in some regions during the summer of 1940, had a hard time finding institutional spokespeople who were willing to put pressure on public authorities.

The euthanasia program provoked action in legal circles. Hitler had ordered the study of a possible law on the issue but finally rejected the idea. The T4 action was thus carried on outside any legal context—that is, with the most complete illegality. Many provincial prosecutors received complaints from the families of those who had disappeared. Unaware of everything that was happening, they did not know how to respond to the requests. For this reason, Bouhler and Brandt summoned the tribunal presidents and prosecutors. During this meeting, on April 21 and 22, 1941, they exposed the program's bases and development with no major opposition from the magistrates.

Reports transmitted by the local Nazi party leaders also conveyed the population's increasing anxiety. Party members themselves showed their incomprehension about the program's merits. Some thought Hitler should be informed about it, whereas others thought a law would resolve the problem. The military was also concerned, since handicapped and incurable veterans fell into the category of patients to be eliminated. Dissension appeared within the Reich's General Staff itself. Heinrich Himmler, in particular, was never completely in favor of the action. Josef Goebbels feared reactions from the Catholic community. A study of his diary shows that he thought that in order to win the war, they should not tangle with the church (on this point, he disagreed with Martin Bormann). From Goebbels' perspective, the church would keep up the population's morale, an important task toward victory. Once victory was assured, there would be time to settle their accounts with the worthy fathers.

Goebbels was right. Still, religious authorities, who were informed early on about what was happening in the psychiatric institutions, were not the first to react. The protest movement came instead from the grass roots of the church organization. Some of the pastors of the Internal Mission of Evangelical Churches approached the authorities. Pastor Paul-Gerhard Braune, director of the Bodelschwingh institutions in Lobetal, tried several times to approach high officials and even ministers; they admitted their impotence. He then decided to write a memorandum based on incontestable facts that he and several of his colleagues had gathered. This text, addressed to the Chancellery on June 9, 1940, emphasized the military's concern and set forth the problem of defining the concept of incurability: "Who is abnormal, asocial, ill without hope of being cured? What shall we do with soldiers who have become incurably ill or maimed while fighting for their fatherland? This is already being discussed in army circles."[27] Acting on his own, Theophil Wurm, the Protestant Bishop of Wurtemberg, sent a detailed letter to the Minister of Interior on July 5, 1940. He wrote other letters afterward to the Minister of Justice. Cleverly using Nazi phraseology and referring to the Führer's declarations in favor of a "positive Christian faith," the first of these texts was circulated without the author's knowledge in party and army circles and had a major impact. In the fall of 1940, some pastors tried to make the Protestant churches take a common stand. Pastor Ernst Wilm, who was the mainspring of the project, still had to admit that even within the confessing church, people were divided over what tactics to use. Other pastors took different initiatives, but none resulted in anything concrete, except the arrest and sometimes deportation of their authors. Germany then won a military triumph. Indeed, between the months of April and June 1940, its considerable territorial conquests relegated the country's internal problems to the background. All in all, the church hierarchy applauded this impressive string of victories. During this time, T4 continued on its infernal course.

It took public protests by several Catholic prelates to suspend this deadly enterprise. During the summer of 1940, an increasing number of priests and nuns pressed their bishops to react openly. In the beginning, the bishops refused, preferring to adopt the same confidential procedures as their Protestant colleagues. On August 1, 1940, the Archbishop of Freiburg, Konrad Grober, the author of an anti-euthanasia work published in 1937, wrote a letter of protest to the Minister of the Interior. On December 15, 1940, Pope Pius XII received a letter from the bishop of Berlin, von Preysing, who was determined to act publicly and forcefully. At that point, the Pope firmly condemned euthanasia and pressed the German bishops to react. But the bishops still hesitated to make an open declaration. The president of the episcopal conference, Adolf Bertram, archbishop of cardinal of Breslau, slowed everything down with a confidential letter that he wrote to the Chancellery on August 11, 1940; in it, he recalled the Catholic Church's condemnation of euthanasia. But he still refused to confront the regime directly, since he was worried about preserving the church's assets that were under his care.[28]

From then on, however, putting "incurably" ill patients to death took on public notoriety. Comforted by the supportive letter that he had received from the Pope, von Preysing decided to speak. In his sermon on March 9, 1941, he openly criticized the "murders that have been christened euthanasia." On July 12, 1941, after much hesitation, the episcopal conference sent the government a text that stated its position against euthanasia in very general terms. The sharpest attacks finally came from Westphalia in the sermons of the Bishop of Münster, Clement-August von Galen. He was not fundamentally hostile to the regime. A great aristocrat, a convinced patriot, and a veteran, he simply thought that Nazi ideology indulged in some excesses that should be combatted. With sometimes sharp words, his sermon on July 13, 1941, condemned Gestapo brutalities. On July 20, he called upon Christians to be firm with respect to the regime's practices. Then on August 3, in his most famous sermon, he strongly denounced the "assassination" of the mentally ill. He recalled that he had lodged a complaint with the tribunal against the crimes committed in his diocese, based on article 139 of the penal code, which stipulated that "he who has real knowledge of a murder plot and does not warn anyone about it, either the authorities or the person threatened, within the required time, will be punished." Since his complaint had not been followed by any legal proceeding, he called upon Christians to resist.

We must avoid any sustained contact with those who want to continue to provoke divine justice, who blaspheme against our faith, who steal and chase our priests and nuns and who send innocent men to death, brothers and sisters. We want to remove ourselves from their influence so as not to be contaminated by their impious thoughts and actions, so as not to be accomplices or share with them the punishment that only God must and will pronounce on all those who, like the ungrateful Jerusalem, do not want what God wants.[29]

After von Galen, other bishops also denounced euthanasia publicly, including Machens, the Bishop of Hildesheim, and Bornewasser, the Bishop of Trier, but the sermons of the "Münster Lion" had the most impact on opinion and the regime.

They were often reproduced and distributed across the country and throughout Europe. In France, the underground newspaper, *Les Cahiers du Témoignage Chrétien*, published them. These texts circulated within the German army as well and went as far as the Russian front. Christian communities, who had remained expectant until then, pressed the regime to deny the incriminating facts publicly or to put an end to the program. Werner Molders, one of Germany's aviation heroes and a fervent Catholic, whom Hitler had just decorated with the Iron Cross (the highest military honor), also protested against euthanasia. Finding out that Molders risked being arrested because of this position, Marshall Hermann Goering spoke personally with Hitler so that he need no longer worry.

In fact, Nazi leaders no longer knew quite what to do. The T4 operations were no longer really secret, and their effects on public opinion were becoming disastrous. At the head of the SS, Himmler favored taking a break from the program while the military criticized it sharply. The war wounded were sacred to the German people. Marshal Keitel also intervened to stress the presence of World War I veterans among the targeted patients. The Nazi party itself was divided. Should they keep quiet or have von Galen arrested? At the head of state, Bormann declared that he favored von Galen's physical elimination, but Goebbels opposed this plan. He wrote in his personal diary that if anything happened to the Bishop of Münster, the Westphalian population would be lost for the duration of the war. Two months before, Germany had joined battle against the Soviet Union, and all the nation's forces were needed. Hitler decided that he could no longer run the risk of dividing the country just when all its forces should be united. On August 24, 1941, a Chancellery "leak" intimated that Hitler had ended the euthanasia program.

It seems that Hitler interpreted this decision as a personal defeat. He wanted revenge. He figured that once the war was won, he would reactivate his lists and settle his accounts with the hated church. He knew that his regime needed the church's support, but the day would come when he would get rid of those Christians. The T4 program resulted in between 70,000 and 100,000 victims in a little under two years. It was thus Germans who died in the first gas chambers of history.

The program did not end completely, however. Soon the extermination camps began operating in Poland, where the T4 staff had been transferred. It is still true that Hitler experienced this episode as his first important setback since his accession to power. He had no doubt about it. The very German people whom he thought he was serving had made him fail. As Léon Poliakov has pointed out:

the program's evolution shows us the limits of Germany's leader. His gift was galvanizing the masses, leading them down new and disconcerting paths. But in this particular case, having presumed on his possibilities and having come up against a spontaneous and deliberate resistance, he found himself compelled to reverse his course. But it took a unanimous refusal, a true reflex of horror, to shake up most of his people. Even though German opinion was muzzled by the Nazi rod of iron, it thus managed to express itself and to pressure its leaders. The mobilizing of certain church representatives as symbols of moral legitimacy played an essential role in this area. This mobilization lent more weight to civilian public opinion movements, which had been deprived of their own means of expression.[30]

This episode should not make us forget that the mobilization of the religious community was slow, disorganized, and fragmentary. Protestant Church leaders did not encourage it at any time. These events are of interest because they show that a public protest by the Catholic prelates, even a limited one, was enough to make Nazi leaders reverse their policy. As long as there were no authorized voices to express a mobilized opinion and mobilization was limited to individual initiatives by important religious personalities, the public authorities were able to equivocate. They were forced to withdraw only when some of the Catholic Church's highest representatives broke the silence. The bishops' protests had all the more weight since there was no doubt that a major portion of German opinion was behind them. Mobilized opinion found institutional expression only when the prelates who spoke knew that their parishioners supported them. This mobilization of civil society, from both the bottom and at least partially from the top, became a real force that Hitler's regime could no longer ignore. Still, one wonders if such a protest could not have come earlier. Konrad Adenauer reproached the German churches for this after the war. In a letter dated February 23, 1946, to a pastor in Bonn, he wrote:

> I think that if the bishops had taken a public stand together from their pulpits on an agreed on date, they could have prevented many things. This did not happen, and we cannot excuse it. On the contrary, if the bishops had been sent to prison and concentration camps, then that would not have been wrong. But that did not happen, and that is why we would do better to keep quiet about it.[31]

On September 1, 1941, at the very moment when the Nazis stopped killing the mentally ill, Jews were forced to wear the yellow star. The first mass executions started in Poland and the Soviet Union. Since 1933, neither the churches nor general opinion had ever opposed the persecution of Jews, with a very few exceptions, such as the Reverend Dietrich Bonhoeffer. Herein lies one of the main weaknesses of the opinion phenomenon: its limited character. Vast opinion movements usually mobilize over a single issue and forget the others. An opinion movement usually results from a collective emotion about a problem that suddenly appears serious to many people. It is a fact that German society tolerated attacks against Jews while it did not tolerate attacks against the mentally ill. There was an opinion movement in favor of the latter, but not of the former.

Opinion is also unstable. It can change within a few days or a few months. Like the sea, opinion is mobile, drifting like the tide. But opinion is not necessarily continuous. Power can be submerged by a wave of hostile opinion and then, without apparent reason, the wave can recede.

One might say that opinion is the emotional expression of civil society. The state of opinion is a fluctuating index of the relationship between the regime and civil society. As a result, opinion needs to be worked on and stabilized in the struggle against a *de facto* regime, in order for it to become a stable political element against the regime. That is the task of resistance movements.

THE POLITICAL WALLS OF CIVIL SOCIETY

In politics, nothing is ever definitely won. Each party, each adversary must always strive to improve its position or, at least, to keep its advantage. Granted, as we have seen, evolving opinion is a factor determining the development of resistance and its public expression. At the same time, this does not mean that resistance is entirely dependent and passive toward opinion. On the contrary, resistance must constantly work toward opinion. Indeed, if we accept that resistance can develop only in the context of an opinion that is increasingly in favor of its cause, the main work of resistance is to continue convincing popular opinion of its merits. The more that resistance can rally opinion, the more it will guarantee the conditions of its existence and growth. That is why propaganda work played such an important role during the war, through radio broadcasts and underground newspaper distribution. There is thus a dialectical movement—from resistance toward opinion and from opinion toward resistance.

In countries where opinion was not initially in favor of fighting against the occupier, some representative political leaders became involved in a collaboration process. In these countries, the main task of the resisting groups was to conquer opinion by sensitizing and organizing populations. Claude Bourdet's distinction between the network oriented toward military intelligence and the movement oriented toward action by the population is illuminating:

A network is an organization created with the aim of specific military work, essentially intelligence, secondarily sabotage, and frequently aiding the escape of war prisoners, especially pilots who had landed in enemy territory. By definition, a network is in close contact with an organ of the leadership of the forces for which it works. . . . A movement, on the other hand, aims first of all to sensitize and organize the population on the broadest level possible. It also has concrete objectives, of course . . ., but basically one could almost say that it fulfills those tasks *in addition*, because each of its members needs to feel concretely involved. Above all, a movement undertakes these tasks as part of a *relationship with the population*. The population is the objective and most profound concern.[32]

Actually, the resistance was trying to win its own legitimacy through its various movements. It hoped to impose itself on the population and become the only representative of the population's true aspirations.

In countries where the legitimate leaders were not involved in a collaboration process, the resistance had an opposite problem. It had to keep the occupied country from legitimizing the occupier's power, whether such a fear was founded or not. Its action was, paradoxically, more dissuasive than offensive, in that it tried to preserve the collective identity of the attacked society from any contamination by the aggressor. It had to act so as to keep away or isolate collaborationist inclinations from general opinion. This does not mean that popular opinion was disposed spontaneously to support resisting actions. Resisting presupposed collective preparation and an organization that had not existed at the beginning of the occupation. One of the main tasks of the first resistance groups was thus to convince popular opinion that struggle and organization were necessary.

All things considered, depending on the initial power struggles, the goal of the resistance was either to reconstruct the collective identity of an attacked society that was more or less involved in a collaboration process or to preserve a collective identity by trying to keep its population from being willing to collaborate with the occupier. The goal of the resistance was thus mainly political—at stake was the legitimacy of power of the adversaries. In most countries, resistance to Nazism was based on the defense or revival of national and patriotic values. As resisters themselves have often said, ''We were patriots above all.'' Roderick Kedward's concise definition applies to both rationales of resistance described above: ''Resistance was thus a political response to political provocation, as well as a patriotic response to a 'national crisis.' ''[33]

One could perhaps criticize this point of view for minimizing the occupier's presence. Indeed, everything that has just been said puts more emphasis on the relationship between opinion and resistance than on the direct confrontation between the resistance and the occupier. Is this so surprising? In the countries studied, the resistance was never in a position to represent a true military force that could realistically challenge the occupier's physical presence. Therefore, the resistance was compelled to develop what we call an indirect strategy today.

Such a strategy has two dimensions—*armed* and *unarmed*. The first aims at tormenting the occupier and obstructing his movements using guerrilla tactics. The second defines ''civilian resistance'': more globally, it tries to involve the whole civil society. When it is impossible to get rid of an invader militarily, civilian resistance aims first of all at ''maintaining political distance'' between the occupier and the occupied. That is why it is so essential to preserve or reconstruct a country's political identity. The effort resembles digging an impassable ditch between the occupier and the occupied, cutting off all bridges to collaboration. In this sense, the civilian resistance struggle is comparable to the fight to defend a besieged citadel. Even though militarily beaten, civil society must remain or become a fortress with impregnable ''political walls.'' This is the only way it can remain or become uncontrollable by the opposing power, even if that power has an army at its disposal. This difficult struggle, like a state of siege, is played out in time. It presupposes good preparation, which is certainly not easy.

THE THEORY OF THE THREE CIRCLES

One thing becomes clear from all this. One cannot deal with internal resistance without also dealing with the accompanying movements of opinion, and vice versa. In countries that had collaborating governments, opinion and resistance progressed by fits and starts, moving down a path that made them a major influence over society. In countries where the legitimate political power refused to collaborate, opinion and resistance exerted a strong influence over society relatively early. Their problem was to avoid slipping from this plateau if collaborationist movements increased.

Combining opinion and resistance under the same heading challenges the widespread idea that opposition to Nazism was a fringe activity. Granted, if one considers only *organized* political opposition in the context of institutional resistance, it appears not as a fringe activity, but as a *minority* activity. Resistance follows the general rule that minorities make history. Those who made up this active minority were not ordinary people. Most research shows that they represented diverse social milieus and currents of opinion; resistance thus represented the broader civil society in miniature.[34]

It is absurd to think, however, that a *whole* society can become a resisting organization. It is clear that there are *degrees* of military involvement: for personal and psychological reasons, not everybody is necessarily ready to take the most serious risks. One can be fundamentally opposed to a regime without necessarily being in the right circumstances to fight against it in a concrete way. In this sense, one cannot make a moral judgment about everyone's past behavior, at least not as easily as we sometimes do. Moreover, society's mobilization against a particular political regime follows rules that anyone seriously intending to study the resistance to Nazism must take into account.

From this point of view, we can distinguish three "circles" of social mobilization. The first is the circle of institutional resistance as an organized political force. Institutional resistance unites all militants from various movements and all their activities. The second circle is the broader one of active complicity—the occasional "helping hand" or the "providential" aid spontaneously offered to a resister about to be arrested.[35] Finally, there is the third, much more far-reaching circle of passive complicity. It represents currents of opinion that favor the resistance and that approve or financially support its actions. Simply because this last circle seems "inert" does not mean that it is less important than the two others. The opposite may be true, since there is no lasting and effective resistance without a state of opinion that favors it.

Actually, the roles of opinion and resistance have to be seen as dynamic and complementary. Without supporting opinion, resistance is bound to fail. At the same time, opinion cannot change the course of events without a resistance embodying its will. In a certain way, opinion protects resistance, while resistance acts in the name of the opinion that supports it.

NOTES

1. Jean-Pierre Azéma, *De Munich à la Libération* (Paris, 1979) 168.
2. Paul Struye, *Évolution du sentiment public en Belgique sous l'occupation allemande* (n.p., 1945).

3. Pierre Laborie, *Résistants, Vichyssois et autres: Évolution de l'opinion et des comportements dans le Lot de 1939 à 1944* (Paris, 1980).

4. Laborie, *Résistants* 2.

5. It is in the nature of opinion that it modifies itself with the course of events; chronological adjustment is fundamental.

6. Étienne Dejonghe, "Le Nord isolé: Occupation et opinion," *Revue d'histoire moderne et contemporaine* (January-March, 1979) 48–81, and "Le Nord et le Pas-de-Calais pendant la premier année d'occupation," *Revue du Nord* 51:203 (October-December, 1969) 678–708.

7. Quoted by Dejonghe, "Le Nord isolé" 50.

8. Dominique Veillon, "La vérité sur le STO," *L'Histoire* 80 (July-August 1985) 106.

9. *Les Voix de la Liberté: Ici, Londres (1940–1944)* vol. 2 (Paris, n.d.).

10. Quoted in Jacques Evrard, *La Déportation des travailleurs français dans le IIIe Reich* (Paris, 1971) 63.

11. Evrard, *Déportation* 103.

12. Veillon, "La vérité" 108.

13. Jean-Pierre Vittori, *Eux les STO* (n.p., 1983) 99–100.

14. Laborie, *Résistants* 253. See also by the same author: "Les maquis dans la population," *Colloque sur le maquis, 22–23 November 1984* (Paris) 33–47.

15. See chapter 8.

16. E. Leclef, *Le Cardinal van Roey et l'occupation allemande en Belgique* (Brussels, 1945).

17. Struye, *L'Évolution* 30.

18. Quoted by Henri Haag, *Rien ne vaut l'honneur: L'Église belge de 1940 à 1945* (Brussels, 1950) 29.

19. Haag, *Rien*.

20. Struye, *L'Évolution* 61.

21. See the seminar essays from the 1984 Berlin meeting devoted to research on German resistance to national socialism. These are collected in *Der Widerstand Gegen den Nationalsozialismus—Die deutsche Gesellschaft und der Widerstand Gegen Hitler* (Munich, 1985).

22. Leonore Siegele-Wenschkewitz, "Les Églises entre l'adaptation et la résistance sous le IIIe Reich," *Revue d'histoire de la Deuxième Guerre mondiale* 128 (October 1982).

23. Klaus Scholder, "Politischer Widerstand oder Selbstbehauptung als Problem der Kirchenleitung," *Der Widerstand* 261.

24. See Heinz Huerten, "Selbstbehauptung und Widerstand der katholischen Kirche," *Der Widerstand* 243.

25. Robert Lifton, *The Nazi Doctors* (New York, 1986).

26. Kurt Pergande, *Bodelschwingh, der Einsame von Bethel* (n.p., 1968).

27. Quoted in Georg Denzler and Volker Fabricius, *Die Kirchen im dritten Reich: Christen und Nazis Hand in Hand?* vol. 1 (Frankfurt, 1984) 119.

28. Gunther Levy, *L'Église catholique et l'Allemagne nazie* (Paris, 1964) 261.

29. Yves Ternon and Socrate Helman, *Le Massacre des aliénés: Des théoriciens nazis aux praticiens SS* (Tournai, 1971).

30. Léon Poliakov, *Le Bréviaire de la haine* (Paris, 1983) 210.

31. Quoted in Scholder, "Politischer Widerstand" 262. See Konrad Adenauer, *Briefe 1945–1947* (Berlin, 1983).

32. Claude Bourdet, *L'Aventure incertaine* (Paris, 1975) 96.

33. Roderick Kedward, *Resistance in Vichy France: A Study of Ideas and Motivations in the Southern Zone (1940–1942)* (Oxford, 1978) 230.

34. Dominique Veillon, *Le Franc-Tireur: Un journal clandestin, un mouvement de résistance (1940–1944)*, (Paris, 1977).

35. Counting militants and active sympathizers, Jean-Pierre Azéma has estimated that about a million French citizens were involved in the resistance by the spring of 1944. See his article "Résister," *L'Histoire* 80 (July-August, 1985).

Chapter 7

Civilian Resistance Against Repression

It is hard to imagine how an unarmed fighter can stand up to an adversary who is determined to use armed force. Both the experience of history and the logic of strategy seem to confirm this difficulty. Repression is considered an absolute weapon against all forms of civilian resistance. The study of certain forms of resistance against Nazism, however, reveals that we cannot accept this so quickly. Indeed, a somewhat paradoxical thesis can be defended; research on one of the most extreme forms of violence known to humanity uncovers a resistance based on avoiding the adversary's violence.

In themselves, arms are inert objects. The power relationship between two adversaries is not, therefore, simply the result of one being armed and the other not. Arms become dangerous only when their possessor has the will to use them. Anyone who reflects on the concept of dissuasion is familiar with this problem. The determination to resort to the arms at one's disposal will most likely put the person without weapons at a concrete disadvantage. Still, whenever human will is concerned, potential fluctuations, uncertainties, and variations come into play, because a multiplicity of parameters comprises the human factor. Psychological, sociological, political, and other considerations can cause an occupier to modify his repression of the occupied.

Indeed, the debate over the options that a civilian resistance has against repression is often obscured by our seeing the relationship between an occupying army and a conquered civilian population as a confrontation between two individuals. Between individuals, it may appear that the one who has a weapon automatically has the upper hand over the one who does not, even though such an assumption itself deserves further exploration. In any case, *group* confrontations, involving thousands of people, change the dynamic of this collective confrontation completely. In the context of a face-to-face confrontation between occupation authorities and an occupied civil society, it is possible to discern psychosocio-logial or political factors that regulate the behavior of the parties present and that influence the force of each camp's particular means of action. Some of these complex factors—largely unexplored until now—are likely to intensify repression while others limit its scope.

PROVOKED REPRESSION

Resisting eventually leads to confronting repression. There is no resistance without repression. As with war, resistance follows a logic of sacrifice, because to win a war, one must pay the price. A strategist's cold calculations might make him think, for example, that by sacrificing 1 or 2 percent of his own population, his side will be able to win the war. In this respect, military strategy is similar to that of a chess game. A player can decide to sacrifice one or several of his pieces in order to get into a winning position.

A study of the forms of resistance to the Nazi occupation shows that, in certain cases, reprisals were so harsh that they eventually made populations wonder whether their actions were justified. In particular, this was the case with the practice of the "individual attacks" that were executed by various European communist parties against German soldiers during the summer of 1941. The occupier responded with the mass execution of hostages out of proportion to the action they were trying to repress. Civilian populations were therefore the main victims of this form of armed resistance, which was, furthermore, carried out in their names. One can unfortunately see quite clearly what was lost—"sacrificed"—in this case, but it is difficult to see what was gained.

The tactic of individual attacks therefore provoked continual debates, especially in France, from both the moral and the political points of view.[1] After 98 hostages were executed as a reprisal against the assassination of a German officer in the streets of Nantes, General de Gaulle quickly condemned the principle of the tactic in a speech on October 23, 1941.

Beyond the understandable rivalry among the actors of the period, regardless of who was for or against the communists, these debates posed a riveting question: what effective actions can civilians take in a crisis situation such as a foreign occupation? In the context of war, this discussion was simplified to two extremes: on the one hand, those who thought that populations could do nothing but wait for the final victory of the conventional allied forces—the *attentistes* or "waitists"—and, on the other those who insisted that civilians must not simply wait for this hypo-thetical moment without fighting against the occupier here and now—the supporters of "immediate action". One side thus declared that soldiers had the supreme, if not exclusive, role in leading the conflict (General de Gaulle expressed this view very clearly in his speech on January 23, 1941: "There is one tactic in war. War must be led by those in charge."[2] On the other side, the supporters of the individual attacks maintained that rejecting "waitism" would bring civilians into the armed struggle, which they considered the most effective action against the occupier.

This position was clearly developed by Charles Tillon, the main founder of the armed groups controlled by the French Communist Party, the *Francs-Tireurs et Partisans* (FTP), in a letter addressed to de Gaulle on November 20, 1942: "The struggle against such a formidable invader cannot be limited to ideological propaganda but must take on the character of armed action."[3] The problem was not so much deciding whether civilian populations should participate in the struggle against the invader but to know how they should take part in it without needlessly exposing themselves to repression. The debate, therefore, was not really between waitism and activism, for the history of the resistance shows that there were many kinds of civilian opposition. The debate was also not really about whether there should be armed struggle; the practice of sabotage with explosives, for example, was not generally criticized. What was discussed was one very particular idea of armed struggle—individual attacks. This tactic was criticized for generating ferocious repression, and its goal was strongly contested. In other words, the sacrifice being asked of activists and populations did not always seem in proportion to its supposed "benefits."

Indeed, the military effectiveness of individual attacks was practically nil. The death of a few hundred German soldiers in France did not change the outcome of the war at a time when Hitler was throwing millions of men into battle. This kind of harassment may have helped to make the occupation forces feel insecure, but if so, we do not know whether the insecurity sapped the occupier's morale or made him more defensive and thus more brutal toward the population. A book by Stéphane Courtois has assessed the results of the first year of individual attacks in France in a reference book on the French Communist Party:

Militarily, the blows struck against the Germans are infinitesimal. Granted, German soldiers will get orders to be cautious in their nightly peregrinations through Paris. Their tranquillity as occupiers may be disturbed. But not enough, frankly, to disrupt their activities. They are even tending to close ranks and become more efficient in their repression.[4]

If these petty annoyances did not worry the occupier militarily, then the only justification for their practice is political. This was Tillon's main argument in the letter already quoted, in which he concluded that individual attacks mostly "helped to develop our peoples' spirit of resistance, to paralyze attempts by collaborationists and "waitists," to prevent any atmosphere of agreement between the Germans and the French."[5] This text contains the two main political arguments justifying the FCP actions of this period, which some historians still put forth today; on the one hand, by imposing a "strategy of tension," the practice of individual attacks made the occupier reveal himself while taking charge of the repression himself; on the other hand, this radicalizing of the confrontation helped to stir up the popular opinion that had been anesthetized by Pétainism, thus pushing the mass of French people toward resistance.

The most recent historic research does not seem to confirm such an opinion. In the context of the period, one can understand how members of the resistance movement might have believed this kind of action to be effective. After the fact, however, its political usefulness seems doubtful at best. Opinion seems to have condemned the practice of executing hostages from the beginning and became increasingly hostile toward the occupier. A report by the French police, written after the executions of December 1941, declared:

Faced with this situation, Communist leaders decided to react energetically and exploit the population's indignation as much as possible. They are going to try to get all French people involved in their terrorist action by inciting them "to avenge the innocent victims of German repression and punish the murderers." This propaganda is likely to find favorable echoes among the population because of the discontent and hostility provoked by the repressive methods of the German authorities, so we have to expect an increase in terrorist acts.[6]

This popular condemnation of the occupier's overly thorough methods, however, to which French opinion was already hostile, does not mean that French opinion approved of the practice of individual attacks. As Jean-Jacques Becker has emphasized: "Going along with General de Gaulle's opinion . . . , opinion was hostile to attacks that it considered premature, without real effect on the outcome of the war, and likely only to provoke terrible reprisals."[7] An in-depth study of how opinion reacted to the cycle of "provocation-repression" triggered by the series of individual attacks would be useful.

In any case, the facts speak for themselves. Following the first such attack in Paris on August 21, 1941, in which a Communist militant assassinated a German soldier, the series of attacks did not incite the French to armed combat. The FTP organization remained a tiny minority until the spring of 1943 when the mass disobedience movement against the STO began. The increasing collaboration by French and German repressive forces by the end of 1942 decimated the FTP, which proved they were unable to find the necessary support for their cover, and thus their security, within French opinion. More than a year and a half after the individual assassinations started, this continuing gap between the action's perpetrators and French opinion proves the FTP's failure to reach the political objective it had assigned itself. The struggle took on a mass character starting in the summer of 1943, but, as we know, the phenomenon developed because of other factors. These included the general direction of the war and the rejection of the very unpopular STO.

Actually, it has now been established that the decision of the French Communist Party (FCP) leaders to move on to armed struggle was dictated by party orders from Moscow. The main contribution of Courtois's book is his demonstration of the extent to which Soviet strategy determined the French communists' "national" line, an analysis that has been confirmed by more recent research.[8] The FCP's involvement in the struggle against the German occupier actually started only in July 1941 after Germany attacked the Soviet Union. Stalin was completely taken aback, having thought that he had nothing more to fear from Germany after the signing of the German-Soviet nonaggression pact of August 23, 1939. This serious error in appreciating Hitler's true intentions risked leading the Soviet Union into catastrophe. That is why Stalin, still under pressure from the 2 million German soldiers penetrating Soviet territory, seized the strategic importance of the opening of a second front in Western Europe. This goal became a permanent request by Soviet diplomacy toward first England and then the United States from then on. In the same perspective, Stalin tried to rely on the international communist network to incite European communist parties to fight in the rear of the German forces. This explains why he called on communist parties to engage in armed struggle in his famous speech of July 3, 1941.

The leaders of the FCP and other international communist sections thus had to engage in an entirely new line of action almost immediately. In some countries, like Yugoslavia and Greece, civilian armed struggle developed to such an extent that it took an original form of combat: guerrilla warfare. In the Soviet Union itself, the action of partisans behind German lines was also very intense. But in France nothing had prepared the communists for this. Since the Paris Commune in 1870, neither the workers' movement in particular nor the French public in general had had the experience of armed struggle. As Albert Ouzoulias, another FTP leader, reported with great candor:

during the whole second half of 1941, the whole year of 1942 and the beginning of 1943, FCP leaders had to struggle against the current in the Party and in the population to overcome hesitations, even resistance. . . . During three long years, but especially at the beginning, armed combat posed many and complex problems. One does not go from ordinary activities like distributing tracts and newspapers, work stoppages, strikes, and all sorts of demonstrations to a whole new form of armed combat.[9]

Jacques Duclos, who was in radio contact with Moscow, stayed on the course of individual attacks, even though Leninist teachings recommended against armed struggle except when the "mass consciousness" supported it.

It had been maintained that the FCP strategy was that of a terrorist organization. Such an indictment warrants discussion. Granted, it behooved the Vichy authorities and the Germans themselves to call communist militants "terrorists" and all others "resisters." It is clear that the practice of individual attacks lent credence to this type of argument and led to the even more brutal repression of all forms of opposition to the regime.

From an analytical point of view, however, the FCP's fight cannot be reduced to the practice of individual attacks, since it also developed other tactics: propaganda, sabotaging production, derailing trains, and so on. The so-called "protest struggle," defended notably by trade-unionist Benoit Frachon, aimed at provoking strikes and demonstrations for better living and salary conditions after a temporary lull, returning to the party's earlier plan at the beginning of 1943. One could thus read in the January 8, 1943, issue of *L'Humanité* (the FCP's newspaper), three general aims for the protest struggle, one of which—rather surprisingly—was an appeal for civil disobedience in the paying of taxes; the others included raising salaries and improving food supplies.[10] In 1943, armed struggle was generally considered complementary to protest struggle, with both aiming toward national insurrection.

Strategically, it is not clear whether individual attacks should be associated with terrorism. They certainly have elements in common: the lack of participation by the masses, which makes it an ultra minority action, as well as concomitant determination to limit state power through violent and spectacular actions that are emotionally shocking to the population. Terrorism, however, is characterized mostly by its indiscriminate targets. In order to make potential victims as tense as possible, this tactic makes them understand that anyone may be targeted, anywhere, any time. We cannot claim that the French communists followed this line of action. Their targets were always German soldiers—preferably officers—and certain well-known collaborationists. It therefore seems fairer to say that the FCP leaders tried to apply a guerrilla strategy whose primary goal was to take the enemy, not the civilian population, by surprise. Because of reasons inherent in the nature of French society and even more in the societies of Western and Scandinavian Europe, this strategy could not grow extensively. Briefly, it was a problem of trying to engage in guerrilla tactics without enough support to succeed.

Civilians still paid dearly for the communist leaders' attempts to impose such a strategy on France, and in retrospect it is legitimate to wonder about the "usefulness" of the deaths of the sacrificed militants and the hundreds of executed hostages. The most certain effect of the individual attacks was the triggering of vicious cycles of provocations and reprisals, each adversary being unable to back off without seeming to change its mind. The occupier's executions of hostages were reason enough to justify committing more assassinations of German soldiers, which, in turn, led to further executions. In both cases, the adversaries' responses followed a mechanism of vengeance, since each camp used the other's violence to legitimize its own. The communists could justify their actions by stating that they had to avenge the executed hostages, whereas Vichy and the occupier could argue that their struggle against "terrorists" was to maintain order. The result was the increased efficacy of the Franco-German repressive system.

Nonetheless, although society paid the price of these isolated acts, not only in terms of civilian deaths but also in the increased harshness of the occupation regime, eventually the image of the FCP was strengthened in the eyes of French opinion. Indeed, the Germans turned everyone against them, thanks to the brutality of their absurd "logic" of disproportionate repression. Censure against individual attacks was nullified by the even greater censure against the executions of hostages. Among those executed were many Communists who, as the executions multiplied, were perceived more and more as martyrs of the resistance. Repression thus led to sanctifying the French communists' actions. At the same time, the Soviet Union was penetrating German lines in the East, and the closer they came to Berlin, the higher hopes rose of finally putting an end to Nazism. The communists thus acquired great prestige in popular opinion, because of both their sacrificial actions within the country and their military victories abroad. That is why Courtois has emphasized the radical change in the FCP's political position during the year of 1943. "During the fall of 1943," he has observed, "in a France where resistance is becoming a real force listened to and followed by the population, the FCP appears in all its rediscovered power like the great patriotic party, friend of this Soviet Union that is crushing Hitler to the East."[11]

In an international context that was becoming favorable to them, the French communists thus knew how to take advantage of the particularly severe repression that they had to endure. As Jean-Pierre Azéma has emphasized, not all the executed hostages were communists. Still, the FCP called itself the "Party of the Gunned Down" (*fusilés*), because its leaders had seized on the political value of garnering the sympathy generally inspired by those who sacrifice their lives for a cause. And it is true that the communists were especially persecuted. Political factors specific to pre-1939 France were already making them "internal enemy number 1," and this was even truer after the Vichy government was formed. Of course, the communists brought on their own increased repression by developing the tactic of individual attacks during the summer of 1941.

Insofar as this tactic's efficacy remains questionable, its only ultimate justification is that its logic of sacrifice benefited the communist party rather than French society. It made many people, including noncommunists, respect the FCP. In this regard, it is significant that the FCP's reputation as the most active resistance organization, especially after the war, is based more on the repression that its activists suffered rather than on the real successes they won. This shows that, in some circumstances, it is possible to exploit a situation of military inferiority for one's own advantage in order to reap political benefits.

RESTRAINED REPRESSION

The above discussion of communist strategy brings out an often forgotten truth. The repressive factor must not be considered in the abstract; its intensity depends on various tactical and strategic conditions that undergo variation. Generally, three types of factors can be distinguished: those due to (1) the politics of the occupier (strategic objectives and forms of the occupation regime), (2) the attitude of the occupied (general behavior of the population and perhaps modes of resistance), and (3) the influence of a third party partially mediating the occupier-occupied relationship (moral, national, or international authorities or states allied with the occupier). The combination of all these factors, which is often highly complex, always produces very different concrete historic situations.

From this point of view, the idea that civilian resistance would be possible only against an adversary whose moral qualms made it willingly limit its repression seems rather simplistic, given the complexity of factors influencing the parties involved. Let us agree that the tenets of Nazi ideology made a mockery of any moral discretion; and yet, the intensity of Nazi modes of repression varied considerably from one country to another, from one population group to another, and from one year to the next. Their racial considerations played an important role here, of course. Slavs were much more harshly repressed than were Scandinavians, for example; Hitler was hoping to convert the latter to the virtues of national socialist ideology. He therefore had to deal with them tactfully, since a tyrant must not eliminate the people he wishes to reeducate. We still should not forget that both the nature of the strategic objectives toward the occupied countries and the populations' reaction toward their occupation also influenced the intensity of the repression. It is interesting to look for factors that helped to restrain repression rather than intensifying it (like the individual attacks).

First of all, it is important to understand the differences, other than racial considerations, between Germany's occupation politics toward Western and Eastern Europe. From all points of view, Western European societies had reached a higher level of development in 1939 than had Eastern European societies. The economic riches and technological know-how of countries like France, Belgium, and the Netherlands were highly desirable to Germany as supplementary rewards for winning the war. The victor could get many of their specialized workers and technicians from numerous fields to work for the Fatherland; this labor source could not be found elsewhere, at least not in this quantity. The objective of economic exploitation, pushed to an extreme, was a general factor that moderated repression. As the chief of Belgian administrative services, General Eggert Reeder, wrote in a report to Berlin: "Although it may be possible to force a worker to go to his workplace, it is impossible to obtain high productivity from him against his will."[12]

This high level of economic development went along with an already very complex social system. The efficiency of state services, from the ministry to the community, was based on the cooperation of competent agents, which was not available to the occupier. Since the occupier's main concern was that society continue to "function"—in other words, that life would continue—the occupier had to avoid going too far in its repressive politics. It had to intimidate opinion without antagonizing it with too much brutality. That is why the method of state collaboration fit so well with German objectives for Western Europe, even though Berlin had not thought the policy out ahead of time. State collaboration was actually the best way to assure minimal compliance in the occupied countries, without which exploiting their economic wealth and human resources would have been far less effective.

The German attitude was completely different toward Eastern Europe. There Hitler saw only a *Lebensraum* for his people, with the Slavic populations presenting an obstacle to his project's achievement. There was therefore no moral restraint in the politics of repression in Poland or the Soviet Union. On the contrary, the rule was to eliminate these *Untermenschen* or, at best, to enslave them. Room had to be set aside for the arrival of the German colonists. According to this same logic, the collaboration formula held little interest for the occupying power that thought it more advantageous to administer these new "colonial territories" by itself.

To analyze repression, one first has to take into account the global context of the occupation. The general level of repressive politics is determined initially by the nature of the occupier's objectives toward the occupied. In other words, everything depends on what the occupier expects from the occupied. The more that the occupier believes the occupied to be potentially useful in some way, the greater the interest in skillfully managing the occupied population. Generally, the occupier's dependence on the occupied is a factor that moderates repression.

Since the occupier's objectives vary with respect to the political, economic, and social structures of the occupied countries, there are as many politics of repression as objectives of repression. These initial objectives define a given, so to speak, on the basis of which the "average" level of repression toward a given occupied society is formed. This level of repression results from the occupier's preliminary calculation. But this repression policy undergoes fluctuations with respect to the populations' concrete attitude and, more generally, to the way in which the occupier-occupied relationships evolve.

Occupation walks in step with repression. There is no occupier that is not prepared to put down possible resistance movements, and no resistance movement that does not expect to be repressed. As we have already said, resistance always has a price—a human cost. In this perspective, one would have to agree that the best resistance strategy is the one that brings the most gains with the fewest losses. When one examines this problem with regard to repression, one concludes that the concern of any resistance movement is to score the most points against the occupier without feeding into more repression. In other words, it is a question of knowing how far one can go while remaining determined about resistance objectives. Beginning down such a path is to start thinking about the new field of nonprovocative resistance strategies, which are the exact opposite of the strategy of individual attacks.

Research into the Nazi occupation period shows that the means of action specific to civilian resistance are those that allow this strategy to develop. Of course, we have seen that such actions, especially spontaneous strikes, were sometimes put down severely. Still, we must compare these actions with all other forms of opposition. This general examination suggests that the modes of civilian resistance led to milder repression than guerrilla action. If the strike as a tactic made victims, it seems to have made fewer than did the reprisals after sabotages and especially after attacks on German soldiers. We can thus propose, with Henri Michel, that demonstrations were put down less harshly than strikes, and strikes less harshly than sabotage and individual attacks.[13]

If this was indeed the case, the first possible explanation is that the stakes of the civilian resistance actions were lower than the stakes of guerrilla action. A symbolic demonstration seemed less important in terms of the occupier's principal concerns, for example, than an attack with explosives against its own troops. It could tolerate the first, if need be, but certainly not a repetition of the second. In the latter case, its repression could not fail to be ferocious.

But this observation should not conceal other elements of an explanation that are certainly less obvious but perhaps more important. If civilian resistance provoked less repression, it may also be because of the nonprovocative nature of the *means* of action. Psychologically, civilian resistance does not arouse the fear of dying since, by definition, it does not resort to armed struggle. This simple fact of not physically threatening individuals is a considerable factor in deflating repression. Furthermore, we know that violence follows a pattern of imitation whose cycle of "provocation-repression" illustrates the unavoidable chain of events perfectly. Sociologically, this spiral of reciprocal violence is broken as soon as one of the adversaries does not resort—or no longer resorts—to armed struggle. Finally, as René Girard's works have shown, violence needs to justify itself: it needs a pretext.[14] Politically, not resorting to armed struggle deprives the occupier of the argument that it needs to justify its repression. This triple approach makes it possible to maintain this paradox—that unarmed struggle offers less that repression can get a grip on, or at least interferes with the application of repression.

Basil Liddell Hart's opinion on this subject is particularly illuminating. When he had the opportunity to interrogate German generals during their captivity in Great Britain after the war, he asked their opinions on the different forms of resistance that they had encountered:

Their evidence also showed the effectiveness of non-violent resistance. . . . Even clearer, was their inability to cope with it. They were experts in violence, and had been trained to deal with opponents who used that method. But other forms of resistance baffle them— and all the more as the methods were subtle and concealed. It was a relief to them when non-violent forms were mixed with guerrilla action, thus making it easier to combine drastic and suppressive action against both at the same time.[15]

This commentary by a man who was one of the greatest military historians of his time challenges those of us who want to understand in depth the dynamics of the different forms of resistance to the German occupation. Liddell Hart was certainly not completely in favor of civilian resistance. He concluded in the same passage that guerrilla tactics were the best adapted and most effective resistance method in mountain regions like the Balkans. But his opinion brings out one important element of civilian resistance—repression against it was not easy.

An analysis of the consequences of a developing civilian resistance in the general dynamic of the occupier-occupied relationship also supports Liddell Hart's statement. We must keep in mind that repression risks creating an emotion within popular opinion that can sometimes be considerable. With regard to the French department of Lot, Laborie has accorded major importance to the death of the first resister killed by the Gestapo; his funeral in Cahors, on December 2, 1943, inspired a public anti-German demonstration by thousands of people from across the whole department.

General intelligence services estimated that there were 7,000 participants (5,000 men and 2,000 women) in the procession, not counting the enormous crowd gathered on the procession route who marched in impressive silence. All the city's stores were closed, the German troops were confined to their barracks, the militiamen and others were not to be seen. The popular rumor claimed that the Resistance leaders were there, hidden in the crowd and protected by their men.[16]

Several comparative studies give the impression that repression against unarmed resisters was likely to arouse public indignation even more than repression against armed resisters. Even if their struggle was legitimate, the regime could always imply that armed victims were guilty precisely because they acted with violence, and this type of argument can hold sway over part of public opinion. A population can still accept repression in the name of a certain fatalism: "In war, everyone gives knocks and knows he will get some back."

But when repression strikes unarmed resisters or people who are not even implicated in opposition activities, it is much more difficult to justify, although it is still possible, of course. History abounds in examples of police and military operations against unarmed individuals and groups, carried out for political, union, religious, and other reasons. Repression is harder to apply then, however. It is more difficult to convince public opinion that victims "get what they deserve," unless opinion is already predisposed toward the repression, which facilitates its application. Repression becomes a "naked act" that cannot be covered by any justifying argument. A sympathy movement within public opinion is therefore much more likely to form toward unarmed victims than toward armed ones.

The importance of the public opinion factor is evident in both the unleashing of repression and the degree of its intensity. Repression can never be reduced simply to a relationship between persecutors and potential victims. There are always witnesses. Even when repression is carried out in secret, it always ends up being known. Repression is thus played out with three actors: the persecutor, his potential victims, and a "third party"—(public) opinion. It is usually said that repression's goal is to intimidate opinion and thereby discourage resistance. But the significant role that opinion itself plays in repression has not been emphasized enough. If opinion approves of repression, then repression is more than likely to be ferocious. If, on the contrary, opinion hangs back or protests against it, repression is likely to undergo moderating influences or even an interruption. The witness or third party thus regulates repression.

In some circumstances, the witness/third party expresses itself openly in favor of the victims by mobilizing certain civilian institutions. When not directly connected to the conflict, these institutions are in a mediating position. Their intervention among the public authorities, especially when performed openly, is likely to limit repression. But their third-party function can be effective only if these institutions count in the eyes of the persecutor. In other words, it is because the persecutor needs to control them that he can show himself willing to revise his repressive policy. In the context of the Nazi occupation, Christian churches were generally in a situation where they could play this role. The occupier knew that it had to deal with religious authorities because of their influence over the population. This is why the higher clergy were likely to be heard if they protested, in various circumstances, against the repression led by the occupier or the collaborators.

Opinion that is mobilized against repressing victims who are perceived as "innocent" has another possible effect: undermining the persecutor's political unity. All power carries within it internal contradictions among the forces that comprise it. The Nazi state had its own contradictions, torn as it was by struggles for influence among various personalities in the regime and the ministries, by the claims of the Wehrmacht versus the Gestapo, and so forth. It is the nature of war to wipe out these kinds of divisions, so that all energies can be channeled toward the final victory. Armed resistance also tends to reinforce unity as the occupying forces must "close ranks" to take on the threat. Civilian resistance, by its nature, offers less of a stimulus for this type of *esprit de corps*. Quite the contrary, its effect is often the opposite, encouraging latent contradictions to appear within the enemy camp. The differences between Bormann and Goebbels over the Catholic bishops' protests against euthanasia, like those between Terboven and Quisling in the teachers' controversy, illustrate this.

It is often declared that a particularly ferocious regime does not allow for a choice of resistance methods. Armed struggle is the only option. "Soft" resistance methods are appropriate only against regimes with a certain "softness" about them and would thus not be appropriate for completely brutal regimes. This somewhat static assessment does not take into account the interactive nature of the "repression-resistance" dyad. Repression tends to radicalize resistance methods, of course, but those methods also can help to intensify or influence it.

Using a study of the feedback from resistance to repression, Gene Sharp has proposed a general strategic concept based on the systematic use of civilian resistance methods of nonviolent action. Assuming that the adversary has armed force at his disposal, Sharp's basic principle consists of consciously refusing all confrontation on the terrain where the adversary is strongest. It is wiser to exploit the adversary's errors, by playing on the emotional shock that repressive acts are likely to arouse in popular opinion and that the adversary will have a hard time justifying. The progressive mobilization of civil society that can result will then allow the confrontation to move to the political realm, where civilian populations have an imposing advantage: the strength of their numbers against the minority who possess armed force. Such a strategy is based on the asymmetry of the means of action available. The effects resulting from repression perform a central and driving function, since it is anticipated that repression will end up turning against those who wield it. Finally, the goal of this strategy is to conquer the adversary by forcing it to reveal itself, to throw the adversary to the ground by using its own strength against it and making it lose its balance. Sharp's image of a kind of "political jiu-jitsu" seems appropriate.[17]

OTHER FACTORS OF VULNERABILITY

On the whole, this analysis shows that physical repression is not necessarily the most important factor of vulnerability of civilian resistance. The drama of physical repression generally makes us overestimate its impact, although the emotional shock that it provokes in the population can offer new resources to resistance. Still, we must not consider physical repression as "the absolute weapon" against all civilian resistance. This does not mean, obviously, that its importance should be minimized. It is rather a question of making its weight relative, so that we can examine other factors and understand the vulnerability issue in all its complexity.

Economic repression is very important, for example. It appears to be the most formidable weapon in many respects. It consists of interrupting salary payments, for example, or firing personnel to end a strike. It can aim at organizing a food shortage so as to undermine all spirit of resistance within the population. This method of repression, which is more insidious and less spectacular, is much more likely to exhaust civilian populations. The blackmail of job loss is often one of the most decisive arguments to sap all inclination to resist. Auguste Lecoeur has reported that after the Houillères leaders decided to suspend salary payments in the big mining strike of the Nord-Pas de Calais, the strike continued longest in the region of "Ligny-les-Aires in the far west of the basin: there the miner has the greatest possibility of replenishing supplies between the mine and the fields."[18] Without economic resources, there can be no lasting civilian resistance. The occupier can plan a system of food scarcity to undermine all spirit of resistance in civil society from within. This system of scarcity encourages competition between individuals, forcing each one to spend considerable energy and time to nourish himself. Moreover, the system engenders parallel supply networks, often accompanied by different forms of corruption. This "every man for himself" policy is detrimental to developing collective resistance practices. It is even more effective when it physically exhausts the populations.

Actually, everything depends on how the occupier uses the range of repressive weapons to achieve his goals. More than the factor of repression taken in isolation, it is the general concept of his occupation politics that may or may not help to destroy or wipe out all significant forms of resistance. In this perspective, Jan Gross's work on the German and Soviet regimes of political occupation in Poland between 1939 and 1941 are particularly informative.[19] One of the most important clauses of the Russo-German nonaggression pact had involved the partition of Poland. The Germans and Soviets developed very different occupation policies, so the reactions of the populations concerned differed as well.

In the General Government territories controlled by the Germans, the occupier had only a plan of terror. So, "the population quickly recognized the new logic of the situation: whether one tried to meet German demands or not, one was equally exposed to violence."[20] Gross has developed several interesting thoughts on the relationship between obedience and terror. According to him, no power can make populations obedient by using only negative sanctions. Rewards are also necessary to get people to obey. A regime must therefore give positive reinforcement to the conduct it expects and desires. All in all, in education as in politics, obedience is an apprenticeship to a code defined by both negative and positive sanctions. Since the Germans seemed to expect nothing specific from the Poles, the latter could hardly be expected to find rewards for obeying them. Under Nazi discipline, the population quickly realized that terror was applied indiscriminately. Obeying the occupier's "law" brought no benefits, since the politics of repression applied in all directions and equally against the entire population. In other words, it was no more risky to resist than to obey. That is probably one of the major reasons for the mass nature of the Polish resistance.

The development of underground education, which expanded considerably after 1941, must also be interpreted in this context. We must wonder why the occupier failed to eliminate this method of resistance, when one of its clearest goals was to destroy all forms of Polish culture. Hundreds of intellectuals from all professions were arrested. One of the most spectacular arrests—that of the professors from the university of Cracow—triggered such international protest that the majority of the academics were freed in the spring of 1940. But after the French campaign, German domination spread through Europe, and international public attention no longer focused on Poland. If the underground education movement could not be stifled, it was mainly due to resources inherent in Polish society.

An examination of these facts leads us to conclude that the occupier's helplessness to fight underground education effectively was due mostly to a balance of forces. On the one hand, the movement was too massive to be put down effectively; on the other hand, the Germans rarely knew where the underground courses, the *komplety*, were organized. The occupier remained in such ignorance because too few informers were willing to reveal the times and places of the courses. Classes could therefore continue under fairly good security conditions.

The occupier's politics led to the opposite of what it had hoped. Instead of dividing Polish society, the policy increased the cohesion among the Polish people and thereby created the conditions for mass noncooperation. There is no doubt a threshold beyond which a mass civilian movement can no longer be repressed. If the goal of repression is to dissuade resistance, a civilian resistance movement can become so massive that it ends up dissuading repression.

For the situation to be otherwise, the Germans would have had either to get help from collaborationists, which they did not want, or to make their repressive policy less severe. The Soviet occupation of the Eastern part of Poland in 1939 (the territories of the Ukraine, Byelorussia, and Lithuania) was much shrewder in this respect. The experience that they acquired since 1917 in controlling populations must have played a large part. The basic principle of their occupation strategy in this region of Europe, which was already prey to fierce tensions between Poles, Ukrainians, Byelorussians, and Jews before the war, was to encourage populations both to collaborate and to increase their internal divisions simultaneously.

As soon as they arrived in October 1939, the Soviets organized "elections," whose only goal was to involve the local populations in running the new regime. Likewise, the Soviets acceded to some of the Ukrainian nationalist demands, especially in the field of education, and held out the possibility of major agrarian reform to the peasants. In short, the Soviets raised hope among various groups from the beginning and played on the local populations' own demands. They thus provided themselves with supports within the society that would become obstacles to developing opposition movements.

At the same time, the Soviet occupiers tried to stir up conflicts between communities; these were often expressed through personal or neighborhood quarrels. According to Gross, the Soviets exploited these personal animosities in such a way that anybody could denounce anybody else. They thus set up a "revolutionary" social system that came from abroad and was based on denunciation.

In this connection, Gross has proposed an original perspective on Stalinist totalitarianism. The political terror of a totalitarian state is not efficient when it remains *outside* civil society. Terror does not become functional until relayed by the individuals themselves within the society that is targeted to be terrorized. Stalinist totalitarianism succeeded in putting the state at everyone's disposal to settle private quarrels, so that individuals would be permanently at odds with each other. "The idea that Stalinist power is based on a gigantic centralized bureaucratic machine is false. Its power is made up of a myriad of individual and spontaneous contributions."[21] The actual power of the totalitarian state comes from each person being able to appeal to the police to exercise coercion on his neighbor. A "privatization" of the state results, and the main consequence is the shattering of civil society.

In this context of general suspicion, the Soviets succeeded in wiping out all large-scale resistance. The underground education movement, in particular, was insignificant. Starting in February 1940, the Soviets proceeded to mass deportations to the Soviet Union and the collective execution of prisoners, of which the best know was the execution of Polish soldiers in the Katyn Forest, probably in April 1940. The collective executions shocked the populations considerably, but they were too divided to react effectively to this cataclysm that they had not foreseen. The result was that Soviet repression in this atomized society was more effective than the German one. About 23 million inhabitants were then under German control and 13 million under Soviet control. According to Gross, the German occupation resulted in some 120,000 victims before June 1941, if those who died during deportation, mostly Jews, are counted. The Soviet occupation, by contrast, resulted in more than 300,000 victims—Poles, Jews, Ukrainians, and Byelorussians—in a population roughly half the size of the one in the German part.

Granted, possible extrapolations based on these two different but simultaneous occupation policies in Poland are very difficult. On the one hand, the two regions involved did not have the same histories, the eastern part of the country having a much more heterogeneous social fabric. On the other hand, there was an element of indecisiveness in the German policies that was absent from the Soviet side. Berlin did, of course, have some specific goals for Poland: to eliminate the Jews and the intelligentsia and to exploit the Poles for cheap labor. But nothing about the political status reserved for the Polish territories was clear, and contradictions may have emerged in the application of German policies in Poland. By contrast, Moscow had a precise plan for "sovietizing" the region. But when one puts the two situations into perspective, one sees that, in order to wipe out all significant forms of resistance, the occupier's repression can be really effective only in a context of collaboration and dissension within the occupied population. That is why collaboration and social dissension seem to be actually more dangerous to civilian resistance than repression in and of itself. A society that has a high level of social cohesiveness can probably tolerate the ordeal of even an intense repression. A divided society that is prey to collaboration cannot offer any mass resistance. Even if the emotional shock of repression might create the conditions for noncooperation, the insidious presence of collaboration in a context of social dissension wipes out all possible dynamics of resistance. Whether there is collaboration with the occupier, either at the top or the bottom of society, determines to a large extent the nature of the relationship between occupier and occupied.

NOTES

1. See chapter 10 in Henri Noguères, *Histoire de la Résistance en France*, vol. 2 (Paris, 1969) 145–192, and "Le point de vue de Jean-Louis Vigier," in the same volume, 671–674.

2. Quoted in Noguères, *Histoire de la Résistance,* 155.

3. Quoted in Stéphane Courtois, *Le PCF dans la guerre: De Gaulle, la Résistance, Staline . . .* (Paris, 1980) 307.

4. Courtois, *PCF* 224.

5. Courtois, *PCF* 307.

6. Quoted in Denis Peschanski, *Vichy 1940–1944, Quaderni e documenti inediti di Angelo Tasca, Archives de guerre d'Angelo Tasca* (Paris, 1986) 132.

7. Jean-Jacques Becker, "La ligne du Parti communiste," *L'Histoire* 80 (July–August, 1985) 37.

8. One can consult, for example, the papers of the seminar organized in 1983 by the Center for Research on the History of Social and Labor Conflicts, the Foundation of Political Science and the Institute of Contemporary History (CNRS): Jean-Pierre Azéma, Antoine Prost, Jean-Pierre Rioux, eds., *Le Parti communiste français des années sombres (1938–1941)* (Paris, 1986). Also note in this volume the articles by Roger Bourderon, "Une difficile articulation: Politique nationale et appartenance à l'Internationale," 227–249, and Stéphane Courtois and Denis Peschanski, "La dominante de l'Internationale et les tournants du PCF," 250–273.

9. Quoted in Courtois, *PCF* 252.

10. Courtois, *PCF* 314.

11. Courtois, *PCF* 399.

12. Quoted in J. Gérard-Libois and J. Gotovitch, *L'an 40, la Belgique occupée* (Brussels, 1976) 381.

13. See "Sabotages, attentats et grèves," in Henri Michel, *La Guerre de l'ombre: La résistance en Europe* (Paris, 1970) 226 and following.

14. See all of his work, but in particular René Girard, *Le Bouc-Émissaire* (Paris, 1985).

15. Basil Liddell Hart, "Lessons from Resistance Movements," *The Strategy of Civilian Defense*, ed. Adam Roberts (London, 1969) 205.

16. Pierre Laborie, *Résistants* (Paris, 1980) 298.

17. See Gene Sharp, "Political Jiu-jitsu," *The Politics of Non-Violent Action*, vol. 3, (Boston, 1973) 657–703.

18. Auguste Lecoeur, *Croix de guerre pour une grève* (Paris, 1971) 72.

19. Jan Tomasz Gross, *Polish Society under German Occupation: The General-government (1939–1944)* (Princeton, NJ, 1979); Jan Tomasz Gross, *The Revolution from Abroad: The Soviet Conquest of the Poland's Western Ukraine and Byelorussia* (Princeton, NJ, 1987).

20. Gross, *Polish Society* 212.

21. Gross, *Revolution* 232.

Chapter 8

Civilian Resistance to the Genocide

It is difficult to understand how the systematic extermination of 5,200,000 Jews could have taken place on the highly civilized continent of Europe. Their genocide in the course of World War II reveals the most hideous side of humanity. It indicts not only the German people, who were its principal architects, but the human conscience in general. It shows that supposedly "normal" and "cultured" family men can easily become obedient agents of blind violence. Many authors have pointed out that Nazism confounds human intelligence. We now know in detail how this rationally planned industrial enterprise of death functioned. The questions still remain as to why. Historians are divided between the "intentionalists," who think that Hitler had planned the extermination of Jews much earlier and was able to realize his plan because of the war, and the "functionalists," who think that this goal emerged progressively among the Nazi bureaucracy that worked it out as the most "rational" solution to the "Jewish problem."[1] Highly complex debates have occurred over the nature of the Nazi regime. Well-known German historians have called for a "normal" historical treatment of Nazism.[2] What features make Nazism a totalitarian regime similar to others? What features differentiate it from others—Stalinism, for example? These are formidable questions that make us question the uniqueness of the Jewish genocide with respect to a long series of mass exterminations, of which history has, unfortunately, many examples.

The goal of this chapter is not to recall known and incontestable facts.[3] Rather than describe the methods of genocide one more time, this study focuses on the resistances that the Nazis might have encountered here and there while carrying out their program. Indeed, the terrible toll of the millions of deaths in Poland's gas chambers hides significant disparities in the percentages of victims by their countries of origin. Major differences exist between Poland (where most Jews were eliminated) and Bulgaria (where they were spared), between the Netherlands (84 percent of the Jews killed) and Belgium (50 percent), between Norway (50 percent) and Denmark (5 percent). Why was the "final solution" limited or even prevented in certain countries? How should we interpret these data?

The first explanation that comes to mind is that the extermination camps stopped because of the German military defeat. Without the liberation of the camps, the extermination of Jews who had not yet been arrested in 1944 or 1945 was only a question of time. In the long run, those who remained would have been taken, and almost all European Jews would have been eliminated. But this "military" interpretation risks distorting the political and sociological analysis of how the Nazis carried out their program. Wherever Hitler was master, he intended to execute his plan—destroy "the Jew." Whether Slav or Latin, a Jew remained a Jew and had to be wiped out. Annie Kriegel has maintained that, in this sense, the master of Europe waged a private war against the Jewish populations he meant to destroy, even at the price of hindering the wider war.[4] Still, during the four years when the Nazis applied this policy wherever they could, the results of this extermination program were uneven.

Many variables must be taken into consideration: the degree of integration of the Jewish communities (their social and cultural assimilation); their distribution throughout the territory (their urban concentration); the status of each country's occupation; the amount of warning time (whether or not they had knowledge of their eventual fate); the proximity of a welcoming country; and so on. The overlapping of all these data makes it futile to attempt any general interpretation. As Léon Poliakov told me one day, quoting Alexander Zinoviev, "since the event had manifold causes, it is impossible to know the cause of the event."[5] Still, as my knowledge of the facts increased, it seemed to me that the concepts used throughout this work (collaboration versus noncooperation, cohesion versus social division, public opinion, etc.) offer analytic tools that are sufficiently relevant to lend coherence to my ideas. I see in them a confirmation of the functional character of such ideas insofar as they allow us to comprehend very different problems: the relationship between the occupier and the occupied (a classical case of a foreign power occupying another country) may yet resemble the relationship between persecutor and victim when the collective extermination of the victims is foreseen (the genocide case). The implication of such an approach is limited, to be sure, since correctives would be needed to account for the local situation in each country. We cannot expect more from these concepts than they can give, only a frame of reference allowing us to describe overall tendencies beyond national and regional differences.

At the risk of being criticized, I therefore propose an analytic grid that, in my opinion, will help us to understand why, in some cases, the "genocide machine" encountered obstacles that it could not always surmount.

THE STRATEGY OF VICTIMIZATION

The genocide of the Jews can be interpreted as the irruption of a vast sacrificial crisis of which Jews were the main scapegoats. The main ones, but not the only ones; we must not forget that other groups were also exterminated, such as Gypsies and homosexuals. Historical, economic, and cultural factors contributed greatly to the victimization of the Jews. German anti-Semitism did not start in 1933. Other European countries also experienced strong anti-Semitic currents, especially in Eastern Europe. In the 1920s, pogroms had broken out in the Ukraine, Poland, Hungary, Rumania, and Slovakia had likewise been theaters of violence against the Jews. In the West, anti-Semitism was less virulent but just as real, notably in France. Therefore, Hitler and Germany should not be considered as solely responsible for the extermination of the Jews. To be sure, the historic persecution of the Jews had not yet gone so far as the horror of Auschwitz. Exclusion, forced conversion, and exile had, until then, been the most frequently used methods of their persecutors. Nazism too resorted to ancient behavior, but at the same time, it was completely new in that it effected a radical, never yet imagined solution: a systematic plan for the extermination of the "Jewish race." In this respect, October 23, 1941, can be considered a turning point. From that day on, throughout all of Nazi Europe, Jews were forbidden to emigrate; they were completely immobilized in order to be arrested and exterminated.

Before the war, Jews were in an extremely vulnerable situation, because of their lack of social assimilation in various European communities. The fact that the Jews of the East were more persecuted than those of the West sheds light on this issue. In 1940, there were important social differences between the Jews of the East and the West. Poliakov has pointed this out emphatically:

In the invaded territories of the West, there are many fewer Jews than in the East. The equality of rights between citizens—Jews and non-Jews—is in effect. They live spread out among the population from whom they are indistinguishable by their appearance. We understand why the persecution in the West proceeded at a different pace and why the measures were more difficult, applied later, and seemed crueler, especially in the beginning.[6]

In Eastern Europe, Jews constituted an easy prey in a very tense social and political environment. As Ezra Mendelsohn emphasized during a colloquium organized by the École des Hautes Études en Sciences Sociales:

The deterioration of the Jewish condition was not the result of the rise of Nazism, although this event certainly had considerable influence. Starting in the thirties, most citizens of Eastern Europe considered Jews as obvious second-class citizens without rights or nearly so, thus constituting a legitimate target for organized offensives.[7]

In other words, the more Jewish communities turned inward, submitting to the more or less patent hostility of their social environment, the more they were decimated. The absence of social cohesion between Jews and non-Jews against the persecutions of the former is the direct consequence of their victimization. From this perspective, Helen Fein has convincingly shown the close correlation between the intensity of prewar anti-Semitic currents and what she has called the "rate of victimization" of the genocide.[8]

The basic principle of the Nazi strategy was thus to rely first on local anti-semitism. It aimed at increasing or strengthening the exclusion of Jews in order to create the conditions for their deportation. The objective was to break all their former social connections before physically tearing them from the places where they were still trying to survive. That is how we must interpret the chain of increasingly harsh anti-Jewish measures experienced by most countries under German domination: their identification, professional exclusion, dispossession of their property, exclusion from public places, regrouping into ghettos, marking (the yellow star) and, finally, deportation. In Eastern Europe, this strategy did not pose serious problems. The visibility of the Jews facilitated their rapid elimination or their temporary transfer to ghettos.

In Western Europe, however, these operations were more complicated. These countries had a democratic tradition, and it was difficult to explain why generally well-integrated, Jewish citizens presented a mortal threat. "Everywhere in western Europe," Michael R. Marrus and Robert O. Paxton have written:

Nazi leaders worried what would happen when the deportations would affect the local Jews, those who had been citizens of the countries they were living in for a long time. The occupation authorities knew full well that the civil servants and the police of the western countries often established a distinction between well-assimilated, completely integrated Jews and foreign Jews.[9]

Actually, it was primarily the sometimes massive influx of Jews from the East toward France, Belgium, or Holland that made public opinion consider the existence of a "Jewish problem" more or less explicitly. Out of the 57,000 Jews counted in Belgium by the Gestapo, only 6.7 percent were of Belgian nationality. In Holland, more than half of the 120,000 Jews were of foreign origin. As for France, it had experienced the largest immigration in the world following the end of World War I: out of the 350,000 Jews residing there in 1941, mostly taking refuge in the southern zone, fewer than half had French citizenship.[10] None of these new arrivals was integrated into the social fabric of their new countries. Immigrants from Germany, Austria, Poland, and Czechoslovakia in particular encountered suspicion, even hostility, in their new environment. Because of this, they were Adolf Eichmann's first target in Western Europe. To make it easier to seize German Jews, Berlin even published a general decree in November 1941 that stripped those living abroad of their nationality. These Jews found themselves in the lowest of categories—that of people without a country—a status that would make it easier for the national police to arrest them.

Local resistance was strongest to the deportations of small, well-integrated communities. Because of their size in comparison with the general population of the country, general opinion did not feel there was a "Jewish problem" in these cases. In this respect, Denmark and Norway, where tiny Jewish communities had been living for a long time, appeared *a priori* to be the countries that would resist the deportations the most strongly. Martin Luther, the representative of the Foreign Affairs Ministry, predicted difficulties in Scandinavia during the Wannsee conference (which had gathered to coordinate the activities of German ministers in reaching the "final solution") on January 20, 1942.

The Nazi strategy also took into account the possible reactions of public opinion to the promulgation of the anti-Jewish measures. This has to be considered along with the preceding point: the less the Jews were integrated socially, the less public protests were to be feared, and vice versa. Poliakov was one of the first to show how "tightening the net" around the Jews depended directly on how opinion evolved. Germany progressively perfected the method by observing populations' reactions to increasingly severe anti-Semitic measures. At each new phase, when a population did not seem very moved, the Germans took this passivity as a tacit authorization to escalate the persecution. In this spirit, public opinion polls were organized in France and Germany.[11]

Still this practice of taking public opinion into account was relative. Indeed, wherever the Germans ruled alone, Jews were generally threatened very quickly. Specialists have pointed out this finding as well: in countries under direct German administration, the death toll of the genocide was generally higher. This was true, unfortunately, for a long list of countries that were very different from each other and may or may not have had puppet governments. Their common trait was that they were placed under Berlin's direct control. These included Germany itself, of course, Austria, Bohemia-Moravia, Poland, the western regions of the Soviet Union, Norway, Holland, Belgium, Croatia, Serbia, Greece, and Albania. This situation of direct political domination did not prevent the Nazis from depending on citizens who agreed to be more or less active and zealous participants in the deportations, whether as convinced collaborationists or "neutral" public administrators. Quite the contrary. The important thing was that since the Nazis ruled as absolute masters over these territories, Himmler's departments could operate without having to surmount already existing obstacles. Within the satellite countries, however, the Nazis did their best to get the local authorities to collaborate. This tactic had the advantage of being a good propaganda argument. By involving national public authorities, Germany could propagate the idea that other countries, which were also aware of the "Jewish problem," had taken it on themselves to resolve it on their own. The disadvantage was that things progressed more slowly. The result was that in countries like Italy, Finland, Denmark, Bulgaria, and, to a lesser degree, France, the numbers of the victims of the final solution were small, compared to those countries under direct German administration. Thus the fact that Berlin most often delegated measures of arrest and deportation within the collaborating or satellite countries was generally beneficial to the survival of Jewish communities.

The Nazi leaders displayed a perfect Machiavellism in trying to induce other future victims to cooperate as well. In both Eastern and Western Europe, they encouraged the creation of "Jewish councils," which they intended to deal with as representatives of the communities. This solution had many advantages for them, in particular, by forcing the Jews themselves to appoint leaders through whom the Nazis could dictate their conditions. These organizations had to have a "charitable façade" in order to inspire confidence in everyone. They had to provide for the needy and generally manage the communities gathered in the ghettos. They had to make people believe that the best way not to make their lot worse was to follow the recommendations of the Jewish council. So the Nazis created "charity organizations" led by eminent Jewish citizens who, under the cover of bringing aid to the Jews, allowed the Nazis to control them all the better so that they could then arrest them. Adam Czerniakov, the president of the *Judenrat*, the Jewish Council of Warsaw, committed suicide on July 23, 1942, when he at last understood that this organization had been an instrument of the exterminating apparatus. The *Judenrat's* counterpart in Holland was the *Joodse Raad* and in Belgium, the *Association des Juifs de Belgique* (ABJ). In France, it was the *Union Générale des Israélites de France* (UGIF) created by the Vichy government.

The role of these organizations is still highly controversial. Historians are still developing divergent analyses about them. Hannah Arendt triggered a flood of protests, when she declared in her famous essay, *Eichmann in Jerusalem*, that through them, the Jews participated, so to speak, in their own extermination.[12] More recently, Lucien Lazare has noted in a book published in France that, on the contrary, the French Jewish institutions were able to defend the Jews under the occupation[13]; his book has also provoked much criticism. At the core of these divergences is the interpretation of the actions of the UGIF. Serge Klarsfeld has stated that the UGIF played an "underestimated, positive role through its assistance work"[14] whereas Jack Adler has insisted that "those who received official aid from the UGIF, as precious as it was at the time, became dependent on an organization formed for the sole purpose of controlling the Jewish population more tightly."[15]

Can one really have an objective point of view on this intensely emotional subject? The mood of the period was to accommodate the occupier. Why would the Jewish communities have escaped, *a priori*, from this general tendency? Dealing with the persecutor could have been a way to defend themselves, to wait for the storm to pass. Some Jewish leaders, for example, thought that the best way to survive was to work efficiently with the Germans, since theoretically people have no interest in destroying what profits them. But this understandable tactic was unfortunately not adapted to the nature of the threat.

In reality, in spite of their own historical experience of past persecutions, nothing could have prepared the Jews or anyone else for the idea that their lives would end in extermination camps. Jewish councils may have saved people or sometimes allowed the misappropriation of funds and goods for Jews in hiding. Still, we have to consider this assistance with respect to the cooperation by official organizations with the German authorities, which seems to have had fatal consequences for future victims. How can we distinguish between such opposing effects caused by a completely artificial situation? Since the Jewish councils were in charge of managing goods and people, they inspired confidence and thus delayed people from going underground. The situation required radical decisions that were difficult to make: to leave one's property and friends in order to flee the country or to hide or to break the taboo of illegality—so powerfully anchored in everyone, Jews and non-Jews alike—to live as rebels. The very existence of the Jewish councils postponed these choices. The Jews could always think that the council would work things out. In good faith, the council leaders put their hands to the machinery but they did not have the means to stop the infernal motion. As Randolph Braham has pointed out:

Without power, the councils were quickly transformed into German-controlled involuntary and unconscious instruments, at the very time that they were still trying to preserve the interests of their communities with constantly diminishing resources and possibilities of choice. Even this devotion toward the community served Nazi interests. Once the councils joined the German game, they had no choice: they had to cooperate. [16]

This critical conception of the role of the Jewish councils should not leave any doubt as to the nature of responsibilities. Morally, the genocide calls for an absolute condemnation of its Nazi instigators; there is no sharing of the wrong-doing. But it is normal that historians, sociologists, and psychologists should question themselves in depth about the conduct of the victims of the holocaust. We have been astonished, for example, that even while walking toward their own deaths, the victims did not distrust their persecutors. The persecutors intended to deceive them, making them believe until the very end that they were on their way to work camps. The conduct of the victims—Jewish or not—can hardly be explained as voluntary submission. Sometimes they actually did rebel. Some of the most important extermination camps experienced desperate revolts that were put down with great cruelty: Treblinka (August 2, 1943), Sobibor (October 14, 1943), and Auschwitz (October 7, 1944). There were numerous attempts to escape. [17] Furthermore, the historical literature clearly shows the reality of a diversified Jewish resistance. Important debates developed in France, among other countries, over the nature of this resistance. [18] The fact is that, everywhere in Europe, with or without weapons, Jews resisted.

The best-known rebellion was the 1943 uprising of the Warsaw ghetto. The Jews joined with underground movements that they themselves had sometimes created. Like other resisters, they participated in the patriotic fight against the German occupation. They also participated in rescue activities like those by the *Oeuvre de secours aux enfants,* which specialized in camouflaging Jewish children. [19]

The apparent absence of resistance by holocaust victims can probably be explained by the extraordinary pressure that the violence of genocide placed on them, a violence that provoked strange and ambiguous attitudes. The victims reacted with behavior that was not appropriate for their concrete situation. The brutality of their persecution, accompanied by their social uprooting, put them in a state of permanent shock. They were thus incapable of analyzing their situation rationally. They were convinced that their situation could not get worse, a position that became more and more rigid as the situation worsened. They acted "as if" the situation would improve (consider, for example, the phenomenon of ghetto rumors: "They say that . . . "). This denial of reality was an ultimate defense mechanism in a destructive universe.

In the exciting work that he devoted to the state of knowledge about the genocide during the war years, Walter Laqueur showed the difference that existed between credible information and believed information.[20] The author has declared that by late in 1941 and even more during the year of 1942, many people—both Jews and non-Jews—knew what was going on in Poland. That does not necessarily mean that they believed it or had drawn the necessary conclusions. Actually, at the time, the human mind could not bring itself to conceive that such a thing as Auschwitz could exist. The unspeakable reality was beyond comprehension for anyone, Jewish or not. For the potential victims, this denial was fatal.

It is human to close our eyes to the lot awaiting us, but this action was unrealistic and unworkable with respect to the gravity of this particular situation. Shutting out the terrifying vision could not prevent death from seizing its prey. In many respects, we see the same phenomenon among dying patients who act "as if" they are not going to die, because they cannot integrate the idea of their imminent expiration. This defense mechanism can be seen in any human being confronted with the anguish of his or her destruction, whatever that person's sex, race, or religion. Louis de Jong wrote on this subject with great subtlety:

Hitler had said it plainly: let war come and the whole of European Jewry will be exterminated. And the war had come. Why then did no one draw the correct inference? It is easy for us to wonder, looking back as we do at the German extermination camps and gas chambers . . . free as we are of the tremendous psychological tensions of the war, above all free of fear, of mortal fear in its most naked form. . . . The gas chambers, however, spelled death—and what a death!—not only to individuals but to all those they held dear: their parents and grandparents, their children and grandchildren, their relatives and friends. Small, indeed, must have been the number of those among the millions driven to death who could face that awesome truth. And we should commit an immense historical error were we to dismiss the main defense mechanism employed by the victims—not constantly mind you, but by way of intermittent distress signals—as mere symptoms of blindness or foolishness; rather did these defense mechanisms spring from deep qualities shared by all mankind—a love of life, a fear of death, and an understandable inability to grasp the reality of the greatest crime in the history of mankind.[21]

THE SCREEN OF STATE

Everything that helped to put distance between the persecutors and their victims generally had favorable consequences for the victims. The main problem was the attitude of those governments that enjoyed a degree of internal autonomy within the German orbit. In the countries allied or collaborating with Germany, the Nazis had to obtain the agreement of the political authorities to initiate the deportations. The need to gain this approval, which alone would be able to command the national and local police, was in itself a slowing down, indeed a blocking factor, of the genocide process.

It is therefore possible to say that the states allied with Germany or practicing a policy of collaboration were able to offer real protection to the Jews residing in their territories. This does not mean that nothing more was possible to save Jews in the countries under the direct control of Berlin. Too little is known about Poles who took considerable risks to save thousands of Jews, despite the predominant anti-Semitism. And the example of the Belgian administrative authorities which were less cooperative than their Dutch counterparts, shows that there was a margin for maneuvering. But the margin was much narrower than in countries that had some degree of internal autonomy. Within these countries, the state could become a kind of protective screen against the direct persecution of the Jews. Still, those countries had to want to take protective action, and this was far from always the case.

The governments' attitudes were generally determined by the degree of anti-Semitism within local opinion—that is, the extent of social division on the "Jewish problem" within the countries. The more Jews were already the object of bitter complaints, the more local governments were inclined to promulgate anti-Semitic laws and then to organize deportations. When anti-Semitism was weak, however, that is, when countries showed good social cohesion on this question, governments tended to display firmness. The more Jews were considered to be full members of the nation, the more governments were reluctant to promulgate anti-Semitic laws and organize deportations.

A country's military alliance with Germany did not necessarily mean that its population shared the Nazis' opinions about anti-Semitism. Fascist Italy is a good illustration. Anti-Semitism was never deeply rooted in the Italian population nor even within its Fascist party, which Jews had supported in the 1920s, and 1930s. In 1938, Benito Mussolini promulgated laws directed against 50,000 Italian Jews, but these laws were "moderate," compared to their German counterparts. In November 1942, at the time of the German invasion of the south of France, the Italians occupied eight French departments that became places of refuge for Jews. "Not only did the Italian occupation officers refuse to give the Jews over to Vichy or the Germans, but they even impeded the application of French anti-Semitic legislation."[22] During Joachim von Ribbentrop's visit to Rome, he tried in vain to convince Mussolini to modify his position. When Italy capitulated to the Allies in early autumn 1943, the German armies invaded the peninsula and the Jews' situation worsened immediately. Those who had hidden in Italian-controlled French departments were captured and deported. In Italy itself, despite more and more serious military reverses, Himmler insisted that the "final solution" be carried through: 8,000 Italian Jews were deported before the Germans capitulated in 1945.[23]

In fact, there was a potential contradiction for the Nazis between maintaining a good relationship with the states allied with the Reich and strictly applying the deportation measures by those same countries. As long as the governments of these countries agreed with the policy of anti-Semitic persecution, everything was all right: Germany won on both counts. But when these countries proved reluctant on the Jewish question, there was a dilemma. Should Berlin favor a good relationship with the rebellious country (for strategic, military, political, etc. reasons) or increase the pressure so that it would commit itself more strongly to "resolving" the Jewish question? It seems that the Nazis generally opted for the first solution. That still did not keep Himmler from repeatedly asking that the reticent governments deal with the problem of Jewish deportations. The Nazis figured that a favorable opportunity would appear with time, especially if Germany won the war.

Denmark continually expressed a desire for national independence in its internal politics, which contributed to saving its small Jewish community. The Danish population's admirable help in bringing about the escape of 7,000 Danish Jews to Sweden in October 1943 is well known. One cannot understand this act, however, without referring to the initial intransigent attitude that Copenhagen tried to maintain on the Jewish question during the occupation period. If the program of arresting the Jews was delayed, it was because the Danish government did not want to collaborate in this area. In October 1942, Berlin tried to introduce anti-Jewish legislation in Denmark, as they had in other countries. But Germany came up against the categorical refusal of Prime Minister Erik Scavenius who threatened to resign along with his entire cabinet. On the one hand, Berlin was trying to meddle in Danish internal affairs, in spite of the German memorandum of April 9, 1940, that recognized Denmark's authority in internal politics. On the other hand, the assimilated Danish Jews were considered complete citizens. In this respect, it is clear that the Danish government was not manifesting "pro-Semitism." Its attitude was based more on a fundamental political position: going against the Jews meant attacking a basic element of the Danish constitution—the equality of rights for all citizens. When he took office, the new Commissioner of the Reich, Werner Best, described the situation intelligently in a report that he sent to Berlin:

Any anti-Jewish legislation copied from the German model would encounter the strongest opposition from the entire population, the Diet, the administration and the king. . . . Introducing the yellow star would provoke protests by thousands of Danes of German extraction. Denmark considers the Jewish question a constitutional issue. Equality of all citizens before the law is a basic pillar of the present constitution. In the eyes of the Danes, any discriminatory treatment of Jews of Danish nationality would amount to starting to abolish the present constitution.[24]

Perhaps it is because of this firmness that some people still tell the story today of how King Christian X wore the yellow star. The story is apocryphal. The yellow star was never introduced in that country. It is true, however, that the king threatened to wear one if it were introduced; his threat made the Danish government's dissuasive position even more believable.

Not far away, Finland, a country allied with Germany, proved itself to be just as intransigent. In 1942, Himmler tried hard to pressure the Finnish government to deport its 2,000 Jews, but the government refused. According to Braham:

This attitude was due less to the "high esteem" Hitler had for the Finnish people, as Hannah Arendt said, than to political strategy: the Führer no doubt figured that it would have been unwise to compromise his relationship with an independent Finland that was also one of his most reliable allies in the war against Russia, when the only benefit was the elimination of a few hundred Jews.[25]

Other countries interrupted acts of anti-Semitic persecution that they had authorized or even incited up until then. They also openly slowed down the deportations in which their governments were involved. Such decisions had varying motives, such as the desire for national independence by new administrations or the reactions of public opinion to the prospect of disengaging from Germany now that it was losing the war.

The case of Romania, where Jews were much less persecuted in the second part of the war, was typical of such a change in attitude. In 1937, Romania was the second country in Europe (after Germany) to establish an authentic anti-Semitic regime. Fascist groups instigated pogroms there. Although King Karol had formerly tried to calm tensions, he strengthened his anti-Semitic policy in July 1940, hoping to get closer to Germany. When the general and dictator Ion Antonescu (who had made an alliance with the Garde de Fer fascists) took power in September 1940, a period of terror broke out against the Jews. A brief period of calm ensued early in 1941 after the failed coup d'état by the Garde de Fer, which was then kept from power. But when Romania decided to participate in the war against the Soviet Union, massacres began again, the most famous of which was the massacre of Jassy. During the second half of 1941, thousands of people died in the new province of Transnistria. Jews from the provinces of Bessarabia and Northern Bukovina were deported. The Germans then occupied Bucharest. Plans to deport the 440,000 Romanian Jews were drawn up during the fall of 1942.

At that point, well-known political, intellectual, and religious personalities, who had supported Antonescu until then, had the courage to speak out against the deportations. Opposition politicians also criticized the policy. Furthermore, the war against the Soviet Union was not popular, and support for the Allies was growing. All these factors together changed the administration's attitude. The singular personality of the Romanian dictator also played a significant role. An obstinate man, Antonescu decided out of opportunism to thwart German deportation plans and show his fierce desire for independence. He actually favored the mass emigration of Jews and suddenly decided to act in this direction. Thus, at the end of 1942, when the war was still raging and the concentration camps were intensely active, Bucharest authorized its Jews to emigrate to Palestine, in return for a financial consideration. In 1943, Romania developed contacts with the Allies and prepared to switch alliances. That is what saved most Romanian Jews who, until then, had been on the brink of deportation. As Bela Vago has said:

A strong desire for independence, strong pressures by both the opposition and public opinion, in addition to the population's intense anti-German feelings, all led Antonescu to go against German pressures and take control of the extremist minority in the country. A cold-blooded *Realpolitik*, a traditional pragmatism, a healthy dose of opportunism, and even widespread corruption, along with the population's authentic and deeply rooted humanitarian sentiments, especially among the peasants, explains the survival of hundreds of thousands of Romanian Jews.[26]

Hungary's situation was similar to Romania's although the final dénouement was fatal for the majority of Hungary's Jews. Virulent anti-Semitism had been common in Hungary since the 1920s and 1930s. Allied with Germany during the first months of the war, Hungary was governed first by Teleki, then by Bárdossy, both of whom followed Nazi methods, step by step, to exclude Jews from public life. In August 1941, 18,000 foreign Jews were deported to the Ukraine, and 16,000 among them were massacred in Kamenetz-Podolsk. In January 1942, the Hungarian army and police force massacred about 2,600 Serbs and 700 Jews in Hungarian-occupied Délvidek (a region in northern Yugoslavia) without the administration's authorization. Although the Kamenetz-Podolsk massacre went practically unnoticed by Hungarian opinion, the second one triggered intense protests within political circles. In March 1942, Nicholas Kallay's new administration officially accused those responsible for the killing in Délvidek. A moderate politician, Kallay then tried to block the process that would lead inexorably to the deportation of the Jews, going against the popular sentiment that approved their marginalization. He obtained the support of Admiral Miklós Horthy and tried to resist pressures from entrenched national-socialist organizations in the population, especially the *Croix Fléchées* of Szálasi. When the Nazis demanded at least 100,000 Jews during the summer of 1942, Kallay held firm. Like Antonescu, he was determined to assert Hungary's independence from Germany. The progress of the war could only strengthen him in this political stand, and he established various contacts with the Allies.

But Kallay's regime was caught between insurmountable contradictions, between external pressures from the Nazis and internal pressures from a very anti-Semitic public opinion. Kallay had to resign in March 1944. The Germans then took control of the country. The Jewish community, which had known two years of relative calm, was immediately worried. Hungarian police, supervised by a handful of SS men, deported 600,000 Jews within a few months. After the Normandy landing and the very insistent Allied warnings, Horthy made the deportations stop; for the first time, the Hungarian Catholic and Protestant churches protested against them. But in October 1944, the Germans again took control of the country with the support of the *Croix Fléchées*. They committed new atrocities, and deportations started up in Budapest in the presence of Eichmann. For the first time, the international community also tried to act to save the future victims. Several foreign legations delivered thousands of visas and other administrative papers in order to put the Jews under their protection. The Red Cross also did remarkable work. But it was especially Raoul Wallenberg, special envoy of the King of Sweden, and Victor Ludz, the Swiss consul, who stood up for the international conscience. They rivaled one another in their energy and ingenuity to save as many Jews as possible, as if the intensity of their mobilization was proportional to the international passivity during the preceding years.[27]

THE SCREEN OF OPINION

The tragedy of the Hungarian Jews shows that the "protective screen" that a satellite country might be able to provide was powerless against the combined pressures of an influential anti-Semitic public opinion and well-established local Nazi organizations. In this case, Berlin could wait for a favorable opportunity to push forward against the fragile opposition of the political leaders. This reveals the importance of the role of public opinion as either an accelerator or a brake in the process leading to the "final solution." When hostility toward the deportations was expressed openly in a given society, this public expression was sometimes able to form a second kind of protective screen against the increasing victimization of the Jews. When a truly public opinion intervened as a "third party" between the persecutors and the victims, deportations often slowed down and were sometimes even broken off.[28] This mediation mechanism, which was eventually able to deflate repression (see the preceding chapter in the context of the relationship between occupier and occupied), also appears in the particular context of the genocide.

Churches again played a determining role. As moral authorities in a mostly Christian Europe, with access to all social circles, their influence on minds was considerable. As we know, Christians manifested contradictory attitudes toward the persecution of the Jews; there was little similarity, for example, between German and Danish Protestants and between Polish and Italian Catholics. It is inappropriate to judge the behavior of the whole Catholic church by the silence of Pope Pius XII whose attitude provoked numerous debates. We must at least distinguish between the behavior of the Rome that led the hierarchy of national churches and the Rome consisting of faithful Christians belonging to several political families.[29]

Whatever these debates may conclude, we can maintain that when the foremost religious authorities openly expressed their opposition to the increasing marginalization of the Jews, that opposition was likely to challenge the process leading to their deportation. Here we must distinguish between confidential protest (for example, a secret letter addressed to the authorities) and public protest (for example, a bishop's pastoral letter read in the churches of his dioceses), whose impact was obviously much greater. But, as important as their role was, churches were not alone in forming public opinion about the Jewish question. All those who had some political, moral, or intellectual legitimacy were potential third parties in support of the Jews. This category must also include public protests by non-Jewish populations in solidarity with the Jews.

This role as a protective screen, which mobilized opinion was sometimes able to play, depended on the general level of repression that was practiced by the Germans or their allies on the whole of the population. Regardless of their respective degrees of anti-Semitism or their other motives, it was much more difficult for the Poles to manifest their disapproval publicly than it was for the Danes or the French. As we have already pointed out, the efficacy of public opinion was weak in countries governed directly by Germany. Unfortunately, in Bohemia-Moravia, although the population was not very anti-Semitic and the Czech police did not participate in the deportations, protests by Monsignor Kaspar, the Archbishop of Prague, and by other personalities of that city had no influence. In the part of Greece occupied by the Germans, the deportations of 1943 triggered important reactions, particularly the open disapproval by Archbishop Genadios and various intellectuals. Nothing made a difference.

In Germany proper, however, the work undertaken by Nathan Stoltzfus[30] has shown German opinion was in a position to restrain the genocide as soon as that opinion expressed its disapproval of the persecution of the Jews. By the end of 1942, most German Jews had been exterminated, except those married to non-Jews, the *Mischehen*, and their children, the *Mischlinge*. The logic of the Nazi doctrine should have made these 20,000 Jews the first victims of the deportations. On the one hand, the offspring resulting from a mixed couple of an Aryan and a Jew were to be banished. On the other hand, the loyal attachment of the non-Jewish spouse to the Jewish spouse went completely against Nazi propaganda, which outlawed all contact with Jews. It was precisely this particularly intense emotional connection that made taking spouses difficult. The authorities therefore openly encouraged such couples to divorce in order to be able to arrest the Jewish partner more easily. This process, sometimes accompanied by intimidating threats, led to few results. At the beginning of 1943, more than half of these Jews lived in Berlin; they worked mostly in factories that had special workshops for Jews. On February 27, 1943, members of Hitler's personal security force burst into these workplaces and arrested hundreds of Jews. At the same time, members of the Gestapo and the Berlin police went into homes to take the children. They took the Jews to five detention centers situated in the center of Berlin to await their imminent deportations.

Several women, declaring that their husbands had not come home from work as usual, decided that same evening to go stand across the street from one of those buildings, at 2-4 Rosenstrasse, where they thought their husbands were incarcerated. The next day, Sunday, other women had spread the word, and hundreds of them stationed themselves in front of the same building, chanting "Give us back our husbands." Hearing the crowd's clamor, some prisoners screamed through the windows, asking to be let out. By coincidence, the Gestapo headquarters for Jewish affairs was on the corner of that street, in Burgstrasse, so that its members could see the protest from their own windows. They looked to see who the leaders were, but the movement was obviously spontaneous. In spite of the interventions of the Berlin police and the SS brigade, who threatened to shoot into the crowd, the protest continued. The police managed to disperse the group, but it gathered again every day. From February 27 to March 5, 1943, in the coldest weather, this group of women, joined by up to 600 men, protested in the streets of Berlin until their spouses were released, starting on March 6. On this date, Goebbels wrote in his journal that the action had stopped temporarily because of public protest. A month later, a report by the American legation in Berne, Switzerland, reached the same conclusion, noting that: "The action begun by the Gestapo against Jewish husbands and wives must have been interrupted because of the protest it provoked."[31]

In the countries with some degree of internal autonomy, the complex relationship between opinion and victimization appears quite clearly, as can be seen in the cases of Bulgaria and France. These countries were completely different—in terms of the size of their populations and of the Jewish communities living there, their geographies, and their histories. But in spite of these differences, it is striking to notice how their two governments, which had been more or less taken over by Berlin, could be sensitive to open pressures from their own internal public opinions.

In prewar Bulgaria, anti-Semitism was trivial. The small Bulgarian community of about 50,000 Jews was well integrated in this country of 6 million inhabitants—a surprising fact in a region of Europe where anti-Semitism was common. But the rapprochement of Bulgaria and Germany had quick negative consequences for the Jews. In February 1940, the new administration of Bogdan Filov, an ardent admirer of Germany, instituted a moderate anti-Jewish policy with the support of King Boris. In November 1940, the government filed a bill aimed at excluding Jews. Fairly moderate in contrast with the statutes already in effect in Hungary and Romania, this law, which was called "Defense of the Nation," provoked intense protests within public opinion. The Orthodox Church let its disapproval be known, as did various intellectuals and members of liberal professions. Nonetheless, the Bulgarian parliament, the Subrania, functioning as a ratifying chamber for government decisions, passed the bill on January 21, 1941. Bulgaria then entered the war on Germany's side, helped to dismember Yugoslavia and Greece, and benefited from this choice immediately by annexing Greek Macedonia and part of Thrace. Internally, the situation became tougher for Jews. From August 1941 on, some were enrolled in work camps where they had to wear the yellow star. This measure actually touched a limited number of people, and we cannot say that as of that date the Jewish community as a whole was seriously persecuted. Berlin pressed Sofia to show more determination. A new step was taken in August 1942, when Filov created a Jewish Affairs Commission directed by a convinced anti-Semite, Aleksandur Belev. All Jews without work were directed to leave the capital on September 1, 1942, at which time the wearing of the yellow star was applied to the entire community.

These measures in the summer of 1942 provoked a new protest movement. In particular, the metropolitan bishop of Sofia, Monsignor Stephan, delivered a disapproving sermon on September 27. Representatives of the Subrania thought that the administration was going too far. A civil disobedience movement against the wearing of the yellow star developed, with the support of the population. A group of about 350 Jews protested to the Ministry of the Interior and, surprisingly, the minister, Petur Gabrovski came in person to announce appeasement measures to them. Commenting on these events in a report sent to Berlin on November 7, 1942, the head of the German counter-espionage department, Walter Schellenberg, wrote that he had reached the conclusion that "with the latest anti-Jewish ordinances the 'point of toleration' (*das Mass der Erträglichen*) had already been exceeded."[32] This pressure by popular opinion made the administration take a first step backward in October 1942. It asked the press not to attack the Jews anymore and stopped producing yellow stars.

From then on, the Nazis doubted that Bulgaria was willing to "solve" the Jewish question. In January 1943, Theodor Dannecker was sent to Sofia to accelerate things. His mission was to obtain the maximum from the government—that is, to deport the maximum number of Jews. "Negotiations" with Belev led rapidly to the deportation of 20,000 Jews, with priority given to Greeks and Yugoslavians living in occupied territories. From March 4 to March 10, 1943, almost 12,000 Jews were deported from these regions without the decree ordering this operation ever being published. In addition, more than 4,200 Bulgarian Jews were arrested. But this last operation mobilized opinion once again. The vice-president of the Subrania, Dimitur Peshev, led a parliamentary opposition movement and succeeded in persuading 43 delegates, several of whom were close to the administration, to sign a petition. In the province of Plovdiv, a bishop, Monsignor Kiril (later the Patriarch of Bulgaria) threatened to launch a "campaign of civil disobedience including personally lying down on the railroad tracks before the deportation trains, if the planned operation was carried out."[33] These new pressures by public opinion led to the rescinding of the deportation order for Bulgarian Jews. King Boris was determined from then on to prevent deportations, once the international situation after the battle of Stalingrad made him distance himself from Germany. After meeting in Berlin with von Ribbentrop, who expressed his great dissatisfaction, the king agreed only to order the expulsion of Jews from Sofia to make them build roads in the Bulgarian countryside. Hundreds of Jews protested in Sofia on May 24, 1943, and went to the royal palace where they were intercepted by the police. Various Communist, Christian, and democratic organizations appealed to the Jews not to leave the capital.[34] At the heart of the highest political circles, they thought that the administration should reverse itself, so once again the expulsion order was rescinded. In an embittered report, Adolph Heinz Beckerle, the German embassy attaché in Sofia, wrote to Berlin on June 7, 1943: "I would like to assure you that we here are doing everything in our power to arrive in a suitable manner at a final liquidation of the Jewish question." Unfortunately, "The Bulgarians had been living with peoples like the Armenians, Greeks and Gypsies for so long that they simply could not appreciate the Jewish problem."[35] This was absurd, of course, since the same was true for the Hungarians and Romanians.

The mysterious death of King Boris in August 1943 and the formation of the new Dobri Bozhilov administration changed nothing in the situation. Jews continued to escape from deportations. Bulgaria was not Denmark, however. The labor camps to which they were sent had rough conditions. A unique event in the history of occupied Europe occurred on August 25, 1944; the government abolished all anti-Semitic texts in Bulgaria. In the already cited reference book about these events, Frederick Chary has challenged the claim that King Boris was the person mainly responsible for saving the Jews. According to Chary, the king's changes in attitude resulted from pressures by public opinion every time. In the process of forming a counter-power, the author has emphasized the institutional translation of opinion-based protest, whether it occurred through stands taken by religious authorities or through actions by parliament.[36]

In France, as noted above, prewar anti-Semitism was a reality that the Vichy regime strengthened in the context of the "national revolution" that aimed especially at giving Jews a "particular status." During the first two years of occupation, opinion barely reacted to the flood of anti-Semitic measures; these included those of October 3, 1940 (the first Jewish statute); October 21, 1940 (the circular excluding Jews from public office); March 29, 1941 (the creation of a commissary for Jewish questions); June 2, 1941 (the second Jewish statute); June 21, 1941 (*numerus clausus* in universities); and May 29, 1942 (a German order on the obligatory wearing of the yellow star in the Northern zone).

During the summer of 1942, however, when the deportations began, opinion started to react. The introduction of the yellow star in the occupied zone had already provoked displays of sympathy toward the Jews. Georges Wellers has reported stories of young non-Jewish partisans who tried to ridicule this measure; some of them made paper stars and wrote "Negro" on them. Others put yellow stars on their dogs and took them out for walks.[37]

These were spontaneous reactions that, although limited, already showed a change in opinion toward Jews. Emotions became more intense after the first big organized roundup in France on July 16 and 17, 1942, by the Paris police. The sight of entire families being taken from their homes by French police was clearly enough to overwhelm many minds. This memorable action, called the "Vel d'Hiv" roundup because the victims were gathered at the "Vélodrome d'Hiver" (winter cycle-racing track), crystallized and intensified the growing solidarity of French opinion in favor of the Jews. Out of the 22,000 Parisian Jews scheduled to be apprehended, the police managed to seize only 12,884 during the first two days: "There were many friends, neighbors, and strangers who hid or warned the designated victims. And among the police, there was a lack of enthusiasm and even sometimes a failure to do their duty."[38]

How should we interpret this change in attitude, which is somewhat surprising in its contrast to the former passivity of the French? Should we conclude that the French were suddenly expressing a repressed pro-Semitism? Their lack of reaction during the two preceding years testifies to the opposite. The French accepted quite easily that Jews should be set apart as second-class citizens. If opinion reacted at the final dénouement, it was probably because people got scared. Scared for the Jews: we cannot doubt the humanitarian feelings that some experienced in agreeing to help them. But also scared for themselves, since the nature of the roundup was indeed frightening. Its massive, brutal, conspicuous character spectacularly demonstrated the power of a country that seemed out of control. Who could say that tomorrow or in a year, for one reason or another, it might not be my turn to be taken? The powerful emotional shock provoked by this unprecedented, monumental roundup quickly made it a symbol; one could say that there was a pre-Vel d'Hiv and a post-Vel d'Hiv attitude in France with respect to the Jewish question. At the same time that the roundup marked the peak of the victimization process of the Jews in France, it also led to a growing mobilization of a part of French opinion in favor of the Jews.

During the summer of 1942, several police reports noted the population's general disapproval of the deportations. Similarly, various religious authorities both relayed the changes in opinion and, as in Bulgaria, expressed them institutionally. On the first day of the Paris roundup, Cardinal Suhard, archbishop of Paris, wrote to Laval telling him of his emotions. During the month of August 1942, Marshall Pétain also received indignant letters from Cardinal Pierre Gerlier, the archbishop of Lyon, and Pastor Marc Boegner, President of the Protestant Federation of France. Fearing new mass arrests in the southern zone similar to those in Paris, chief rabbi Jacob Kaplan beseeched the administration, in the name of the Consistory, to put a stop to them. When the collaborating press openly announced more roundups in the unoccupied zone, many Catholic leaders felt compelled to speak out *publicly*. The archbishop of Toulouse, Monsignor Saliège launched the movement by having a resounding pastoral letter read throughout his diocese on August 23, 1942, in spite of pressures upon him during the preceding days. This intervention quickly became famous, because it was the first public protest by a high official of the French Catholic church against the deportation of Jews. It was followed by others: on August 23, by Monsignor Theas, the bishop of Montauban; on September 6, by Monsignor Delay, the archbishop of Marseille; and by Cardinal Gerlier himself. So, after having condoned the entire process of Jewish exclusion, influential voices took up their defense just when the French police were preparing to lead them to their deaths. As Wladimir Rabi has observed, the Catholic hierarchy "became indignant only in July and August 1942 because it suddenly realized that discrimination led to physical persecution."[39]

Early on, these reactions do not seem to have had any effect on the politics of Vichy. At the beginning of August, 3,000 Jews from the southern zone were transferred to the occupied zone. On August 26, roundups took place, predictably in the free zone, during which 6,000 Jews were arrested. This number, which fell far short of the predictions, was another indication that there were acts of complicity to help the Jews. But, on September 2, 1942, during a meeting between the head of the SS in France and Karl-Albrecht Oberg and Helmut Knochen, the leaders of the SS and the German police in France, Laval spoke of protests by the church and specifically named Cardinal Gerlier as "head of the anti-government opposition." As a result of these internal difficulties, Laval explained that it would be hard from then on to hand over the regular numbers of Jews to be deported. Oberg and Knochen took this position as well and let Berlin know it. This was not the case, however, with all German authorities in France. Eichmann's staff tried to work out new arrest plans. But on September 25, Himmler decided in favor of Knochen and Oberg; it was better to preserve the hard-working docility of Vichy in order to maintain the strategic and economic interests of the Reich in France.

This still does not mean that the deportations stopped. Nonetheless, the Nazis were forced to operate more and more on their own, and the French police, especially the local police, grew less and less sure about this kind of operation. The numbers indicate decreasing deportations starting in the fall of 1942; out of a total of 76,000 deportees, more than half (more than 40,000) were deported during the five months of 1942 when Vichy participated fully in the arrests. Michael R. Marrus and Robert O. Paxton are certainly right to connect Vichy's hesitancy to carry out the deportations with the evolution of the war.[40] We must also take into consideration the specific role of the pressure of public opinion at a time when the fate of the war was far from decided. According to Serge Klarsfeld: "confronted with the reactions of public opinion in the free zone and with the influential interventions by church leaders . . ., Vichy saw itself forced to restrict . . . its massive cooperation and to refuse to fulfill its delivery of Jews in October 1942."[41] Vichy had trouble resisting pressures from the Church, to which it owed much of its legitimacy, and the Germans had a hard time doing without Vichy, to which it owed so many benefits. Consequently, we can state that France was in a political position to be able to resist Nazi pressures, especially concerning the deportation of the Jews.

It has sometimes been claimed that Vichy "saved" the Jews, since "only" 76,000 out of 350,000 were taken. Such an argument relies, more or less implicitly, on our already developed observation—namely that the collaborating government, as an intermediate political power, put distance between the Nazis and the Jews that was able to benefit them. In this sense, it is true that creating the free zone offered a temporary refuge for all those who were being pursued by the Germans, Jewish or not. But this thesis obscures the issue of Vichy's will. Instead of taking advantage of this intermediary position and showing firmness on the Jewish question, the French government did exactly the opposite: it put its administration and its police at the service of anti-Semitic persecution. In the southern zone, where Vichy theoretically enjoyed a certain sovereignty, the government, on its own, duplicated the German anti-Semitic legislation of the northern zone, even though it was not really pressured to do so. If Vichy had really been determined to defend the Jews, Berlin would probably have had to accept deferring the final solution, either temporarily or permanently, as they did in other European countries. But then, Vichy would not have been Vichy.

THE SCREEN OF SOCIAL NETWORKS

The above discussion should not make us forget the concrete physical protection provided by anonymous families and militants who sometimes risked their lives "simply" to protect the victims and, especially, the children. These individuals often had the impression they were only doing their duty and that even this was not enough. Their resistance was noble nonetheless: it saved lives.

This interwoven fabric of individuals and groups constituted the third "protective screen" that shielded Jews from arrest through networks of social solidarity. All things considered, the opposition of a satellite country or public protests against the persecutions amounted to a kind of political dissuasion against the Nazi will. On their own, these two factors, discussed above, slowed or even halted the process of victimization.

By contrast, the concrete assistance given to Jews took place on a very different level: that of a battle, which was, literally in this case, the struggle involved in the potential victims' defensive deceptions or flight. It had to do with organizing a resistance against the effects of the victimization process. The goal of this resistance movement was thus to construct a kind of social cover to envelop the Jews and to make them invisible or inaccessible. As Annie Kriegel has pointed out: "We must seek the secret of the most effective grass-roots survival strategies in the nature of the daily interpersonal relationships between Jews and non-Jews."[42] Whether or not a country was under Germany's direct control, whether opinion in favor of the Jews was expressed more or less openly in this country, the victims were always in a vulnerable position as long as they were without the social cover that alone could camouflage them. This circumstance demonstrates the importance of the concrete solidarity networks that surrounded the Jews in keeping the genocide in check.

In France, priestly residences, convents, and schools took in Jews. In the heart of the Cévennes region, in Huguenot country where the population was familiar with persecution, the Protestant village of Chambon-sur-Lignon accomplished a remarkable feat throughout the duration of the war. Led by pastors André Trocmé and Édouard Theis, the townspeople of Chambon carried out one of the most significant acts of nonviolent resistance (they openly declared this term) at the local level.[43] They formed welcome or escape channels abroad through either the Comité Inter-Mouvements Auprès des Evacués (the Inter-Movement Committee For Evacuees or CIMADE),[44] which was created at the beginning of the war to help refugees from Alsace and Lorraine, or *l'Amitié chrétienne* or Christian Friendship, run by Father Chaillet out of Lyon and supported by Cardinal Gerlier. Some claim that 12,000 Jews fled to Spain and 10,000 to Switzerland thanks to them.

The proximity of countries that offered shelter to Jews clearly contributed to the success of this kind of operation. Nevertheless, it seems that what we could call "geo-demographic" factors (the concentration or dispersion of communities, the proximity of countries of refuge, etc.) played a determining role only when factors of "political dissuasion" did not function. Indeed, when there was no satellite country, or when the latter showed no desire to defend the Jews, or when public opinion turned out to be powerless to stop the process of victimization, the last recourse was battle. It is in battle that geography plays a determining role. The tactic of camouflage assumed that the victims were hidden in the thousands of interstices of the social fabric. The tactic of flight assumed a welcoming country nearby. In either case, it was better for the victims not to be concentrated in one place.

The example of Holland, where more than 80 percent of the Jewish community was exterminated (out of a population of 120,000 Jews in 1940), illustrates this analysis tragically. The mechanisms of political dissuasion could not function in that country for various reasons. Holland was placed under the direct control of the occupier, and the Dutch administration *did* cooperate. Either of these elements alone already implied considerable vulnerability. In particular, a Dutch civil servant early in the occupation invented an identification card that was almost impossible to falsify; with authorization from his superiors, he rushed to show it to the Gestapo in Berlin. "From 1940 to 1945," Dutch historian Louis De Jong has written, "there was no scourge from which the Dutch received bloodier wounds than from this execrable identity card—the invention of an over-zealous civil servant, himself not a Nazi."[45]

Furthermore, the reactions of popular opinion did not succeed in influencing the direction of decisions. There were various spontaneous manifestations of sympathy toward the Jews, but these did not coalesce into a concrete network of assistance. Holland's major problem was the weakness of the social cover available to the Jews. Holland did, however, have an unbelievable network of hiding places for those persecuted by the regime. This generalized assistance movement appeared mainly after the major strikes of April and May 1943, when Germany laid claim to young Dutch citizens for forced labor. By that point, most Dutch Jews had already been exterminated.

When the first anti-Jewish laws were promulgated in the fall of 1940, Jews received some support, especially from the teaching corps from which Jews had been excluded. Students at Leiden University and the Polytechnical School of Delft went on strike, and instructors signed petitions for the reinstatement of their colleagues. Then, in an atmosphere of growing tension between groups of young Jews and pro-Nazis, Himmler ordered the first roundup of 400 Jews in the streets of Amsterdam on February 22 and 23, 1941. This spectacular operation triggered a series of strikes, especially by city workers and employees. The roundup was not the only cause for the strikes. After the discovery of what Nazi occupation was really like, the exasperation of the population was at its peak; the deterioration of the economic situation, numerous unpunished exactions by pro-Nazi groups, and the occupier's arrogance all contributed to the Dutch reaction. The transit workers and municipal employees of Amsterdam organized a strike in the capital that reached a few other Dutch cities on February 26 and 27, 1941. Thousands of people stopped work to take part in sporadic demonstrations sometimes accompanied by gestures of violence by the demonstrators. Even though partially organized by the Communists, this action had no real direction and was quickly put down by the Germans. Its main result was to reinforce German repression over the Dutch in general and the Jews in particular.[46]

Dutch churches—both Protestant and Catholic—were far from inactive in supporting the Jews, but they did put off expressing their disapproval publicly. In November 1940, they sent an unpublished text protesting the banning of Jews from certain professions. In 1942, at the time of the deportations, they again sent protest telegrams, which they threatened to make public, to the Commissioner of the Reich, Seyss-Inquart. In response, Seyss-Inquart warned them that he would then deport Jews who had converted to Christianity. The Catholic Church refused this extortion and published its declaration; those Jews were indeed deported.[47] This affair demonstrated once again the weakness of public protest in a country under direct Nazi control. We must add, however, that it was easy for the Reich's commissioner to exploit the divisions within the churches of Holland. Things might have turned out differently if the Dutch Reformed Church, which was actually quite close to those in power, had decided to publicize its text as well. Whatever the case may have been, the lack of unity among the churches in this affair was an important factor in their powerlessness.

In this very difficult situation, in which the two "protective screens" of the satellite country were nonfunctional, the only ways left to limit the victimization of the Jews were to hide them or to help them flee. In 1942, this became practically impossible. The great vulnerability of the Dutch Jews was that the majority of them had lived in Amsterdam before the war. Once the ghetto was surrounded by the occupier, it became impossible to hide them among the rest of the citizens. Since the famous identity cards made them easily identifiable, their situation became desperate.

Still, we should not exaggerate the importance of "geo-demographic" factors, because nearby Belgium, which was comparable to Holland (also under direct rule, also a small territory with a very dense population), succeeded where Holland failed. Other factors differentiated them, of course. The Belgian Jews were more dispersed, with the majority of them living in Antwerp and Brussels, but with smaller communities living in Liège and Charleroi as well. The Catholic Church had great influence over the consciences of its followers, and the church hierarchy encouraged its parishioners to help the Jews. The Belgian government—and even the Germans—showed less enthusiasm in implementing the persecution process.

Nonetheless, the anti-Semitic laws were passed there at about the same time as in Holland, and deportations were also on the agenda for 1942.

Actually, the main difference between Holland and Belgium was that Belgium had the best organized national civilian resistance movement to help the Jews—the Committee for the Defense of Jews (CDJ), whose history was traced by Maxime Steinberg.[48] Founded by Hertz Jospa, a Communist Jew of Romanian extraction,[49] the CDJ was directly connected to the Independence Front, one of the most important national resistance movements. After the war, the Belgian government gave the CDJ the official status of a "civilian resistance" movement. Because of this and its links with the Independence Front, and in spite of its autonomy, the CDJ was able to reach into a variety of social circles, which helped considerably in hiding Jews. When the Nazis introduced its typical Jewish council under the name of the Association of Belgian Jews (AJB), the CDJ succeeded in getting one of its members on the council, so that the organization was informed about what was happening. The CDJ's work was sometimes supported by the armed actions of a resistance group, the partisans, who, for example, destroyed the AJB's index-card cabinet on July 31, 1942.[50]

The CDJ conducted a massive propaganda effort to convince Jews not to give themselves up voluntarily at the Malines Center (the deportation departure point), as the AJB had ordered them to do. Wherever there was an AJB office calling for departures, there was also a clandestine CDJ cell advising the Jews not to go. The organization then developed an entire network of hiding places across the country. Temporary shelters often became permanent. A sort of entrenched resistance against deportations progressively took root over the expanse of Belgian territory. The Catholic Church played an essential role in building this network with its schools, convents, and priestly residences often becoming places of refuge, especially for the hundreds of children.

Young women called "visitors" helped the Jews regularly, risking their lives to take care of the latter's daily needs. The organization furnished false papers and ration cards, thanks to different kinds of help within the government. This multifaceted work succeeded in reducing the deportation numbers significantly. Out of the 50,000 Jews living in Belgium after the arrival of the Germans, about 25,000 were deported. And out of the 25,000 remaining, it is estimated that 15,000 owed their lives to the work done by the CDJ; of these, 3,000 were children.[51] This would tend to prove that this third protective screen—the social cover of a concrete solidarity movement—could accomplish quite a lot, even in countries under direct German rule.

The most remarkable solidarity movement in history of the genocide was unquestionably the saving of the Jews in Denmark. This case is well-known because of both its almost complete success (more than 95 percent of the community was saved) and its resemblance to an adventure story (the evacuation of the Jews to Sweden by boat). "The history of the Danish Jews is very particular, and the behavior of its people and government toward the Jews is unique," wrote Hannah Arendt. No other European country—whether occupied, an Axis member, neutral, or truly independent—reacted this way. One is tempted to recommend this story to any political science student interested in measuring the strength of nonviolent action and passive resistance when the adversary possesses violent and more powerful means.''[52]

Nonetheless, various authors have been determined to diminish the importance of this unprecedented rescue by developing the thesis that its success was due to particular circumstances. They have mentioned the special affection that Hitler was said to have felt for the Danes, even though for him Jews remained Jews, whatever their nationality. They have emphasized the date of this event—October 1943—a period when people finally "knew": even so, many Jews were still exterminated after this date. They have claimed that the rescue succeeded because Denmark was so close to Sweden, while forgetting to add that no similar event happened in Norway. They have also stressed the small size of the community and the fact that with 7,500 Jews, rescue was easier. We have only to compare this episode with comparable phenomena. Norway's community of 2,000 Jews was even smaller than Denmark's, but half of them were caught in a sweep by Quisling's police in October 1942—an event that the Norwegian resistance could not prevent.

Denmark's case is not exceptional for the reasons usually given. Its rescue was unique in that the three protective screens were present at the same time. These screens manifested the firmness of the satellite country in discouraging attacks against the Jews, the support of public opinion for this policy (role of the Protestant Church was considerable), and choices of the so-called solidarity movement that organized the rescue. Another factor was the consequence of the first three and should be included: disagreements among the occupying authorities themselves.

The rescue of the Jews from Denmark took place in August 1943, shortly after the major political crisis between Berlin and Copenhagen that led to the fall of the Danish government and the establishment of martial law. The Germans planned to deport the Jews as soon as they took control of the country. On August 31, they stole the files on the members of the Jewish community in Copenhagen, where most of Danish Jews lived. The chief rabbi and his son were arrested within the next few days. On September 18, Hitler ordered his plenipotentiary minister of the Reich, Werner Best, to proceed with the deportation of the Jews.

But the plan met with difficulties from the beginning. Since it was impossible to count on the collaboration of the Danish police, Best asked Hermann von Hannecken, the commander of the Wehrmacht in Denmark, for men. Conflicts between him and Best made him refuse. Best thus had to have German police come specially from Germany for the operation. Actually, some of the Germans within the general staff in Denmark who were informed thought the plan was mistaken, given the tense climate in the country ever since the government had fallen. An attaché from the German embassy, George-Ferdinand Duckwitz, tried in vain to convince Best to give up his plan. Duckwitz went to Berlin and then to Sweden to get the latter to use its influence with Germany. Stockholm did intervene, but it was of no use. On September 28, several days before the roundup that was planned for the night of October 1–2, Duckwitz warned the leaders of the Danish resistance.[53]

The information was immediately communicated to the leaders of the Jewish community and to some high officials of Denmark. The next day, September 29 and the eve of Rosh Hashana (the Jewish New Year), the rabbi of the Copenhagen synagogue warned his congregation during the morning service. The news spread quickly by word of mouth. Channels of information peculiar to the Danish resistance, both social-democrat and Christian, played an important role in warning all those who could be warned. Professional organizations and associations of all kinds also spread the word. Danes mobilized quickly to help and hide the Jews.[54] The recent resignation of the administration had radicalized many people who were then ready to "do something," not necessarily for the Jews but against Germany, in hopes that the values of Danish democracy would survive.

On the morning of October 2, Best succeeded in having 475 people arrested, 6.2 percent of the 7,695 Jews in Denmark. They were deported to Theresienstad, more a transit camp than an extermination camp.[55] Public protest against the roundup was quickly made by the primate of the Danish Church, the bishops, the main political parties, and various union, professional, and other organizations. But the Jews were not yet out of danger: hidden in Copenhagen and its environs, their security remained precarious. It became imperative to evacuate them by boat to nearby Sweden.

Outside the context in which this plan was produced, it might appear completely unrealistic because of its technical difficulties and potential dangers. But within a few days, saving the Jews became a national affair for many Danes, a concrete way to defy the Nazi order. Thousands of people from all levels of society mobilized spontaneously to make the operation succeed. One of the most important leaders, a teacher named Aage Bertelson, recounted the details later.[56] He described how men and women who had absolutely no experience working with the resistance spontaneously became involved doing all kinds of jobs; how they had to recruit fishing boats and make sure the fishermen were paid; how they had to ensure the security of the Jews when they went to their embarkation points, and so forth. Members of the resistance guarded the main routes leading there in order to guide those who got lost. Even the Danish police took part in the rescue, guiding people in the right direction. Private citizens and even banks advanced large sums of money to cover costs, since many people did not have the money to pay for their trip.

The rescue of the Jews owes its success to the strength of this social cohesion among the Danish population. Some people could easily have denounced the Jews and those who helped them. Even though there were not many, the Germans did have some sympathizers. "It was impossible to hide an operation involving thousands of people from the eyes and ears of the population," observed Leni Yahil.

There was a certain element of security in the general nature of the action; even if he was inclined to be pro-German, a neighbor would certainly hesitate to stir up the anger of the majority of the population who supported the rescue operation. This would explain the fact that there were so few informers.[57]

That is how the rescue of the Danish Jews became one of the most remarkable events of the war, a testimony that human solidarity on a large scale could still exist in Nazi Europe. It shows that a small disarmed people was capable of breaking the infernal logic of the genocide when anti-Semitism was absent.

THE TERMINAL STAGE OF CANCER

Genocide is not an accident of history. It is the most serious syndrome of the worst disease of mankind: violence. Like war, genocide is the spectacular manifestation of man's ability to destroy man. It is comparable, in this respect, to a form of cancer that eats away at the social body. In spite of the abundant literature devoted to the subject, rare are the efforts to comprehend genocide as a disease of humanity. But if we start to learn about genocide as a pathological phenomenon that can affect any human society, we may be able to come up with some therapeutic ideas.

Man's tragedy is that he seems able to shape his social identity only by denying that of someone else to varying degrees. The formation of a human group generally leads to a social hierarchy at its core, with the group taking shape based on the designation of a common enemy. War is traditionally the way to affirm the identity of the belligerent group against this "Other," this dangerous designated enemy. Generally, historical observation shows at least three forms of this affirmation of self—a collective Self—through the negation of the Other. These can be interpreted as reductions of the Other to the Self.

- *Assimilation*: the dominant group makes the dominated one adhere to *its* values; that is, embrace *its* culture, religion, and so on. If they obey, the dominated group's members can retain certain limited rights. This is a kind of absorption of the Other by the Self.

- *Enslavement*: the dominated group is placed in a position of total servility, its members deprived of all rights. This is a kind of "instrumentalization" of the Other.

- *Extermination*: clearly the most extreme way of "reducing" the Other—eradication.

It is important to note that this form is illogical in terms of the self-interest of the dominating group. Indeed, in the first case, one might think it would be in the dominating group's best interest to deal tactfully with the dominated group in order to prolong its domination. In the second case, the enslaving regime completely profits the dominator but risks provoking rebellion because of the brutality of its yoke. In the final case, the dominating group seems to derive no apparent profit. It is in this sense that the rationale of genocide is purely irrational. One can say in this respect, with the cold objectivity of analysis, that enslavement is a protection from extermination. As long as the dominating group profits from exploiting the dominated one, it does not occur to the former to destroy the latter.

It might commit massacres against it, but only in order to maintain the rule of terror through which the enslavement can continue. Here we see the profound difference between the nature of enslavement and extermination. The persecutor obviously offers pretexts (racist, nationalist, ethnic) for extermination, but basically genocide is an insane undertaking.

Genocide is thus a syndrome of a collective mental pathology, a pathology of the collective Self that reveals a profound identity crisis within the group. For historical, cultural, and economic reasons, the group experiences the crisis as uncertain and fragile and thus questions its origins. As has been pointed out, war is the classic process by which a society that feels divided and shattered can close ranks and reassert itself once again. The focus of social energy against a foreign body—the enemy—is likely to reestablish its unity and identity.

The particular nature of genocide (stemming from the same need to assert the collective Self) is that this foreign body is not outside but inside the social group. In this sense, genocide is a war directed within a society. The two processes— war and genocide—are interconnected, the whole phenomenon revealing the gravity of the crisis within the society involved. Genocide aims at "extracting" the foreign body whose presence is perceived as the basic cause of social malfunctioning. Destroying this foreign body then becomes a priority so that the group can recover its identity. It must be destroyed on the inside but also on the outside, since, clearly, its external ramifications must also be eliminated. Genocide and war are interconnected in that way as well. The extraction of the foreign body includes three processes: identification, uprooting, and annihilation. Insofar as genocide is a process of war that moves to the inside of the society that commits it, it is a form of collective self-destruction. Genocide is the destruction of society by itself.

In this process of "social conflagration," everyone ends up implicated. Genocide certainly has a central focus from which it spreads, but everything happens thanks to at least some degree of indifference on the part of those around it. Everything leads us to believe that the relationship between the designated victims of the genocide and their social environment is very equivocal. Insofar as genocide is a huge sacrificial crisis focused on victims who are already in the scapegoat position, one can say that genocide occurs only with some kind of social consent. The consent is not necessarily expressed openly. People can sometimes claim they did not know the facts or that they were afraid to help the victims because of reprisals. Nonetheless, the dominant impression is that genocide is accompanied by a kind of disguised approval that sanctions it. Genocide does not occur without collective approval.

Genocide is not a spontaneous phenomenon that can appear overnight. It cannot be decreed. It is the result of a series of social, historical, cultural, religious, and economic factors that shake the social body to its core and organize the group around this insane undertaking. Auschwitz was the terminal phase of a long-lasting disease whose roots ran deep. At this phase, the genocide machine was running at full steam, and it was no longer possible to do much about it. Of course, the protective screens were partially effective, but they were clearly quite fragile. There was too much pressure. The genocide had become a runaway train crushing everyone in front of it; the only thing left to hope for was that as few victims as possible would find themselves in its path.

CAN GENOCIDE BE PREVENTED?

Genocide cannot be "resisted"; it can be prevented. Just as it is difficult to save many people in the explosion zone of a natural cataclysm, it is difficult to save many victims of the social cataclysm of genocide. At best, one can limit the damage at this phase, and examples of spontaneous civilian resistance against the genocide of the Jews show that the results are not negligible. But intervention ahead of time is better. It might be possible to forestall genocide in such a way that it does not happen or that it occurs in a weakened form. In this sense, the "treatment" of genocide is similar to the present-day treatment of cancer. The earlier we catch the cancer the better the chances of wiping it out. The question then is to know what therapy to apply in order to prevent the disease from developing.

The only effective therapy against genocide is prevention—that is, everything that helps to avoid the irreversible victimization of a given national, religious, ethnic, or other minority group. This policy of genocide prevention has several facets. Everything depends first on the potential victims themselves and their own attitudes with respect to the community. It is important to know if they want to be integrated or if they prefer to live on the fringes, knowing that in the latter case, the victims are putting themselves in a vulnerable position. A difficult question arises: should the collective identity of a minority group within a given social entity be preserved, given that integration is not necessarily synonymous with the close assimilation of acculturation?

The second element of a policy to prevent genocide lies in how a society itself treats its minorities. Its leaders' political opinions are clearly influential. Will the leaders, for example, encourage members of minority groups to participate in their country's public life or will they, rather, help to isolate them? Grass-roots struggles in favor of those who are the target of a marginalization policy or who are in the process of being marginalized are also useful to prevent genocide. Everything that helps to develop movements and networks of solidarity with respect to the excluded makes the possibility of their collective murder less likely.

Finally, the vigilance of international public opinion as to the way that countries treat their minorities plays a significant role in the prevention of genocide. The struggle for human rights hinges on two components: reference to texts of international law that countries can chose not to apply but that have the merit of existing; and the triggering of public opinion movements that are more or less strengthened by world-wide media coverage. It is clear that these processes are not always effective, but it is also undeniable that their combination has led to successes. The work of Amnesty International shows us that even recalcitrant dictators turn out to be sensitive to criticism, perhaps because of the development of information systems, international finance, commerce, and tourism. Most governments recognize that a deteriorating international reputation has serious political consequences. This offers hope that genocide can indeed be prevented.

But how can we detect the tell-tale "tumor" in a pre-genocide situation? This is one of the weaknesses of a theoretical approach. Genocides can obviously not be predicted; at most, we can make approximate evaluations of their probability if a society's treatment of its minorities deteriorates seriously. It might be useful to establish indicators of pre-genocidal situations. Among these would be the degree of cohesion or divisiveness within a given society, measuring how withdrawn into itself a society is and how it treats its minorities. We could also analyze its ideology and language, since these elements can reveal a plan to eliminate particular social categories. That is what occurs, for example, with ideologies that claim to create "the new man."

This concept of genocide prevention suggests a prospective vision of international relations. Societies running "high genocide risks" should not be allowed to withdraw into themselves and should be made to maintain open and communicative relations with the societies around them. It is also important not to humiliate peoples and their governments, since humiliation can only feed their desire for vengeance. Such a refusal to humiliate other countries does not mean refusing to treat others firmly as soon as they show a disrespect for human rights. Genocide prevention, like other forms of human rights struggles, comes up against the alleged necessity for noninterference in another country's internal affairs. Everything that has been said and proposed amounts to getting around this principle of noninterference that is so firmly defended by modern countries.

Power is a human phenomenon, and it is difficult to conceive of societies without government. But it is also incontestable that the genocide of the Jews was organized from the stronghold of the state, that, to prevent genocide, procedures regulating national policies must be implemented simultaneously from the top (supra-national movements) and from the bottom (internal social movements). We must open up the operations of governments as much as possible and encourage free movement between nations as well as the internationalization of information and solidarity movements. This is the battle we must wage against institutional inertia and all kinds of vested interests. We all know just how fragile the protective mechanisms remain. We can therefore not declare that the specter of genocide is behind us.

NOTES

1. For a presentation of the different interpretations, one should look particularly at an article by Saul Friedlander in which he makes clear his own preferred view: "De l'antisémitisme à l'extermination: Esquisse historiographique et essais d'interprétation," Colloque de l'École des hautes études en sciences sociales, *L'Allemagne nazie et le génocide juif* (Paris, 1985).

2. In particular, two texts that were presented in the popular press stimulated this "polemic": Ernst Nolte, "Vergangenheit, die nicht Vergehen Will," *Frankfurter Allgemeine Zeitung*, June 6, 1986; Jürgen Habermas, "Eine Art Schadenabwicklung," *Die Zeit*, July 11, 1986. These were reprinted in *Der Historikerstreit* (Munich, 1987), and translated into French under the title *Devant l'Histoire: Les documents dans la controverse sur la singularité de l'extermination des juifs par le régime nazi* (Paris, 1988).

3. The key book on the subject is Raul Hilberg, *The Destruction of European Jews* (London, 1961).

4. Annie Kriegel, "Résistance nationale, antifasciste, résistance juive: engagements et identité," *Réfugiés et immigrés d'Europe centrale*, Colloque International, Paris, October 17-18, 1986 (unpublished) 396–397.

5. Léon Poliakov, *Le Bréviaire de la haine* (Paris, 1951).

6. Poliakov, *Bréviaire* 56.

7. Ezra Mendelsohn, "Relations entre Juifs et non-Juifs en Europe orientale dans l'entre-deux-guerres," *L'Allemagne nazie* 170.

8. Helen Fein, *Accounting for Genocide: National Responses and Jewish Victimization during the Holocaust* (New York, 1979).

9. Michael R. Marrus and Robert O. Paxton, "Nazis et juifs en Europe occidentale occupée (1940–1944)," *L'Allemagne nazie* 303.

10. See the article by Rita Thalmann, "L'antisémitisme en Europe occidentale et les réactions face aux persécutions nazies des juifs pendant les années trente," *L'Allemagne nazie* 134–158.

11. See the article by Marc Knobel, "La position de l'opinion française devant le problème juif en 1943 au travers d'un sondage de type Gallup," *MRAX Information* 44 (September 1986) 38–41. This survey of public opinion, taken in September 1943 in the southern zone, sought to gauge the sentiment toward Jews in general and anti-Semitism in particular. Nevertheless, the survey was not based on a representative sample of the population. Among other responses from the 3,019 people questioned, 51 percent declared "ne pas aimer les juifs," while 12 percent declared "aimer les juifs"—this in the context of a period when it took moral courage to make that statement. Here I would like to express my thanks to Mark Knobel for reviewing this chapter.

12. Hannah Arendt, *Eichmann in Jerusalem* (New York, 1977).

13. Lucien Lazare, *La Résistance juive en France* (Paris, 1987). This view is not shared by other writers such as Richard E. Cohen, *The Burden of Conscience: French-Jewish Leadership during the Holocaust* (Bloomington, IN, 1987).

14. Interview with Serge Klarsfeld in *Combat pour la Diaspora* (1988) no. 23–24, p. 89.

15. Jacques Adler, *Face à la persécution: Les organisations juives à Paris de 1940 à 1944* (Paris, 1988) 217.

16. Randolph L. Braham, "Les conseils juifs, un aperçu," *L'Allemagne nazie* 436.

17. See Georges Wellers, "Sur la résistance collective et la 'coopération' des victimes avec les bourreaux dans les camps d'extermination des juifs," *Le Monde juif*, October 1966, no. 10, pp. 1–9.

18. The issues debated revolve mainly around the question of the nature of the Jewish resistance and whether they participated in the resistance *as Jews*. See the article by Claude Lévy, "La résistance juive en France: de l'enjeu de mémoire à l'histoire critique," *Vingtième Siècle* 22, (April-June 1989) 117–128. Also "La résistance juive en France: où en est son histoire?," roundtable discussion in *Le Monde juif* (April-June 1985) no. 118, pp. 37–85.

19. See the writings of Sabine Zeitoun, "L'Oeuvre de secours aux enfants (OSE): Du légalisme à la résistance (1940-1944)," *Le Monde juif* 46 (April-June 1987), 58-65.

20. Walter Laqueur, *The Terrible Secret: An Investigation into the Suppression of Information About Hitler's 'Final Solution'* (London, 1980).

21. Louis de Jong quoted by Walter Laqueur, *Terrible Secret* 155-156. The Dutch historian has published a seminal work that is untranslated in English or French: Louis de Jong, *Het Koninkrijk der Nederlanden in de Tweede Wereldoorlog* (Gravenhage, 1976).

22. Marrus and Paxton, "Nazis et juifs," 307.

23. Meier Michaelis, *Mussolini and the Jews: German-Italian Relations and the Jewish Question in Italy* (Oxford, 1978).

24. Quoted in Jacques Sabille, "Comment les juifs danois furent sauvés," *Lueurs dans la tourmente* (Paris, 1956) 51.

25. Braham, "Les conseils" 423.

26. Bela Vago, "Les réactions à la politique antijuive des nazis en Europe centre-orientale et dans les Balkans," *L'Allemagne nazie* 351.

27. On the genocide of Hungarian Jews, one should start with Randolph L. Braham, *The Politics of Genocide: The Holocaust in Hungary* I-II (New York, 1981).

28. One must underscore the importance of public protest to achieve that result. Private protest messages from key local figures did not have an effect. Only public protests were able eventually to halt it.

29. See in particular Étienne Fouilloux, "Les chrétiens pendant la Seconde Guerre mondiale," *Études sur La France de 1939 à nos jours* (Paris, 1985) 156-161.

30. Research undertaken as part of a Harvard University Ph.D. dissertation.

31. Quoted in Nathan Stoltzfus (unpublished work).

32. Quoted in Hilberg, *Destruction* 481.

33. Frederick B. Chary, *The Bulgarian Jews and the Final Solution (1940-1944)* (Pittsburgh, 1972) 90.

34. Donna Crispin, "Protest Demonstration of the Jews of Sofia on May 24, 1943," *Annual of the Social, Cultural and Educational Association of the Jews in the People's Republic,* IV (Sofia, 1969) 69-103.

35. Quoted in Hilberg, *Destruction* 483.

36. Chary, *Bulgarian Jews* 191, 193-199.

37. Georges Wellers, *L'Étoile jaune à l'heure de Vichy* (Paris, 1973).

38. *Le Monde juif,* October 29, 1979.

39. Wladimir Rabi, "Les interventions de la hiérarchie en faveur des juifs: Une constatation et une question," *Églises et chrétiens dans la Deuxième Guerre mondiale: La région Rhône-Alpes* (Lyons, 1978) 198.

40. Michael R. Marrus and Robert O. Paxton, *Vichy et les juifs* (Paris, 1981).

41. Serge Klarsfeld, *Vichy-Auschwitz: Le rôle de Vichy dans la solution finale de la question juive, 1942* (Paris, 1983) 9.

42. Annie Kriegel, "De la résistance juive," *Pardès* (February 1985) 202.

43. Philipp Hallie, *Le Sang des innocents* (Paris, 1980), and Philippe Boegner, *Ici, on a aimé les juifs* (Paris, 1981), a novel.

44. See Émile C. Fabre, *Les Clandestins de Dieu* (Paris, 1968).

45. Quoted in Fein, *Accounting* 74.

46. In addition to the works of Louis de Jong, see B. A. Sijes, *De Februari-staking, 25-26 Februari 1941* (The Hague, 1954).

47. Werner Warmbrunn, *The Dutch under German Occupation*, (Stanford, CA, 1963) 161.

48. Maxime Steinberg, *L'Étoile et le Fusil*, 4 vol. (Brussels, 1983-1986).

49. See *Le Combat de Hertz Jospa* (n.p., 1970).

50. Unfortunately, the Germans were able to save a second copy.

51. Figures provided by Maxime Steinberg: they appear also in Philippe de Briey, *Le Comité de défense des juifs* (Brussels, 1981).

52. Arendt, *Eichmann.*

53. After the war, Werner Best claimed in his defense that he had intentionally given Duckwitz the date of the arrests to spread the information and that he had been a double agent throughout the matter. There is no written evidence to this effect, however.

54. Leni Yahil, *The Rescue of Danish Jewry: Test of a Democracy* (Philadelphia, 1969). The author estimates that at least 40 organizations were directly involved in the rescue.

55. Due to the actions of the Danish authorities, who delegated an official for the prisoners, only 111, or 1.4 percent of the community, did not return.

56. Aage Bertelsen, *October 1943* (New York, 1954).

57. Yahil, *Rescue*, 266.

Chapter 9

Which Role for Which Results?

The progressive involvement of European civilians in the struggle of World War II is one of the most original aspects of that war. Individuals who had often been outside of the prewar leadership elite initiated the creation of underground structures to challenge the occupying forces. The emergence of these voluntary civilian groups did not conform to the rules governing the conventional warfare waged by regular armies. The Allies observed the armed movements of the European resistance with suspicion and thought them politically unreliable. Little by little, governments in exile took partial control over them. But the question of the role of civilians in the war remained a source of misunderstanding, discord, and divergent analyses. In France, for example, evidence of this confusion appeared in the debates between those who favored ''immediate action'' and the ''waitists.''

Because the Allies did not want to deliver enough weapons to them, the resisting groups did not have adequate access to weapons and were thus limited militarily. Yugoslavia was the exception, since Tito received heavy equipment from Great Britain, allowing it to compete with the German forces. In countries that had made haphazard war preparations, resistance forces endured bitter defeats when they waged battles on their own. The Warsaw Ghetto uprising was the most tragic example.

This does not mean that the resistance did not make a valuable contribution to the war goals. As a support power encouraging the progression of the heavy allied war machine, the work of the internal resistance was very important both in gathering intelligence and organizing sabotage. It is surprising that Basil Liddell Hart, in his voluminous *History of the Second World War*, hardly mentioned the contribution made by the European resistance.[1] Jorgen Haestrup had reason to regret this oversight in his equally voluminous *History of European Resistance Movements*.[2] In a war that had become total, in the sense that all available economic and human resources were put to the service of the final victory, the internal resistance forces were a resource on the very soil where the enemy had to be beaten.

SURVIVING IN AN INDEPENDENT SOCIETY

Not all internal resistance activities were oriented toward the final military victory, which, in any case, remained uncertain. It would be a profound error to "militarize" the resistance phenomenon. The resistance movement developed precisely because the regular armies of the invaded states had been beaten. Civilian populations, left to their own devices at that point, responded in different ways: collaboration, accommodation, or resistance. As far as civilian resistance is concerned, it is significant that most of the examples studied here took place before March 1943, that is, in a period still favorable to Germany.[3] Civilian resistance took place in the here and now. It aimed at saving what could be saved, without necessarily waiting for the military conflict to be reversed.

In this sense, the logic of civilian resistance was fundamentally different from the logic of war. It was the resistance of survival. It aimed not so much to defeat the occupier—it hardly had the means to do that—as to exist alongside it, in spite of it, while waiting for eventual liberation. This applied to the Jewish question as well as to all sorts of other economic, civic, cultural, and political situations in which the civilian resistance predominated. The harsh conditions of life that the French miners in the departments of Nord/Pas-de-Calais endured in this poorly supplied war zone made survival itself precarious during their major strike in May-June 1941. The Poles worked to save their culture and the intellectual leaders whom the Nazis were trying to annihilate. Dutch physicians worked to make the field of medicine survive free from the occupier's control, refusing an official medical order. All of them fought to survive by affirming their dignity, their identity, even if only through symbolic nationalist demonstrations expressing the legitimacy of certain undeniable values. Civilian resistance is above all an *affirmation of legitimacy*, which the language of symbols expresses perfectly and which the force of arms is powerless to destroy.

Symbolic action is the essential expression of the spirit's non-abdication to totalitarianism. Symbols are the prime "weapon" of civilian resistance. Although also used in armed struggle, they play a fundamental role in civilian resistance. Symbols are the language through which an occupied society still expresses its independence of spirit. Whether in the form of a flower, a sign, or colors, symbols were a permanent challenge to the Nazi order. Their apparently laughable character robbed the overarmed colossus of the means to destroy them. Symbols are the rallying points for all those who refuse to bow their heads. Symbols and the demonstrations that accompany them show a society's determination to affirm its values and express its collective identity against the reigning order.

The specificity of civilian resistance in the context of the German occupation probably derived from this. It had other functions, especially its participation in liberation struggles. But as an autonomous force, its main role was to preserve the physical integrity (in terms of people saved from repression) and the social identity of occupied societies (in terms of ethical and political values). The preferred fields for civilian resistance were education and culture, in the affirmation of ethical and political values that were incompatible with the new regime and were advocated by particular professional categories or the whole society. In this regard, civilian resistance would appear to be a unique means of resistance. It is hard to see how the Poles could have managed to preserve their culture and save their intelligentsia without its mass underground education movement.

If civilian resistance crystallized into specific mass movements, it expressed more globally the way in which an occupied society can defend its way of life, values, and institutions on its own. From this perspective, it is fitting to propose a framework for a broader analysis. Indeed, it is as if the shock of occupation and the forming of a *de facto* dictatorial or totalitarian regime eventually provoke the constitution of two societies interwoven with each other: on the one hand, an official legal, and formal society; on the other, an independent, legitimate, and underground society. Daily life thus becomes marked by the existence of ditches and bridges that separate or connect these two societies. The more the occupying regime can manage to legitimize its occupation, the more official society becomes the real one. The more the occupier fails to get its power recognized, the more a "parallel" society incarnating popular legitimacy can develop in the interstices of official society.

The existence of this rebellious society—through the diversity of its social practices, and the variety of behaviors of the individuals who form it—becomes the major obstacle to the occupier's politics. As long as it exists, it is permanent proof of the occupier's inability to take complete control of civil society. Under the German occupation, a whole range of behaviors of increasing riskiness defined the contours of this independent civil society. These behaviors included listening to the BBC, reading the underground press, slowing down production, not obeying orders from the occupiers or their collaborators, refusing the STO, protecting people on the run, participating occasionally or continually in a structured resistance movement, and so on. In the broadest sense of the word, civilian resistance was the whole fabric, power, and life of the independent civil society that paralleled the official society. In this sense, the mass movements studied here were only concentrated and limited forms of this resistance by civil society on a daily basis.

The development of this autonomous society made people take on new attitudes. Indeed, the surrounding social control forced them to base their conduct and language on the expectations of the occupier or its collaborators. This social pressure, which was exerted on everyone by surveillance and denunciation, gave anyone wanting to go against it no alternative but to try to create space inside himself for autonomy and freedom. In the most successful totalitarian regimes, individuals could maintain their psychological integrity by learning this dissociation between the apparent conformity of submission outside and the preservation of their freedom of spirit inside.[4] Their thoughts did not always match their actions, nor did their words always match their beliefs. They had to learn to be vigilant while appearing docile. Just as the dominant order had to act "as if" deviant behavior did not exist, rebels in spirit learned to act "as if" they were submitting—to the extent that in a totalitarian-style society, everyone can see double. Reality is rarely real. What is visible is dissimulated, and whoever is content with seeing what he sees, sees nothing. To understand, people had to decode language and facts. The duplicity of life in this kind of society is coupled with deception and hypocrisy, corruption and lies. Resisting thus means protecting oneself somewhere against this destructive and psychotic universe, preserving a space of internal unity in which one does one's best to remain faithful to oneself.

Not all political regimes resulting from foreign occupation are necessarily as severe with their occupied populations. But whatever the intensity of the coercion, it is not a simple matter to participate concretely in a resistance movement against an occupying power. In administration, for example, mid-level government employees must demonstrate a spirit of initiative and a firmness of character not usually asked of them under normal circumstances. Indeed, administrative resistance means refusing to obey any orders not issued by the country's legitimate authorities. Based on the experience in the Netherlands, Ehring has shown that such behavior appeared difficult for many civil servants.[5] Accustomed to the spirit of discipline, they were asked to demonstrate an entirely different conception of their work. Depending on the importance of their orders, they had to decide either to refuse to apply them, whether openly or secretly, or to postpone carrying them out as long as possible, or even to agree to apply them partially. Left to their own devices, they thus had to interpret the nature of the orders received whereas, in normal times, they could follow orders without making judgments. Such actions implied obvious risks for those who performed them and demanded determination, courage, and a strong commitment to one's country that not everyone has.

One of the most disturbing effects of resistance to an occupying power is the radical modification of a population's relationship to the *law*. People who are brought up to respect rules are not particularly disposed to commit acts of disobedience, even for a just cause. The very principle of resistance to a usurping power leads to the social practice of illegality. Individuals must therefore overcome the taboo of illegality that may hinder the development of a resistance movement. Added to this is the fact that the law is generally perceived as a fundamental element of security. The law usually protects citizens; many people therefore thought that they would not be disturbed if they stuck to doing their own duties and to respecting the laws during the Nazi occupation. As many authors have noted, especially with respect to the Jews, this attitude reflected a total lack of insight into the true nature of the Nazi regime. But the psychological difficulty of the act of disobedience must also be taken into account. Some could experience the act as very disconcerting, even when it was in their own interest to take the plunge, even when it might mean their very survival. This reveals the intensity of the individual's internal conflict as a result of an act of disobedience.

For a person on the run, security could undeniably be found in dissimulation. Two types of dissimulation can be distinguished. The first consisted of seeking refuge in comparatively inaccessible places (mountains, forests) or going to ground in secret hiding places in cities or the countryside. This physical dissimulation forced people not to move and to depend solely on external complicity. The other process consisted of changing one's identity, by getting "false-real" papers (identification and food cards). This second kind of legal dissimulation had the advantage of flexibility but created other difficulties since not everyone was necessarily able to get false papers of official document quality.

One of the major characteristics of independent society is that it functions mostly through underground practices. Living underground is not easy. "Legal" underground resisters, who worked in the resistance movement while keeping a "cover" of normal professional activity, have traditionally been distinguished from "total" underground resisters, who cut off all connections with "normal life." This double life could be bearable for legal resisters, in that they kept up their social and family connections, even though they had to remain constantly vigilant so as not to commit a tiny fatal error. But living completely outside the social system—excluded, so to speak—could seriously disturb the equilibrium of total resisters. This totally clandestine life was practiced by a minority of resisters and is hard to imagine being practiced by the masses because of the severity of its constraints.[6] In terms of technique, moreover, learning underground ways demanded time, particularly in a society where such a practice was unfamiliar before the war, as was the case in most of the occupied countries. Inexperienced resisters therefore committed careless acts. Taking part in clandestine activity assumes respect for a minimum number of rules of prudence; the novice in a resistance movement has no way of knowing these. He must think of his own security and even more of the security of others. This means always anticipating the consequences of one's most insignificant acts. Underground, one must learn to feel responsible for others. The oath that each Polish student had to take before studying at the University of the Western Territories (the former University of Poznań) reveals the urgency of personal involvement. It read:

I swear: (1) to observe the most absolute silence about the place, the people, the university titles, and the content of the courses and practical exercises, not only with respect to foreigners or strangers but also friends who might not be informed. I swear likewise to use the greatest caution during conversations, particularly in public places;
(2) to respect the instructions given by university authorities about the work and life of the university. . . . I swear it before God.[7]

This necessity for clandestine behavior appeared in all the countries of occupied Europe. It was the indispensable condition for developing a society independent of the regime. As a result, inventive communications organizations and networks were formed that were adapted to the demands of the struggle against an extremely dangerous adversary. This organizational infrastructure constituted the technical base on which actions could be developed. Resisters cannot fight without technology and a communication organization adapted to this kind of struggle.

In Norway, after the arrest of some opponents of the regime in June 1941, the resistance structures went completely underground. Its initiators set up a particularly effective communications network throughout the country (using messages written in invisible ink) that the occupier never succeeded in dismantling. Civilian resistance was led by a coordination committee (Koordinasjonskomiteen or KK); this was made up of about 30 members who represented not political parties but all kinds of professional and interest groups. This role of associations in leading the resistance was considerable: very large and well developed in Norway, they acted as relay stations, disseminating the information provided by the coordinating committee of the civilian resistance.

In France, the communists of the departments of Nord and Pas-de-Calais, founded a school based on the organizational formula of the "POM triangle." This consisted of a hierarchical fitting together of completely separate groups formed around three people, each being in charge of one specific sector: "Politics" (P), "Organization" (O), and "Masses" (M). This formula was the best compromise between speed of communications (a condition for effectiveness) and the separation of the cells (a condition for security) that the communist leaders evolved.

All kinds of organizational formulas, often ingenious ones, were created, varying by countries and regions. All had one thing in common: their authoritarian structure. The organizational operating habits common in a democracy, especially procedures of direct consultation, cannot be the same under a dictatorship. Security needs, the necessity of anonymity, the impossibility of large debates to bring many people together—in short, all the rules of underground life—made resisters give up the elementary principles of democracy for the benefits of authoritarianism. Claude Bourdet has described his own experiences as a French resister with respect to this issue: "It was impossible to lead an underground movement democratically."[8] Like many others, Dutch doctors had this difficult experience, even though, in the beginning, the founders of the resistance organization, *Medisch Contact* (MC), explicitly wanted their professional group to continue operating just as it had before the war—democratically. That plan turned out to be unrealistic. In particular, they had to give up their principle of sovereign meetings of tens or even hundreds of physicians, after one such meeting led to the arrest of several leaders of the organization. This discontinuation had important consequences for the group's internal functioning. The leaders of the *Centrum*, the movement's headquarters, could no longer consult with the grass-roots members and could contact them only through delegates or "couriers." They therefore adopted increasingly authoritarian methods, giving instructions that grass-roots members were not always able to understand but nonetheless had to carry out blindly.

This need for the underground movement to operate in an authoritarian way meant that institutions that had already been very hierarchical before the war found it easier to resist than did the more democratic organizations, at least so long as their leaders wanted to mobilize against the regime. Thus, Leonore Siegele

Wenschkewitz thought that the hierarchical structure of the German Catholic Church allowed it to resist Nazi pressures better than his country's Protestant churches whose decentralization tended to separate them into cells.[9] In Belgium, where the Catholic Church was influenced by the country's political divisions due of the strong collaborationist current, Jean Chelini concluded that: "only the solidarity of the Belgian Catholic hierarchical and associative fabric limited the damage."[10]

Finally, one indispensable element of an independent society and its resistance activities must not be overlooked: its financial means. In Poland, underground teachers were paid mostly by their government in exile in London. Denmark's Jews could not have been saved without a broad movement of generosity, since many lacked the means to pay for the boat to Sweden; the resistance therefore had to collect millions of Danish crowns to help them all leave the country. In Belgium, the Jewish Defense Committee (JDC) received considerable funds through Switzerland from an American Jewish organization that defrayed the expenses of all of those living underground, especially children, whom it protected. In Norway, teachers did not shrink from being arrested, because they knew that if they did, a solidarity fund, supplied by their own dues and anonymous gifts, would provide for the needs of their families. In Holland, the MC set up a sort of insurance fund provided by the doctors themselves. The organization took care of every practitioner whose professional activity decreased as a result of his participation in the resistance. If a doctor lost his life because of his involvement in the resistance, the organization provided for the education of his children. Financial solidarity with people living underground also took on an impressive dimension in Holland, the most densely populated country in Europe, along with Belgium and one that offered hardly any natural refuge. A National Fund for Mutual Aid was set up to bring assistance to all kinds of people: families of soldiers who had gone to London, prisoners, resisters, Jews, and so on. Recognized later by the government in exile, the administration of this illegal fund resembled a large business employing thousands of people. Its funds did not come from charitable gifts, but from loans contracted from wealthy citizens, with the government in exile answering for reimbursement after the war.[11] In September 1944, the government in exile ran the major strike of the Dutch railroad workers that was to bring support for the airborne operations in Arnhem. The railroad workers were thus paid to go on strike.

This financial support is, of course, a basic condition for the development of resistance activities. It is especially vital in confronting one of the most dangerous tactics used by a regime to strangle an opposition movement: economic repression. This is why civilian resistance must have support, not only from the independent society but also from within the official society (among the government employees, for example), and not only inside the country but also from abroad. An isolated resistance is a dying resistance.

Thus, the success of the civilian resistance in Europe undoubtedly depended on the resources that the resistance could use both inside and outside the occupied society.[12] By resources we mean not only the men and women ready to become involved in collective action but also all kinds of supports that they might or might not use: organizational infrastructures, means of communication and transport, financial means, international aids, and so forth. In the context of the Nazi occupation, it is clear that the technical, financial, and organizational logistics of the civilian resistance were severely limited. This deficiency of means was one of the main causes of its weakness in the face of the much more considerable means of the occupier and its collaborators.

DIRECT, INDIRECT, AND DISSUASIVE EFFECTIVENESS

Civilian resistance started from scratch. It had to invent everything. It needed lots of time to grow and assure its organizational bases. Even in countries where the political conditions encouraged its growth (by not legitimizing the occupier's regime), it took considerable time to organize a structure of resistance. In Norway, the civilian organization of the resistance movement was barely ready before the end of 1941 or the beginning of 1942, more than a year and a half after the occupier's arrival. In Poland, where occupation conditions were much more severe, the underground education structures were really set up only after the summer of 1942, three years after the Germans arrived.

The growth of the civilian resistance movement followed the development of the resistance in general. Throughout this comparative study, we have progressively pointed out the key factors that seem to be correlated with the development of civilian resistance (apart from the variables linked to the evolution of the war). Not all of them belong strictly to this particular form of struggle.

Some result from particular characteristics of the occupied societies. One can thus say that the resistance was more developed in:

1. Countries with a democratic tradition;
2. Zones of high urban or industrial concentration; and
3. Groups with high social cohesion

Other factors were linked to the technical and logistical aspects of the resistance. They depended on:

1. An organization that was structured clandestinely or underground;
2. An equally clandestine communication system;
3. Various resources (food, money, etc.); and
4. International support

Still other factors had to do with the dynamic or the conduct of the action itself:

1. Maintaining or forming a legitimate authority was indispensable for motivating the fight.

2. Civilian resistance needed to develop a language of its own; symbols played a crucial role here in that they were simultaneously a means for expression, recognition, and consolidation, but difficult for repression to destroy.

3. "Triggering" circumstances were necessary, however, to precipitate the choice to take action. The unpopularity of some of the occupier's decisions were the main factor encouraging collective mobilization against it.

4. Not resorting to armed struggle was in itself a protective factor for civilian resistance. When civilian resistance was connected to an armed struggle, it became more likely to be subjected to ferocious repression and thus to be wiped out.

5. The support of a third party (churches, for example) that mattered to the occupier gave more credibility to a civilian resistance movement and, in this sense, strengthened its audience and impact.

6. The support of public opinion in general toward a civilian resistance movement was also a protective factor.

7. Finally, the emergence of potential contradictions and splits within the adversary's ranks, whether caused by the civilian resistance or not, benefited the resistance.

This list of factors is not exhaustive and should be improved. Still, it can probably be used as a guideline for the analysis of other cases of civilian resistance outside the context of the Second World War. For example, this guideline may be useful in understanding contemporary conflicts stemming from dictatorial or totalitarian regimes. Its relevance can be improved by applying it to other historical events and testing its explanatory power.

But it is one thing to identify the factors contributing to the development of civilian resistance and another to evaluate the effectiveness of its procedures. Many authors seem to have a rather confused idea of a "successful" action organized by a resistance movement. An action can be considered a success because it brought together tens of thousands of people, for example. In itself, such an event can indicate the growing mobilization of opinion. But this does not necessarily mean that the action was effective. Evaluating the effectiveness of a form of resistance assumes above all a comparison of the results of a resistance procedure with the objectives pursued by the adversary. It is important to know if these objectives were hindered, limited, or prevented by the forms of resistance that the adversary had to confront. In the situation of a country occupied by a foreign power, it is necessary at least to make distinctions between the occupier's economic objectives (to exploit the conquered country's wealth), political objectives (to install a regime that is favorable to it, for example), and ideological objectives (to win the population's approval for the occupier's values). In this perspective, this research reveals that even if civilian resistance had limited effectiveness, that effectiveness was still not negligible. From this point of view, several forms of effectiveness can thus be distinguished: direct, indirect, and dissuasive.

Civilian resistance had direct effectiveness in the sense that some of its procedures themselves created tangible obstacles to the realizing of the adversary's plans. For example, noncooperation procedures could keep the occupier from exploiting the fruits of its conquest or from realizing its objectives. A mass civilian disobedience movement, on its own, created a power struggle that could thwart the adversary's plans. The movement rejecting the STO was of that sort. In France, Holland, and Belgium, the *sum* of individual refusals finally deprived the Germans of an important part of the manpower requested, especially in the last year of the occupation. The effects of this procedure of direct constraint are depicted in this German report of January 1944, describing the state of mind of the Nord–Pas-de-Calais region with respect to STO:

Obligatory recruitment is not understood at all, and no one is willing to collaborate. We can count on the French only to the extent that the activity asked from them does not go against the supposed interests of their country and does not ask a particular or personal sacrifice that they are not at all prepared to make for the benefit of the occupying power. The failure to transport forced manpower to Germany is the most specific example of this.[13]

Work slowdowns or technical sabotage also had direct effects by decreasing or even stopping production. It is difficult to measure the results of these anonymous procedures precisely, but statistics sometimes give an approximate idea. In Belgium, coal production was said to have fallen by 36 percent in the winter of 1941-1942, attributed mainly to the "bad attitude" that prevailed in the mine pits.[14] Étienne Dejonghe has observed the same phenomenon in the mines of Nord-Pas de Calais. In a detailed study of the Bergamo region of Italy, Stefano Piziali has shown that the decreased production in a factory that was forging steel for the Germans was due to worker-initiated industrial sabotage, and the damage was worsened by Allied bombings.[15]

Diverting orders, funds, or food provisions also damaged German interests. Administrative personnel linked to the resistance were largely responsible for this. Here we must mention the heroic action carried out in France by work inspector Jean Ismeolari. He arranged for official "Board of Appeals" documents that won STO labor conscripts almost automatic exemptions. Jacques Evrard has estimated that these "boards" accounted for about 100,000 irregular exemptions and assignments, which cost Germany hundreds of millions of work hours.[16]

These tactics of noncooperation did not stop Berlin from reaching its main economic goals, especially in Western Europe, whose wealth was essential to the German war machine. But here we must take into consideration the weight of the economic collaboration of Western Europe's business community; by and large, it did not hesitate to do business with the Reich. This industrial collaboration, whether voluntary or compulsory, helped Berlin to reach its goals. Noncooperation techniques (work slowdowns, technical sabotage, diversion of orders, etc.) came into their own in the context of this general compromise with Nazi Germany. Becoming increasingly widespread, noncooperation techniques helped reduce the benefits that the occupier could derive from its conquered territories.

Civilian resistance was also directly effective in protecting Jews, resisters, and STO deserters who were being chased by the German police. This no doubt helped hundreds of thousands of people to escape from the fate awaiting them. Judging from the final solution's overall figures, one could maintain that no civilian resistance procedures—from the lack of cooperation by the Jews themselves to expressions of solidarity on their behalf—were effective with respect to the genocide of the Jews. Still, the event has to be considered in its historical context. The Jewish genocide resulted from the forces of increasing anti-Semitism that were deeply rooted prior to the war. It was a kind of prolonged paroxysm that became ever more hideous as the international environment remained indifferent to the persecution of the Jews. By the time that the genocide exploded in the context of the war, it had become practically impossible to stop it. The only thing possible was to limit the damage. It is from this perspective that we have to judge the results of civilian resistance.

The fact has been established. Although informed very early of the fate reserved for the European Jews, the United States, England, and the Soviet Union did nothing to limit their extermination, not even bomb the railway tracks leading to the extermination camps, as they had been openly asked to do.[17] This indifference on the part of the military leaders may seem shocking or, at the very least, confusing. It does, however, have a certain coherence from a military point of view. The Allies were involved in a total war that they were not sure of winning. Their main goal was to gather as many forces as possible to destroy the German and Japanese war machine. In the context of total war, they did not consider Auschwitz a strategic goal.[18] That is why the resistance was more effective than doing nothing in protecting populations in general and Jews in particular. It is difficult, of course, to evaluate the number of people saved, and the effectiveness of this action cannot be judged on the basis of the case of Denmark alone.

One can argue that it was only the German military defeat that put an end to the genocide of the Jews. In Western Europe, trains were still leaving for Auschwitz in August, September, and even October 1944—more than three months after the Allies landed in Normandy.[19] But during the wait for Germany's capitulation to put an end to the extermination camps, the only effective action was keeping as many Jews as possible from boarding the trains. The prospect of unconditional military victory over Germany would have meant an end to the Jewish Calvary—but in a completely uncertain future—whereas civilian resistance with its skimpy resources could at least bring relative but immediate security.

Civilian resistance also had an indirect effectiveness when its procedures provoked psychological or political reactions that subsequently proved unfavorable to the occupier. Forms of action that had no apparent immediate impact on the occupier's objectives could thus have mid- or long-term consequences that proved detrimental to it. A typical example was the demonstration in France on January 6, 1943, at the Montluçon train station, protesting the workers' departure for Germany. Hundreds of people invaded the station, preventing the train from leaving, and most of the labor conscripts took advantage of the commotion to flee in spite of the police presence.[20] This action was an apparent failure, since all those who escaped from the train were caught. But how the escape took place, how the police were ridiculed, and how a determined crowd took power made this action an important event; stories about it in the underground and international press gave it even more importance. In other words, the Montluçon demonstration had a major impact on opinion, by showing that collective opposition to the STO was possible. This is the first form of the indirect effectiveness of civilian resistance reinforcing the occupied population's cohesiveness, which is necessary, according to historians, to reinforce the population's morale.

Strikes sometimes had similar effects despite their apparent failure. The strikes in Holland in 1941 and 1943 led to no immediate concession from the Germans. On the contrary, they led to a wave of repression. The results of these two decisive strike movements were positive, nonetheless. Thus, Haestrup has written: "Both strikes were pinpricks and nothing more than pinpricks, but their psychological and political effect reached a great deal further than their material importance."[21] The April-May strike of 1943 in which hundreds of thousands of people participated showed that, even after three years of foreign occupation, the Dutch people remained attached to their identity and could conquer their fears. The consequences included the development of the underground press and of an organized resistance movement. This event also awakened the rural population's political conscience and encouraged young people to refuse to go to work in Germany. In short, this apparently unsuccessful strike allowed the population to strengthen its unity against the occupier. B. A. Sijes's analysis has summarized its impact: "The April-May strike was the biggest event since the surrender. . . . The psychosis of fear was broken for a while, and we no longer felt like repressed subjects of a regime of terror but like courageous people pulled along by an invisible and unifying thread."[22] One should therefore not judge the importance of an action solely on the basis of its direct effectiveness (the number of hours lost to the occupier, the number of people saved from repression, etc.). An action like a symbolic demonstration may have zero direct effectiveness and still have a major indirect effect due to its psychological impact on opinion. An action can have a liberating effect on minds even though the population remains in an objective situation of domination. The physical domination of a people does not necessarily imply their political and moral submission. Civilian resistance is precisely the appropriate means of increasing the gap between domination, which is a state of fact, and submission, which is a state of mind. The less submissive a people feels, the more uncontrollable it becomes. When an occupied population learns how to be united and not afraid, the occupier in power loses its authority. So civilian resistance is first and foremost about *minds*; it comes before the combat and the clash of wills.

Civilian resistance was not the only factor responsible for the growth of political currents unfavorable to the occupier's cause. As has been said many times, the evolution of the war modified the population's state of mind radically. Successful guerrilla actions also strengthened the morale of occupied populations by showing that the enemy was not invincible. But "mental liberation" was probably the area in which civilian resistance was the most effective, especially when indirect effects on populations are contrasted with the occupier's political and ideological goals.

Civilian resistance provided a kind of "ideological rampart" against all the efforts of the occupier and the collaborationists to influence the conquered societies ideologically. From this point of view, the Nazi occupier in Western and Scandinavian Europe failed to make the still rebellious populations accept its values and "new order." By permitting mass participation, as opposed to armed struggle led by a minority, civilian resistance was the privileged expression of this collective refusal. In certain circumstances, as in the Norway teachers' affair of 1942, the ideological fight took on strong political significance. It attested to the fact that a militarily conquered society still remained largely uncontrollable politically. Civilian resistance was effective in the sense that it prevented the occupier from "normalizing" the country's political and social life.

A second type of indirect effectiveness was also possible for civilian resistance—the creation of divisions within the occupied forces. This took place several times with respect to the Jewish question. In Denmark, there were disagreements and a personal rivalry between the Commissar of the Reich and the commanding general of the Wehrmacht. There was also the spectacular initiative by a German embassy official in Copenhagen who revealed to the Danish resistance the date when the Jews would be arrested. In France and Bulgaria, the differences of opinion between Eichmann and Himmler's departments have been well documented. Similarly, the Terboven-Quisling rivalry in Norway turned to the advantage of the teachers. In Germany itself, public opinion protests against eliminating the mentally ill divided the Nazi General Staff. At the same time, there is no hard evidence that the dissensions in Denmark, for example, were caused explicitly by that country's particular forms of resistance. One can suggest at most that civilian resistance created a context that encouraged internal dissension among the occupiers.

Many authors have emphasized the internal contradictions within the Third Reich, the power conflicts both among the regime's highest officers and between the various branches of the state. The assassination attempts against the Führer show that Hitler's policies received far from unanimous approval, especially within the army. Not all Germans were Nazis, and that was a major contradiction that had the potential to be exploited. This was an excellent propaganda theme for the "psychological warfare" departments of the Allies. But how can its impact be evaluated?

The problem is that the context of total war did not encourage such contradictions to emerge. The logic of armed struggle seems very different from that of civilian resistance in this respect. While armed struggle unifies an adversary through a group reflex that relegates internal differences to the background, unarmed struggle tends to bring out divisions within the ranks of an adversary that does not feel physically threatened. Thus, civilian resistance can be doubly effective. On the one hand, it can undermine the occupier's regime politically, thereby leading to the regime's ultimate breakdown. On the other hand, activating such contradictions within the adversary's ranks can make occupation politics waver, which in turn can moderate repression. Given the context of the war and the struggle against guerrilla forces in many countries, however, the potential internal dissensions among the Germans rarely became explicit.

Civilian resistance could achieve a dissuasive effectiveness over the occupying power when the pressure from civil society was particularly strong. In this case, the political determination of the occupied society was able to force the occupying or collaborating power to give up a plan or, at least, to delay or limit its execution. Dissuasion was used when an occupied society, either through its institutions or its populations, led the occupier to think it inadvisable to "go too far" in exerting its pressure politics over civil society. A typical example, that has already been mentioned, was the Danish government's firmness in protecting the Jews, which persuaded Berlin to delay arresting the Danish Jews.

Social movements could also exert a moderating effect on occupation politics—after the fact. In the Netherlands, the strike from April to May 1943 seems to have had the effect of limiting the forced recruitment of those who had already been interned to go work in Germany: only a few thousand left, although Berlin had predicted tens of thousands. In Norway, Quisling's failure to control the teachers dissuaded the Commissar of the Reich from launching a similar operation aimed at union workers. Given the state of the society's mobilization, Terboven believed that this initiative would have troublesome consequences that would no doubt trigger a general strike. In France, the repetition of demonstrations on symbolic dates (May 1, July 14, and November 11) finally convinced the occupier that it would be better to grant May 1, 1944, as a day off rather than confront yet another day of protests and strikes.

Showing moderation may serve the interests of occupying forces that are trying to maintain relative "social peace" when civil society is in a position to show its strength. W. Bosseler and R. Steichen have reported the testimony of a German government official on duty in Luxemburg who was very impressed by the 1942 strike:

He had not foreseen such courage and such ferocious will to resist. He thought it possible that there might be still more revolts, and his personal interest and fear of dismissal made him try to avoid measures that were too general and too grand that could make the population of Luxemburg respond collectively.[23]

This testimony has the merit of reminding us that the occupied populations were not the only ones who feared sanctions. The occupation officials were judged by their superiors on their ability to administer the conquered territories. It was in their interest to have no trouble in their zones of authority. Occupied societies could sometimes exercise political dissuasion against occupation officials, to the extent that the officials would defend a relatively moderate line to their superiors to avoid taking measures that would be too unpopular. From this point of view, a stifled civilian resistance movement is not necessarily a failure. Its long-term consequences have to be measured in order to evaluate it accurately. Of course, ferocious repression can demoralize a population for a long time and thus break any dynamic of opposition within it. But conversely, a mass resistance movement can exert a strong influence over authorities, so that they themselves are then careful to limit their pressure over civil society in order to keep such troubles from recurring.

Finally, it would be appropriate to explore the limits of civilian resistance's effectiveness. In the context of the Nazi occupation, only a resistance of survival with limited objectives was possible. The question is whether civilian resistance can claim a more ambitious goal—namely, to liberate a country from a dictatorial or totalitarian power.

If civilian resistance had a limited impact, it is no doubt due to the occupied people's improvisations and their disparity of social behaviors. In this regard, the analogy with the functioning of a soccer or baseball team is illuminating. A particular player can be very effective individually within such a team, but if his teammates do not play well or commit errors that benefit the other team, his team will lose the game. It goes without saying that, to win a game, a team must be united and well-coordinated; it must evaluate its opponents' strengths and exploit their weaknesses.

None of the above characterizes the behavior of these societies toward the occupier. Those who played the noncooperation game could be very effective on their level. The problem was that others were simultaneously playing the collaboration game, taking very personal initiatives, or else waiting on the sidelines for the situation to evolve.

The basic weakness of the occupied societies resulted from this unconnected quality of their game, in terms of both institutions and the populations themselves. Among those who wanted to "do something," no one really knew what role to play or what rules to follow so that his behavior would match his neighbor's. In March 1941, one and a half years after the invasion of Poland, when Cyryl Ratajski, the head of the underground Polish state and deputy of the government, went to London, he explained that the people simply did not know how to behave toward the occupier. Members of all professions—whether doctors, artists, railway employees, city bureaucrats, and others—asked how far they should accommodate the occupier and what would be the best ways to resist at their level. They were all on their own.[24] The reason was simple: neither in Poland nor elsewhere had civilian resistance ever been thought out as such. Everything had to be made up from scratch. In the light of such experiences and given that, unfortunately, populations still risk experiencing occupation situations, can we elaborate a *civil defense strategy*?

NOTES

1. Basil Liddell Hart, *History of the Second World War* (London, 1970).
2. Jorgen Haestrup, *European Resistance Movements (1939-1945)* (Westport, CT, 1981), especially 494-499.
3. See the list of cases examined at the end of the book.
4. See in particular the remarkable analysis by Bruno Bettelheim of his own experiences in a German concentration camp, *Informed Heart* (New York, 1960).

5. Dr. A. H. Heering, "L'administration publique sous occupation étrangère," *Alternatives non violentes*, no. 52, p. 52.

6. Henri Noguères, *La Vie quotidienne des résistants sous l'occupation allemande en France (1940–1944)* (Paris, 1985).

7. Quoted in Werner Rings, *Vivre avec l'ennemi* (Paris, 1981) 217.

8. Claude Bourdet, *L'Aventure incertaine* (Paris, 1975) 134.

9. Leonore Siegele-Wenschkewitz, "Les Églises entre l'adaptation et la résistance sous le IIIe Reich," *Revue d'histoire de la Deuxième Guerre mondiale* 128 (October 1982).

10. Jean Chelini, *L'Église sous Pie XII: La Tourmente (1939–1945)* (Paris, 1982) 175.

11. Other cases of financial solidarity were likewise devised by responsible Catholics and Protestants.

12. The idea of "resources" is used here as it was developed by Charles Tilly in his theory of the mobilization of resources in a society undergoing social change: Charles Tilly, *From Mobilization to Revolution* (Reading, MA, 1978). The approach was also influenced by the work of Mancur Olson, *The Logic of Collective Action* (Cambridge, MA, 1965).

13. Quoted by Étienne Dejonghe and Daniel Laurent, *La Libération du Nord-Pas de Calais* (Paris, 1974) 30.

14. Haestrup, *European Resistance*.

15. Stefano Piziali, "Résistance non armée dans la region de Bergame, Italie (1943–1945)," *Les Cahiers de la Réconciliation* 4 (Summer 1986) 34. Production fell from 109,439 tons of steel in 1943 to 76,747 tons in 1944 and 15,882 in 1945.

16. Jacques Évrard, *La Déportation des travailleurs français dans le Troisième Reich* (Paris, 1971) 141.

17. For example, Léon Poliakov reported that, in 1944, the Jewish Agency in Jerusalem asked the British to bomb the Birkenau camp to slow the extermination of Hungarian Jews. London replied that, for "technical reasons," it would be impossible, although documents show that British planes were able to bomb an arms factory near the camp. See Léon Poliakov, *Le Procès de Jérusalem* (Paris, 1963) 252.

18. See the work of Walter Laqueur, *The Terrible Secret* (London, 1980) and David S. Wyman, *The Abandonment of the Jews: America and the Holocaust (1941–1945)* (New York, 1984).

19. The last train for Auschwitz left from France on August 17, from Belgium on July 31, from the Netherlands on September 9, and from northern Italy on October 24.

20. See the striking account of this in Charles Tillon, *Les FTP: Témoignage pour servir l'histoire de la résistance* (Paris, 1962) 212–213.

21. Haestrup, *European Resistance* 105.

22. B. A. Sijes, *De April-Mei Stakingen in Twente* (Bijlage, 1956) 102.

23. W. Bosseler and R. Steichen, *Le livre d'or de la résistance luxembourgeoise* (Esch-sur-Alzette, 1952) 508.

24. See Jan Tomasz Gross, *Polish Society under German Occupation* (Princeton, NJ, 1979) 135–137.

Conclusion

The New Field of Civilian-Based Defense Strategies

The idea that civilians can participate in their own defense by using unarmed methods is rather recent. We owe it to an English military man, Major Stephen King-Hall, who developed the idea in the late 1950s.[1] Several years later, also in England, the first international conference on this subject was held at Oxford University.[2] A number of works have continued to explore the concept in various countries of Western Europe during the 1970s, bringing out, little by little, a new approach to civilian defense, or, in other words, a civilian strategy of defense.[3] This research has been furthered by authors who seek to call attention to ways in which nonviolent action and methods contribute to resolving conflict. Breaking with concepts of pacifism and moralism, they have tried to show how and under what conditions this kind of struggle can produce a true balance of forces with an armed adversary. Having studied social conflicts in which strikes, boycotts, civil disobedience, and so on played an important role, they have been determined to ascertain the tactical and strategic principles of these forms of action and have proposed applying them within the framework of a national defense policy. The works of Gene Sharp and Jean-Marie Muller in this area deserve particular attention.[4]

The concept of "civilian defense" should not be confused with protective measures taken by populations against the direct effects of war (air-raid shelters, for example). These should more accurately by called "civilian protection," since their mission is precisely to protect civilian populations. The concept of "civilian defense," however, should be taken in its strongest sense: the active participation of civilians in defining, preparing, and implementing a defense policy in which they are fully involved as civilians. To avoid linguistic ambiguity in English with the concept of "civil defense," Sharp proposed the expression "civilian defense" in 1963 and later, to be even clearer, "civilian-based defense"—that is, literally "defense based on civilians."

The historical research undertaken here shows the importance of the study of civilian defense. In case of a serious crisis that may potentially lead to an occupation, it is essential for a nation's civilian institutions and population to know in advance how to behave in order to serve their country's basic interests and contribute to its survival and freedom. This, in our opinion, would be the main purpose of civilian defense in light of the historical events analyzed. When one considers the scope of the disaster provoked by the German invasion in 1940, one wonders if the whole thing might have turned out differently had the governments of the occupied countries seriously anticipated a strategy of this kind in case of a military failure.

In such circumstances, the goal of a civilian defense can evidently not be to block the progress of an advancing army. If the aggressor's sole goal is to conquer a territory that it considers strategic, it is hard to see how civilian defense could prevent it. Civilian defense is not a territorial defense but, to use the German expression, a *social* defense (*soziale Verteidigung*). Likewise, it is clear that such a strategy would not be effective against a war of extermination. Nonetheless, this strategy has the potential to work if the aggressor's goal is political domination, economic exploitation, or ideological influence over the targeted society. Civilian defense is then a response adapted to the nature of the aggression.

In this case, if the military defense does not resist the enemy thrust, then the civilian defense of the invaded society is certainly desirable. Its role would be first to keep the population from panicking, so as to help the authorities maintain control of the country's internal situation. It would then be to engage in political combat in order to keep the invader from taking control of civil society. This fight is based mainly on having civilian institutions and populations implement a strategy of noncollaboration on their own. Civilian defense can be defined as a policy of defense of civil society against military aggression; it aims to plan and prepare collective actions of noncooperation and confrontation with the adversary so that the latter will be unable to reach its goals and set up the political regime that it wishes to impose on the population. Because civilian defense occurs *after* the military battle, one can call it a "post-strategic weapon."[5]

With these limits established, civilian defense can be the keystone of a country's security for the protection of its basic interests. The system's entire credibility is obviously based on working out the strategy ahead of time. Much remains to be done in this area. In order for a government not to be surprised by different scenarios during potential crises, it is advisable for it to determine, first of all, its *political and strategic choices*: staying in place at all costs, fleeing abroad, mixed solutions, having certain key political personalities slip underground, and so forth. According to the possible configurations of an international crisis, different civilian defense plans must be worked out. Noncooperation measures should be defined by ministries (instructions to various government employees) and by key economic sectors (banking, industry, energy, technology, etc.) in order to protect the country's basic interests (by hiding documents, putting machines out of order, destroying information systems, etc.). An alternate communication system must also be designed ahead of time to permit the government to remain in contact with those responsible for civilian defense and the population in general. The importance of economic resources for civilian defense must also be emphasized, since it is essential that certain infrastructures continue to function, particularly in providing food for the people. In this respect, civilian defense is based on two principles: on the one hand, paralyzing the strategic sectors that are of most interest to an aggressor, but, on the other hand, maintaining vital sectors for the survival of the population (ensuring food supplies, in particular).

Research efforts in these different areas would be indispensable to make sure that such arrangements will work. It must be added, however, that preparing for this civilian defense strategy must not be limited to simply elaborating strategic options for a crisis situation accompanied by a list of appropriate technical measures. These arrangements make sense only if the populations have the will to fight in a situation where their society's very foundations are threatened by a foreign power. Although it is possible to prepare civilian defense measures on a voluntary basis, no decree can *force* civil society to mobilize against an aggressor. Defending oneself implies taking risks and possessing certain psychological and moral qualities that not everyone may have.

Our research seems to show that the determining factor for such a mobilization is the degree of a population's social cohesion. A society in which a large part of the population does not perceive the political institutions as legitimate is highly vulnerable to collaboration, as is a society in which social or ethnic groups are kept in a situation of exclusion. From this perspective, the search for consensus on political institutions, the struggle against inequalities, and efforts to develop solidarity among social and ethnic groups are not simply goals of internal politics. They are elements that objectively help to create a social and political consensus that allows societies to defend themselves. In other words, the necessary spirit of defense is linked directly to the degree to which the population is attached to the type of society in which it lives. Human experience attests to this. We defend well only what we hold dear. We are willing to take risks only for what matters to us. The more a society proposes procedures of integration and participation for everyone, the more it contributes to its own internal cohesion, which is a prime strategic factor against potential aggression. Having citizens take responsibility, develop their autonomy, and extend their common life are all propitious factors for civilian defense. This reveals just how strongly the political basis of civilian defense closely correlates with that of the democratic ideal.

Few authors envisage the civilian defense described here as an alternative to armed defense.[6] During the last few years, however, experts on the concept have reached a consensus that it is *complementary* to armed defense. Governments in Western Europe and Scandinavia have ordered studies on the subject.[7] Since 1986, Sweden has officially adopted the implementation of a component of "civilian resistance."[8] In spite of its critical character, Alex Schmid's report, written for the Dutch government, has also come out in favor of complementarity.[9] A study by a Dutch soldier, Lieutenant Colonel A. A. Klumper, had similar findings.[10]

But is this concept of civilian defense too closely tied to the history of the occupation? Although any defensive politics must take this hypothesis into account, the primary goal is to *avoid* occupation, not to resist it after the fact. It is therefore important to investigate the dissuasive capacity of preparations for this kind of civilian defense. The study of occupation situations suggests an interesting line of thought. Indeed, if the forms of the German occupation in Eastern and Western Europe were very different, this is due to both Nazi racial considerations and the different structures of the occupied societies. If the politics of repression were less barbaric in the West, it was because Western European societies were already highly industrialized, had complex bureaucracies, and were modeled on democratic rules, making them harder to control than the Central and Eastern European countries; the recent creation of these latter countries and their undeveloped industrial structures combined to make them more fragile. In this respect, democracy, technology, and urbanization go together, in that they make societies more complex and therefore harder for a foreign power to control. Collaboration by competent officials therefore provided considerable aid to an occupying power. What was beginning to characterize Western European societies in 1940 does so even more at the end of the twentieth century because of the prodigious progress of technology and computer science. From this point of view, it would be much more difficult to occupy Western European societies today than it was in the past.

If these structural factors are added to a strategic determination to prepare political, administrative, technical, economic, and other measures of noncooperation with a possible aggressor, one could reasonably believe that setting up such a system could serve as dissuasion. Of course, at the same time as they have become more complex, modern societies have probably become more centralized as well. This hyper-centralization of technological infrastructures or of administrative systems can be considered an important vulnerability factor of these societies; it offers the potential aggressor convenient strategic points at which to take control of important sectors of the economic and social life of a country. This vulnerability must not be over-estimated, however. Such systems are really highly fragile, in the sense that a defective element with an apparently secondary function can influence the whole of their operation. Recent events have shown that they can experience spectacular breakdowns. Therefore, a strategy of dissuasion would need to figure out methods of paralysis, not only at the top of the system but also on its periphery.

It may seem surprising to hear that preparing a civilian defense strategy helps to dissuade an aggressor. It is true that today we seem to recognize only the nuclear method of dissuasion or deterrence, whose principle is based on the threat of reprisals by weapons of mass destruction. This neglects the older and more general meaning of the term "dissuasion," which applies to all defensive approaches whose goals are to make a potential aggressor perceive that "the game is not worth the candle." In this sense, one can maintain that the specific structures of a society and, even more, the way that a country prepares itself to "welcome" an aggressor can help to discourage aggression ahead of time. We have thus proposed the concept of civilian dissuasion within the framework of a study written at the request of the French government. This study concludes that this would constitute an "added value" in the whole range of dissuasion in France's strategy.[11] Civilian dissuasion aims to increase the fear of a potential aggressor—in this case, the Soviet Union—of failing to carry out the goals of its aggression. The role of dissuasion is thus to convince the adversary to give up the plan of a possible occupation on its own, since it would otherwise find itself plunged into a sort of "social and political *maquis*" from which it would not be able to extricate itself. An aggressor must know that it risks confronting an inextricable situation with slim chances for substantial gains once noncooperation tactics are put into action.[12]

Civilian dissuasion should also help to thwart less extreme threats than military aggression. The occupation of a foreign country is always a dangerous and risky operation. It can sometimes be more advantageous to pressure a coveted society from a distance so that it will eventually fall like a ripe fruit into enemy hands. The methods of psychological warfare, the periodic exercise of diverse kinds of blackmail, and even terrorist-style actions generally accompany this kind of strategy. It is highly doubtful that military defense, whether conventional or nuclear, is really adapted to this type of insidious threat. Faced with the risk of the political destabilization of a society, and especially of its institutions, the counterstroke must be launched from the same field, namely the field of political firmness and social cohesion. As we have emphasized, the entire dynamic of civilian resistance is oriented toward preserving the collective identity of invaded societies. In this sense, the development of an awareness of the stakes of defense among civilian populations is part of the very process of preparing a civilian defense. This focusing of a group on its "existential core" is the best response to all efforts of destabilization. The more a society is aware of what it has to safeguard, the less likely it is to fall prey to different forms of subversion and blackmail. A strategy of civilian dissuasion implies more than preparing planned measures of noncooperation.

The evolution of the relationship between Nazi Germany and the other European powers from 1933 to 1940 poses a basic question to all defense politics, whether based on military or civilian means. When a political regime is so openly turned toward aggression, is it necessary to wait for the attack simply because we are confident that we can rely on an effective system of defense? Staying on the defensive, as France and England did, does not appear to have been the best of strategic positions. The more one waits, the greater the risk of finding oneself in a situation worse than the preceding one.

That is why, after the war, some people thought that they should have launched a preventive war against Germany, that intervention as early as 1936 might have prevented the occupation of the Rhineland and thus stopped the process of German rearmament. But other choices were possible. Given the way the Hitler regime evolved, France and England could have united to isolate Germany internationally instead of trying to deal with the Führer alone. This political line could have been accompanied by different measures aimed at censuring the Nazi regime rather than at giving it signs of recognition or acknowledgment. As early as the mid-1930s, Basil Liddell Hart advocated adopting economic sanctions against Germany. Likewise, before the Munich accords, this British historian and strategist pronounced himself in favor of a total embargo by the League of Nations against Germany in case Germany invaded Czechoslovakia.[13] It would still have been appropriate to support internal opposition to the German regime; although relatively strong in the beginning, it remained without real international support, which encouraged its elimination. Of course, there needed to also be vigorous denunciations of human rights violations, primarily against Jews, as well as committed international campaigns in solidarity with them. When we understand the importance that the Nazis accorded the demonstrations of opinion, we realize that if the international community had expressed a feeling of revulsion toward the treatment of the German Jews, the worst might have been avoided. But all this is only "history-fiction." Europe would have had to be a different Europe from that of the 1930s—divided and riddled with anti-Semitism itself.

Nonetheless, this discussion has the merit of emphasizing an important point: the need to complement a defense strategy with an *offensive* policy toward a potential aggressor. From this perspective, it might be advantageous to implement what we could call an "offensive civilian strategy," since it does not have the provocative character of a preventive war. Its goal is to divert the opposing regime from its plan of aggression by exerting different kinds of indirect pressure on it and even contributing to its internal evolution. One of the main objectives of such a strategy is to stir up and sustain movements of opinion that, within the very ranks of the potential aggressor, would be likely to oppose its bellicose plans. The weapon of information is essential here, since it makes possible direct links with the peoples of the target country. The power and diversity of radio, television, and tape and video recorders allow the media to touch populations who in the past have lived isolated among themselves under the exclusive influence of state propaganda. Another objective can be to work toward *isolating* the potential aggressor. Economic or financial sanctions toward this goal can be considered, even though working them out can be complex. Demonstrations of international public opinion can also apply pressure. In short, a whole gamut of pressure and constraint tactics exist between diplomatic protests and declarations of war. It is in our interest to explore their use in an offensive civilian strategy.

Since the beginning of time, countries have resorted to nonmilitary means to enhance their interests and spread their power. Such means have often been implemented during wartime to facilitate military operations and hasten their success (blockades, embargoes, boycotts, psychological warfare, etc.). Now that nuclear weapons have transformed war, we are observing a large deployment of unarmed means of pressure. Today more than ever, these means can even aim for goals that are independent from war goals. The globalization of commercial and industrial trade, monetary and banking systems, means of information and transportation, sporting events, and so on has created a complex network of relations between countries. Each country has become more dependent on all the others and has simultaneously acquired the means to influence them. This internationalization of economic, financial, cultural, and athletic relations creates a favorable atmosphere for the extension of civilian strategies of pressure and constraint without the danger of triggering war.

We should not overestimate the efficacy of such procedures when a tyrant is determined to go to war. But in most cases, they constitute at least an initial response that is more satisfying than the passivity of complicity. A civilian strategy of pressure and constraint can thus serve as the first step in a society's mobilization against a hostile power. This step prepares it for the next one—resorting to defense itself—should the external threat become a reality. But an offensive civilian strategy must not remain the strategy of a nation state. We must consider it a way for citizens to participate themselves.

Whether offensive or defensive, these strategies are all based on an international balance of forces, on identifying not just the military threat itself, but other forms of aggression that can be practiced economically, ideologically, culturally, socially, or technologically. "In all these sectors, a modern nation can present enough vulnerabilities to diminish its international position and damage its ability to react to outside aggressors. There is thus material for strategic analysis."[14] From this perspective, the basic principle of a defensive civilian strategy is to reduce the economic, political, social, and cultural vulnerabilities of a given society against a potential aggressor. The general goal of an offensive civilian strategy, by contrast, is to *increase* the vulnerabilities of the opposing society. In short, the former strategy aims at limiting the effects of aggression, even at dissuading an aggressor from carrying it out, whereas the latter tries to short circuit the war-generating process that can lead a society to plunge into open aggression. In this sense, both of these nonmilitary strategies can be called civilian strategies of security.

Some people now worry about the demobilization of citizens toward defense; they wonder how to rekindle a "defense spirit" that seems to be dying out in European public opinion. Some experts ask: "What use are the populations of nuclear countries?"[15] The civilian strategies of security briefly presented here open a new path that may lead to the concrete participation of civilians in the security of their countries. Indeed, they are likely to encourage this "defense spirit," whose absence is deplored by many soldiers. It is true that the will of a people is one of the keys to its defense, if not its most effective guarantee.

Civilian strategies are certainly not a panacea against many forms of aggression. They can, however, be an *option* in various circumstances, either accompanying and strengthening a military operation or taking its place. In this sense, recourse to civilian strategies enlarges a country's potential initiatives and political responses on the international scene. In a world where the balance of terror seems to paralyze all direct confrontations between the major powers possessing weapons of mass destruction, civilian security strategies actually cover a large and diffuse field. It is necessary to recognize, however, that no comprehensive research has been done on them. This book seeks to show the importance of such an effort.

NOTES

1. Stephen King-Hall, *Defence in the Nuclear Age* (London, 1958).

2. Adam Roberts, *The Strategy of Civilian Defence: Nonviolent Resistance to Aggression* (London, 1967). The work was reedited two years later in a paperback collection to augment a study of the events in Czechoslovakia in 1968: Adam Roberts, ed., *Civilian Resistance as a National Defence: Nonviolent Resistance against Aggression* (Harmondsworth, 1969).

3. See Anders Boserup and Andrew Mack, *War without Weapons* (London, 1974); Gustaaf Geeraerts, *Possibilities of Civilian Defence in Western Europe* (Amsterdam, 1977); and Theodor Ebert, *Soziale Verteidigung Historische Erfahrungen und Grundzuege der Strategie*, vol. 1; *Soziale Verteidigung, Formen und Bedingungen des Zivilen Widerstands*, vol. 2 (n.p., 1981).

4. Gene Sharp, *The Politics of Non-violent Action* (Boston 1973); Jean-Marie Muller, *Stratégie de l'action non violente* (Paris, 1973).

5. General Georges Buis, "Une arme post-stratégique," *Alternatives non violentes* 59 (April 1986) 18–20.

6. The two best examinations of civil defense that consider it as an alternative approach are Jean-Marie Muller, *Vous avez dit "pacifisme"? De la dissuasion nucléaire à la dissuasion civile non violente* (Paris, 1984) and Gene Sharp, *Making Europe Unconquerable* (Boston, 1985).

7. For an understanding of these studies, see "Défense civile: 15 ans de recherche" in *Fiches Documentaires pour une Autre Défense* 34 (1988).

8. Using our terminology, it would be better to call it "civil defense." The Swedish decision evolved from a long process of parliamentary debate in the 1970s. Nevertheless, little information was made public on the work of the commission charged with developing the "civilian resistance" component of Swedish defense.

9. Alex Schmid, *Social Defense and Soviet Military Power: An Inquiry into the Relevance of an Alternative Defense Concept* (Leiden, 1985).

10. Lieutenant-Colonel A. A. Klumper, *Sociale verdediging en Nederlands verzet (1940–1945)—Ideel concept getoetst aan historische werkelijkheid* (Tilburg, 1983).

11. Christian Mellon, Jean-Marie Muller, and Jacques Sémelin, *La Dissuasion civile* (Paris, 1985).

12. One can get a feeling for the various political, military, and religious reactions to the study in number 59 (already cited) of the review *Alternatives non violentes*. See, in particular, the views of Deputies Bernard Stasi and Christian Pierret, Generals Dominique Chavanat, Claude le Borgne, Étienne Copel, Admiral Olivier Sevaistre, Fathers Jacques Julien and Eugène Ernoult, Pastor Jacques Maury, and Jean Klein.

13. Liddell Hart left World War I with the conviction that the economic power of adversaries could have a decisive role in preventing war. He believed that "the economic army" could be used against Germany to weaken its military preparations and to isolate it politically. See Christopher Kruegler, "Liddell Hart and the Concept of Civilian-Based Defense," diss., Syracuse U., Syracuse, NY, 1984, 73–75.

14. Bertrand Warusfel and Patrick Follea, "Contribution à une réflexion sur les stratégies indirectes," *Stratégique* (April 1987) 40.

15. Dominique David, round table on "Les perspectives réalistes de transarmement dans le cadre de la France," *Les Stratégies civiles de défense* (Saint-Étienne, 1987) 241.

Appendix

Elements of Methodology

The breadth of the field of civilian resistance assumes recourse to *criteria of selection* for the subject to limit the research to a clearly defined number of historic cases. The *criterion of autonomy*, mentioned in chapter 2, offers an initial framework that is indispensable for understanding civilian resistance. Let us think, in particular, about repression by the occupier that is generated not only by the civilian resistance itself but by the fact that repression overlaps with military or paramilitary goals. Insofar as the dominant reality of resistance to Nazism resided in this permanent overlapping between armed and unarmed forms of opposition, the application of this criterion would reduce the field of study considerably. But it is a relative criterion, of course, since it is clear that the context of international events, the general progress of the war, and the operations of the armed resistance can have obvious effects on the triggering, the unfolding, and the conclusion of an autonomous resistance.

In the second place, the only cases of autonomous civilian resistance we have chosen to retain are those that had a *mass character*. It is not possible to take into account the multitude of isolated cases of resistance by small scattered groups. It is no doubt important to devote monographs to them, as has often been done. But my goal is different. I am interested in them only when the actions carried out by small groups became so numerous and so obvious that they then took on a true collective dimension and social significance. In this case, they indicate the state of mind of a people and of the mobilization of a population. Clearly, it is difficult to say where a "group" ends and a "mass" begins. We also have to treat this mass criterion with a certain flexibility. This means that our priority will be to look for actions involving thousands, indeed tens of thousands, of civilians.

These forms of mass civilian resistance may emerge at the base of unorganized groups or be planned by already structured organizations. That is why we distinguish

LIMITS OF THE FIELD OF INVESTIGATION

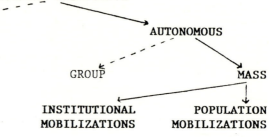

CIVILIAN RESISTANCE

COMBINED WITH OR
INCLUDED IN WAR GOALS
AUTONOMOUS

GROUP
MASS

INSTITUTIONAL
MOBILIZATIONS
POPULATION
MOBILIZATIONS

⟶ Field of Research
- -→ Outside the Field of Research

between population mobilizations and institutional mobilizations. The former term designates collective actions by groups whose bases are generally not organized. The latter includes actions by the institutions that structure society. In this second case, the concept of "institution" has two realities in this study: either state bodies (the political administration, police, courts, etc.) that theoretically embody national unity and determination, or representative organizations of the population (churches, unions, associations, etc.) that express a collective determination more or less limited to a category of citizens.

In summary, my field of investigation could be described as follows: the study of autonomous, mass, civilian resistance, whether mobilized by populations or by institutions, that can be illustrated by a tree-like structure (Figure 1). The expression "civilian resistance" is used in this study to designate, by agreement, the limited meaning described here.

This study is not a work of history in the methodological sense. It is not based solely on the use of new documents. It is more interested in *putting particular events into perspective*. It was influenced more by historical sociology or political science. Its goal is to present an overall study of the phenomenon of civilian resistance and to specify its fundamental problems and parameters by means of a comparative analysis of historical cases

Several hurdles, mostly related to knowledge of the facts and the possibility of comparing them, make this task difficult. The elaboration of a historical work on civilian resistance poses particular historiographic difficulties. All historians of the resistance encountered this problem: how to get documents reliable enough to reconstruct events? The history of the resistance is difficult to write because the resister himself had to learn not to leave any traces. "Rare are the underground workers who kept journals or wrote regular notes," as Claude Levy has pointed out.[1]

But the history of civilian resistance poses a second problem. As mentioned above, historians since 1945 have studied the military or paramilitary aspects of the resistance more than its unarmed aspects. This has created a bibliographic imbalance that biases the collection of data from the start. Cases of civilian resistance are often mentioned but rarely explored. Furthermore, since the research was done within the European context, I had to expand my learning about the different national resistances without being able to claim the erudition of a historian specializing in a particular country. Indeed, treating such a subject in depth would have required common work between several research institutes specializing in European history. My contribution therefore must remain modest.

I first read general works on the European resistance. From there, I started to note examples that would correspond to my criteria of selection. These books include those by Henri Michel, *The Shadow War*; Henri Bernard, *History of the European Resistance*; Gordon Wright, *Europe at War (1939-1945)*; and Jorgen Haestrup, *European Resistance Movements (1939-1945)*.[2] I also did an exhaustive study of the articles in the *Revue d'Histoire de la Deuxième Guerre mondiale*, an indispensable work of international renown. Consulting these texts sent me back to specialized works at the library of the Institut d'Histoire du Temps Présent (IHTP), the laboratory of the Centre National de la Recherche Scientifique, as well as at the Bibliothèque de Documentation Internationale Contemporaine (BDIC) and the library of the Centre de Documentation Juive Contemporaine (CDJC). During my stay at Harvard's Center for International Affairs (1986-1988), I was able to find even more new references at Widener Library. Furthermore, I undertook a correspondence with specialized institutes abroad that obtained documents for me that I could not find in France. This was the case for Belgium, Luxemburg, Holland, Italy, and Norway. Finally, during the course of my studies I could sometimes share my analyses with French and foreign historians, and during a 1985 stay in Poland, I was able to gather information and comments on the spot about the history of the period in that country. I used a translation service several times, which now allows me to present previously unpublished accounts—either in part or in their entirety—in French. In those cases, I indicate the source in the language of the country. But more generally, I have given the main references accessible in French, English, or German.

The second difficulty, given the irregular national situations within Hitler's Europe, comes from the danger of "comparativism." It is true that each situation is unique and must always be situated both in its context and in connection to the world around it. But by over-emphasizing this approach, one risks constructing a splintered history that would not take into account larger sociological or political tendencies at the transnational level. Taking into consideration the particular contexts of the facts studied, I am of the opinion that comparative analyses enrich historical works rather than impoverish or undermine them.

Remembering this, I am always vigilant about keeping the *chronology* of the facts in mind, since chronology is crucial to their interpretation. In the context of the Second World War, *time* played such an essential role that some resisters were called "waitists," whereas others declared themselves fervent partisans of "immediate action." The progress of the war thus weighed heavily on the dynamic of the internal resistances. But other factors must also be taken into account. I adopted the four variables about France enunciated by Jean-Pierre Rioux (aside from some corrections) which seem to offer a good point of reference for other countries:

The rhythm of the war itself during the wait for a clearer vision of the balance of forces. . . . ; the evolution of the attitude of the occupier, its physical contact [with opposing forces in the period] from the *Korrection* in 1940 to Oradours in 1944; the capacity of regions and groups to recreate for themselves a collective identity after the trauma of the debacle; and the moral authority that a resistance movement can draw from radio broadcasting and from groups . . . to unify the French people as a whole.[3]

As the first chapter reminds us, the political regimes within German-dominated Europe, in spite of their heterogeneity, can be reduced to a few basic strategic structures that we will always remember. My intention is not to diminish the differences among countries but, on the contrary, to point them out. I hope most of all to show that the dynamic of civilian resistance changed considerably according to the nature of the occupying regimes.

NOTES

1. Claude Lévy, *Perspectives historiques de la Deuxième Guerre mondiale à la lumiere des études françaises*, Colloque de Côme, September 1975, cited by Henry Rousso, "Où en est l'histoire de la Résistance?," *La France de 1939 à nos jours* (Paris, 1985) 114.

2. Henri Michel, *La Guerre de l'ombre* (Paris, 1970); Henry Bernard, *Histoire de la résistance européenne* (Brussels, 1968); Gordon Wright, *The Ordeal of Total War, 1939–45* (New York, 1968); and Jorgen Haestrup, *European Resistance Movements (1939–1945): A Complete History* (Westport, CT, 1981).

3. Jean-Pierre Rioux, "Survivre," *L'Histoire* 80 (July-August 1985) 98–99.

List of Examples Studied

GENERAL FORMS

Work Slowdowns, 38, 39
Clandestine Press, 85
Infiltration of the Government, 37

MOBILIZATION OF THE POPULATION

Demonstrations

Czechoslovakia (October 28, 1939), 74
Netherlands (June 29, 1940), 74
Belgium (November 11, 1940), 74, 84
France (November 11, 1940), 74
France (January 1, 1941), 74
France (October 31, 1941), 75
France (May 1, 1942), 75
France (July 14, 1942), 75
Norway (August 3, 1942), 79
Germany (February 4-10, 1943), 193

Strikes

Netherlands (February 25-26, 1941), 172
Belgium (May 10-20, 1941), 81
France (May 27-June 9, 1941), 82
Luxembourg (August 31-September 4, 1942), 82
France (October-November 1942), 93
Denmark (August 1943), 91
Netherlands (April-May 1943), 83, 172, 174

Mass Civil Disobedience

The STO Refusal in France (1943-1944), 92-95, 170

Specialized Forms of "Professional" Resistance

Dutch Doctors (1941-1945), 70–73
Norwegian Teachers (1941-1945), 68–70
Underground Education in Poland (1940-1945), 78–80

Movements to Help the Jews

France (1942-1944), 148–149
Belgium (1942-1944), 150–151
Denmark (1943), 151–154

MOBILIZATION OF INSTITUTIONS

Protests

German Churches (1940, 1941), 97–103
Dutch Churches (1940, 1942), 150
Norwegian Associations (1941), 66
The Church and some political authorities in Bulgaria (1940, 1942, 1943) 143–145
French Churches (1942), 146–147
The Church in Belgium (1942-1943), 96–97

Limited Noncooperation

Opposition of the Danish government to persecution of the Jews (1940-1943),
    138–139
Opposition of the Finnish government to persecution of the Jews (1940-1944), 139
Opposition of the Italian government to deportation of Jews (1942), 137–138
Opposition of the Romanian government to deportation of Jews (1942-1945), 139–140
Opposition of the Hungarian government to deportation of Jews (1942–1944),
    140–141
The delivery of Danish ships to Germany (1941), 38
The Belgian Court of Appeal (1942), 43–44

Total Noncooperation

Resistance to the coup d'état of Quisling (1940), 51
The position of the Norwegian government (1940-1945), 50–54
Dismissal of the Supreme Court in Norway, 53
Dismissal of the Norwegian Church (1942), 67
Dismissal of the Danish government (1943), 40–42

Index

About the Author

JACQUES SEMELIN is a historian and political science researcher at the Centre National de la Recherche Scientifique (CNRS) in Paris. A post-doctoral fellow of the Center for International Affairs at Harvard, Dr. Semelin's earlier works include *Pour Sortir de la Violence* and *La Dissuasion Civile*.